New World Dharma

New World Dharma

Interviews and Encounters with Buddhist Teachers, Writers, and Leaders

Trevor Carolan

Foreword by Susan Moon

Published by State University of New York Press, Albany

For information, contact State University of New York Press, Albany, NY
www.sunypress.edu

Production, Jenn Bennett
Marketing, Kate R. Seburyamo

Library of Congress Cataloging-in-Publication Data

Carolan, Trevor, date.
New world dharma : Interviews and encounters with Buddhist teachers, writers, and leaders.
pages cm
Includes bibliographical references and index.
ISBN 978-1-4384-5983-7 (hardcover : alk. paper)
ISBN 978-1-4384-5984-4 (e-book)

10 9 8 7 6 5 4 3 2 1

For Gary Snyder

and for the unknown monk,

The Way is endless . . .

Every stump is sacred.
Every stump a saint
Every silted river a church to which
the pilgrim salmon return.
Every breath of wind a love song.
We worship in the wetlands,
bow to the fern, the rock,
the holy salamander,
the blood of sweet water,
the body of moss.

—Gary Lawless

CONTENTS

FOREWORD

Susan Moon

For thirty years, Trevor Carolan has been wandering around, following Buddhist teachers, poets, and thinkers he admires, and, gracefully and somewhat shyly, getting them to talk to him. This book is the result.

Carolan is a follower of both poetry and dharma in the best sense of the word *follow*. His perseverance, attention, and sense of adventure come through here. He follows his own nose, too, and his intuition, bravely setting forth to find people and their teachings. I admire his respectful curiosity. When was the last time you traveled a long way in order to ask a question of someone you admire, someone to whom you are a stranger?

And that's not the end of it. He writes down what happened and he passes it on, sharing what he learned. He is a translator in the broadest sense. To translate is to carry across, and this collection is all about cross-cultural currents, about wisdom coming from the East to the West and being changed into a new East/West consciousness. Everyone is changed by everyone else, by the animals and the trees and the poets and the Zen teachers they meet. Everyone is creating everyone else all of the time.

My own study of Zen Buddhism has taught me to appreciate the ancestors, the long lineage, the list of names—historically true or not it doesn't matter—from the Buddha all the way down to my living teachers. I value, too, the ancestors of literature—like Shakespeare and Emily Dickinson, to name two who have changed my mind, and the living ancestors, who are transmitting poetry to us right now. These last are the voices making up the weave of *New World Dharma*:

x   FOREWORD

a varied gathering of some of the twentieth- and twenty-first-century Buddhist teachers and poets who have changed the way we think in the West, particularly in the west of the West—the Pacific Northwest and California.

One of the voices here is that of the late Nanao Sakaki, wildman from Japan, nature poet, anti-nuclear activist. (It was Carolan who introduced me to the poetry of Nanao Sakaki many years ago, when I published an interview he did with Sakaki in *Turning Wheel* magazine.) Sakaki exemplifies the theme of interconnectedness that runs through the book. The mountains of Japan and the Pacific Northwest do not belong to separate nation-states as he walks them; poetry and Zen are not two different things in his talking. He understands that he is not separate from all the beings around him. He writes, "Soil for legs . . . mushroom for nose . . . wind for mind/Just enough." He proclaims: "Let's eat stars!"

One of my Zen teachers was the late Maurine Stuart. A couple of decades ago, I went to a weeklong sesshin (intensive meditation retreat) she led at Green Gulch Farm. Sometimes the silence included the sound of the surf a mile down the valley at Muir Beach. At the very end of the sesshin, Maurine asked us to turn away from the wall and face each other, for the last period of zazen. Then, without warning, but gently, the old barn filled up with the sound of a cello, like an empty cup waiting to be filled with water. For forty minutes, sitting still in zazen posture, we listened to Yo-Yo Ma playing Bach cello suites.

Woven together were the Zen practice of thirteenth-century Master Dogen, the composition of an eighteenth-century German composer, the performance of a contemporary Chinese-American cellist, a Buddha hall made out of an old California barn, the distant waves of the Pacific Ocean, and a teacher from Cambridge, Massachusetts. Many ancestors were present, working together to help us see our lives.

In the *EiheiKosoHotsuganmon*, Dogen declares: "Buddhas and ancestors of old were as we; we in the future shall be buddhas and ancestors. Revering buddhas and ancestors, we are one buddha and one ancestor."

Thanks to Carolan for bringing us some of our living ancestors.

ACKNOWLEDGMENTS

Some material in this book originally appeared in earlier versions in the following publications. Grateful thanks to all who contributed to their original and revised production, and who gave permission for written material to appear in this book. Trevor Carolan is the author or editor of record and editor asserts copyright over these works and on this compilation. All rights reserved. If an error or omission is brought to our notice regarding copyright we will be pleased to correct the situation in future editions of this book. For further information, please contact the publisher.

"Dancing with China's Old Masters." Copyright 2016 by Trevor Carolan. Used by permission.

"The Wild Mind of Gary Snyder." Copyright 1996 by Trevor Carolan. Used by permission. Originally appeared in *Shambhala Sun* (May 1996).

"Grounded in Humanity: Gary Snyder on *Back on the Fire*." Copyright 2007 by Trevor Carolan. Used by permission. Originally appeared in *The Bloomsbury Review* (July/ Aug. 2007).

"A Bloomsday Interview with Joanne Kyger." Copyright 2008 by Trevor Carolan. Used by permission. Originally appeared in *Pacific Rim Review of Books* (Summer 2008).

"And So Make Peace . . . Talking Story with Maxine Hong Kingston." Copyright 2008 by Trevor Carolan. Used by permission. Originally appeared in *The Bloomsbury Review* (Jan./Feb. 2008)

"The Bedrock of Practice: Sulak Sivaraksa in Bangkok." Copyright 2007 by Trevor Carolan. Used by permission. Originally appeared in *Turning Wheel* (Fall, 2007).

"A Heart Free to Listen: The Awareness Practice of Thich Nhat Hanh." Copyright 1996 by Trevor Carolan. Used by permission of the author. Originally appeared in *Shambhala Sun* (Jan. 1996).

"Embracing the Responsibility of the Moment: The Zen Politics of Jerry Brown." Copyright 2000 by Trevor Carolan. Used by permission. Originally appeared in *Shambhala Sun* (Sept. 2000).

"*Avanti!* The Dharma Poetics of Diane di Prima." Copyright 2007 by Trevor Carolan. Used by permission of the author. Originally appeared in *Pacific Rim Review of Books* (Fall 2007).

"On Forgiveness and Compassion: H.H. the Dalai Lama." Copyright 2001 by Trevor Carolan. Used by permission. Originally appeared in *The Bloomsbury Review* (Sept./Oct. 2001).

"On the Trail with Nanao Sakaki." Copyright 1995 by Trevor Carolan. Used by permission of the author. Originally appeared in *Common Ground* (Oct. 1995).

"Back on the Trail with Nanao." Copyright 2004 by Trevor Carolan. Used by permission. Originally appeared in *Beat Scene*, Coventry, UK (Summer 2004).

"Dangerous Work: The Retirement Interview with Zen Master Robert Aitken." Copyright 1997 by Trevor Carolan. Used by permission. Originally appeared in *Shambhala Sun* (Jan. 1997).

"Expatriate Passions: Meeting Donald Richie." Copyright 2001 by Trevor Carolan. Used by permission. Originally appeared in *The Bloomsbury Review* (Mar./Apr. 2001).

"A Conversation With Andrew Schelling." Copyright 2003 by Trevor Carolan. Used by permission. Originally appeared in *Beat Scene*, Coventry, UK (Winter 2003).

"Notes from the Gone World: Lawrence Ferlinghetti on Street Smarts and the Poetry Rebellion." Copyright 1996 by Trevor Carolan. Used by permission of the author. Originally appeared in *Common Ground* (Dec./Jan. 1995–1996).

"Beloved Renegade: With Allen Ginsberg at Cortes Island." Copyright 2001 by Trevor Carolan. Used by permission of the author. Originally appeared in *Giving Up Poetry*, Banff Centre Press (2001).

From "Soil For Legs." Copyright by Nanao Sakaki, in the Foreword. From *How To Live On The Planet Earth: Collected Poems*. Blackberry Books, Nobleboro, Maine, 2013. Used by permission.

From "Caribouddhism." Copyright 1998 by Gary Lawless. Blackberry Books, Nobleboro, Maine. Used by permission of the author.

My gratitude to all those in this book who generously gave their time in interviews, conversations, and correspondence. A project of this nature is rarely the effort of one individual, and I am indebted to many for their kindness and hospitality during the writing and compilation of this work. Recollecting the many individuals who assisted me through the years has brought to mind a river of memories and I wish to thank the following: Melvin MacLeod, *Shambhala Sun*, Halifax, NS; Joseph Roberts, *Common Ground*, Vancouver; Marilyn Auer and Tom Auer, *i.m.*, *The Bloomsbury Review*, Denver; Susan Moon, Berkeley, for her past editing and for her gracious Foreword to this edition; Kevin Ring, Binley Woods, *Beat Scene*, UK; Richard Olafson, *Pacific Rim Review of Books*, Victoria, BC; Arnold Kotler, Maui; Dr. Micheline Soong, Hawai'i-Pacific University, Honolulu; Dr. Jan Walls, Vancouver; Vincent Katz, Libellum Editions, New York; Judith Huntera, Naropa University, Boulder; Rex Weyler, Cortes Island, BC; Fred Young, Vancouver; Alma Lee, Vancouver; Mike O'Connor, Port Townsend, WA; John Carroll, UFV. *Tujhe-che* to the Tibetan Community of Portland, Oregon; *arigato gozaimasu* Master Asai, Japan Temple, Rabindra Sarovar, Kolkata. Thanks also to the Asia Society, New York; Dr. Rosita Dellios, Department of International Relations, Bond University, Qld., Australia; Professor Lachlin Loud, State University of New York-Suffolk, for an enduring friendship of forty years; Vincent Varga, museum director, Whyte Museum of the Rockies, Banff, Alberta. As a gesture of love for his wife, Terry Peters generously contributed his photography for the cover image. Jan Westendorp, Vancouver, cordially helped with the cover design. During research visits I received welcome from the late Esteban Ahn, San Francisco; Tae-Sun Kwon, Portland; Jan and Usha Kats, Portland; Dr. Charlotte Franson, London; and Perrine Angly in France—*merci* for La Fauconnerie and all the driving. The Allen Ginsberg scholar Bill Morgan and Peter Hale, the Allen Ginsberg Trust, provided special help in the late innings, as did my UFV colleague Dr. Hilary Turner with an expert manuscript critique. The recorded chanting service from Lotus in the Flame Temple, Zen Center of Denver, Danan Henry Roshi, was often of comfort during long hours of travel and study. Victoria Shoemaker, Berkeley, thoughtfully arranged several of the interviews. Gary Lawless of Blackberry Books, Nobleboro, Maine was a steadfast dharmic ally regarding publishing and creative issues. For their care and attention, special aloha to my editors Nancy Ellegate, Jessica Kirschner, Jenn Bennett, and to Kate Seburyamo and all the team at State University of New York. For sabbatical release time necessary to complete this work, my gratitude to the Office of Research and Graduate Studies, University of the Fraser Valley. As ever, *kamsahamnida* and love to my wife Kwangshik, to my now-grown children Patrick Lennon and Erin Delia, for their patience and support during the journeys and encounters during which much of the book was researched and gathered. It could not have been accomplished without them. To all who put their shoulders to the wheel in many ways, peace under heaven.

Introduction

Five years after the Beatles visited India to study meditation and eleven after the American poets Allen Ginsberg, Gary Snyder, Joanne Kyger, and Peter Orlovsky roamed there in 1962, I was on a journey of my own in Calcutta when I first encountered Buddhism in a living way. Setting off one morning on a day's wandering along the Hooghly River, I heard a voice behind me ask, "Do you know the way to the Japan Temple?"

I turned and saw a pilgrim monk dressed in a simple robe with shaved head, flip-flop sandals, a thin shoulder-sack, and a walking stick. He was bound, he said, for the holy places of the Buddha's life at Bodhgaya and in Nepal and had walked for two years from southern Thailand, through Burma and civil war-ravaged Bangladesh.

Thus began a more than forty-year engagement with the Buddha dharma and the seed of this book.

I explained that although I didn't know the Japan temple and had no knowledge of Buddhism, I'd enjoy helping the monk find it, so we strolled together through the long day and were joined by a retired scholar of Pali, the old Himalayan language of Buddhism's holy texts. I listened as they conversed in English—my first dharma teachers from whom I gained early, useful rudimentary knowledge. At dusk the Pali *babu* bid farewell, and we heard a booming from across Dhakuria Lake. Stepping lively, the monk and I arrived upon a little white and red temple where he hoped to rest for a time.

We entered up the temple steps. The monk whispered, "Follow what I do," and we bowed to the Buddha image on a small altar and took our places on the floor among a group of worshippers, mostly women, in fading light. Copying the monk, I fell into the swaying of the others. The repetitive chanting came easily: *Na-Mu Myo-Ho Ren-Ge Kyo*, over and over, and a thundering drum left the temple dome ringing as a group of Nichiren missionary monks took turns hammering away like *taiko* masters. It was easy to dissolve into the chanting and strangely moving. Darkness fell before I finally left the *puja* ceremony with a silent bow to the unknown monk, my head and heart both ringing.

Without looking for it, I found something deep in Asia that took root in my life. Perhaps the dharma had been looking for me. They say you can't go home again, but I never forgot the small Japanese temple that served the mostly Dalit, once-untouchable Buddhist community in what was then still a city of great suffering. My first dharma home.

Later in Vancouver I read Alan Watts' *The Spirit of Zen* and attended whatever infrequent Buddhist events that took place forty years ago. At graduate school in Arcata, California, a Soto monk from Mount Shasta lectured on why "Zen is Not Zen," and in the school library I found poetry books by Gary Snyder, then enrolled in a creative writing workshop led by Jim Dodge. The cue cards were pointing in a definite direction. Hitchhiking two hundred miles to the Zen Center of San Francisco on Page Street brought some form and shape to the basic knowledge I'd been acquiring, and led indirectly to people I'd meet again and again through the years. Not long after, I met a Korean girl who'd become my life partner for what's already been thirty-five years. That meeting was followed in short order by an encounter with a Chinese master to whom I'd devote twenty-three years in studying meditation, tai chi chuan, and China's *San-Jiao-Gway-Yi*—the Three Treasures syncretic tradition that harmonizes Taoist, Confucian, and Buddhist teachings. Organically and unbidden, I was steadily acquiring a kit of ideas and experience focused on the Buddha dharma.

En route, my avocation for Buddhist culture was also evolving as a significant part of my working life as a freelance journalist through writing about, interviewing, or translating from the various teachers, leaders, and wisdom traditions I'd encounter. I wrote for a number of Buddhist, literary, or cross-cultural journals—*Shambhala Sun, The Bloomsbury Review, Kyoto Journal, Turning Wheel, Common Ground*, and *Nguoi Viet*, among others.

Frequently these encounters intersected with my personal interest in eco-conservation, social justice, and indigenous First Nations issues. As sometimes happens, cross-pollination like this can lead to direct action. After getting involved in a number of fiercely contested environmental campaigns I was elected councilman in

North Vancouver, a metropolitan region that shares one of North America's busiest Pacific seaports. Often in political debate I relied on Green ideas I'd picked up through my contact with thinkers and leaders who work with dharma—people who stood as models of how to say *no* in matters of ethical nature or conscience while aware that this might mean a hard return from powerful special interests. Ironically, several of my colleagues and I would soon be in China negotiating with government representatives on Pacific trade issues and I'd have to summon the courage to look our courteous hosts in the eye and explain my constituents' sensitivities to the situation of His Holiness the Dalai Lama and the people of Tibet. Even in public office the dharma and its obligations were never out of mind.

Pivotal new ages of consciousness require their own specific groundings and ways of seeing both the past and the future—spiritually, ethically, ecologically. Searching for the element that binds us interculturally, it is helpful to recall that Confucius in his *Analects* directs the wise seeker looks for patterns. This advice ripples through the accounts and interviews that follow, as a search for a unifying meta-narrative in tune with a global age, and for the transformations that humanity will need to navigate in keeping our Blue Planet in running order. These things are far from certain as I write. What unfolds is a tapestry of conversations with remarkable teachers, a web of spiritual or ethical ideas, stories and aesthetics in which a commonality is the recognition of "interdependence": our fundamental human interconnectedness with both the sentient and nonsentient world. Their insightful stories explain the process of self-awakening and culture-building that will allow us to continue thriving as we repair our broken world. As the message of the following encounters makes clear, even though it derives from diverse peoples, countries, social backgrounds, and Buddhist traditions, when practiced as an everyday sacrament, the awareness of interdependency—what Vietnamese teacher Thich Nhat Hanh insightfully terms *interbeing*— is more than just a Buddhist teaching: it becomes a living truth.

This is of keen interest to people whose lives are touched in some way by the convergence of classical Asian wisdom paths with newer Western models. Since leaving politics for a teaching job, I've discovered that young people are especially eager to learn from and study many of the traditions I have found myself exploring since that first journey to India. Far from being uninterested or without a cause, a charge often unfairly leveled at them, I've learned that their existential situations are different than those of my own generation during its student years; the economics of housing, transportation, and tuition fees are a big concern, as is the surveillance that monitors their communications and public actions more invasively than ever before, and that constrains their actions. They remain aware, however, that there are some things that are not right in the world, and I've been moved to tears in seeing them travel long distances to march in support of peace, an ecological cause, or for social justice and human dignity. In this process I've come to appreciate their willingness to bring an open mind to ideas and stories from Buddhist and other Asian spiritual traditions, and how even in this notionally secular age, such phenomena morph comfortably with the concept of their own socially engaged community actions. Some find it a compatible, nontheistic adjunct to the predominantly Judeo-Christian ethos in which they've been raised.

If asked, I say simply that my wife and I are devotional Buddhists, happy to enjoy the company of, in no particular order, Zen, Tibetan Vajrayana, Jodo-shin, Chinese Mahayana, Korean Won, Southeast Asian Theraveda, and generic Kuan-yin Goddess of Mercy devotees. Sundry dharma bum literary friends who pass through town, or whom we tag up with on our travels, are a bonus.

The material that follows is the compilation of many years' work. It aims to shed light on what history now shows to have been a significant development in Western cultural and spiritual life—the arrival of Buddhism into these new world terrains. The goal is to present readers with an intimate look into the lives and thoughts of key writers and leaders within Buddhism's steady transpacific flowering.

As a journalist or scribe I've been fortunate to hear great dharma teachers like H.H. the Dalai Lama, Robert Aitken-Roshi, Kalu Rinpoche, and others: consistently their wisdom has urged the cultivation of a deeper relationship with our own human compassion and inherent interconnectedness as sentient beings, ideas that can be perplexing to put into words in any language. Some things we can only comprehend with our heart. Renewing our personal sense of belonging seems to require a new sensibility, a shift from what MIT theorist William Irwin Thompson calls seeing the world in terms of "us and them" to an awareness in which differences are recognized as an ecology of "each and all"—the meaningful web of social connections and interdependencies that customarily gave zest to the lives of our ancestors.

From a Himalayan Buddhist perspective that H.H. the Dalai Lama frequently expounds, all things begin in the mind. Our experience of the world is our experience of our own mind. The words and ideas of an important pattern of thinkers are presented here, responding to the challenge of rethinking citizenship, community, and the sacred in the global age. These are individuals whom various publications engaged me to approach for interviews or to write about critically, or whom I consciously sought out as a journalist and student of the dharma. In some cases I was simply invited to meet with them for reasons of their own, or found myself in the right place at the right time and was able to commit their words and thoughts to paper or recording tape. My approach in compiling this book has been to construct a mandala of consciousness from these thinkers drawn from various cultural, social, political, and spiritual fields, and to place this within context for a lay audience likely possessing at least some prior basic knowledge of and comfort with literary and East-West spiritual inquiry. Included here are encounters with Gary Snyder, Maxine Hong Kingston, Robert Aitken-Roshi, current Governor of California Jerry Brown, His Holiness the Dalai Lama, Thich Nhat Hanh, Red Pine, Joanne Kyger, Allen Ginsberg, and others. Collectively, their ideas and words—their *upaya*, or skillful means—illuminate concrete practices for shaping a better individual and, arguably, societal future. No secret decoder ring is needed. Looking at them in an integrative fashion, it is possible to reflect on how unity may be achieved between the individual, larger *community*, and ecological *place*— between the local and universal, the physical and metaphysical—for a shared global future.

The crisis of faith and the yearning for meaning and purpose this dialogue has generated, which is now a cultural signifier of the Western world's postmodern condition, also challenges what it means to be an ethically and socially engaged citizen. What defines identity in these uncertain times of collapsing liberal and conservative visions, with a secular Western center that encourages shallow lives and endless consumerism? What provides a sense of belonging?

For those whose understanding is tempered by the findings of dynamic systems theory and its groundings in Western cognitive science, the coordinates of these mutualities may be observed as the manner in which Buddhism, Taoism, and Hinduism respectively recognize the concept of "from the beginning interdependence"— China's ancient animists understood it as Tao, and Buddhism understands the idea as *pratitya samutpada*, or codependent origination. Similarly, contemporary Western environmental science now acknowledges ecological "innerconnectivity," a concept that leads organically to the Gaia Theory, the view that Earth itself is a self-regulating biological system—as a sentient being, noun and verb.

Central to this collection of encounters and interviews is the appreciation that one is never a stranger anywhere, merely an interested newcomer—and as any veteran traveler can attest, the difference between these solitudes can be enormous. Accordingly, when encountering distinguished personalities it is possible, as an interviewer, to employ a yin/yang dialectic. On the one hand is an honest level of beginner's mind, acknowledging that before this worthy individual, I'm more or less a rookie, motivated to help share his or her ideas and *darshan*, or presence, with others. On the other hand, I am compelled to prepare for every interview intensively—to read and research, produce searching questions, and move discussion beyond the conventional level toward a depth psychology. It's good to be humble, courteous, and it's critical that one be well-informed, flexible, alert to proceedings, and persistent in directing appropriate questions that lead somewhere. If things go well, interview conversations progress like a flowing stream.

Through the years I've come to call this form of literary encounter an "interview poetics." In this I borrow from Allen Ginsberg, who termed the aesthetics of his decades-long fascination for photo-documenting meetings and public occasions with friends and colleagues a "snapshot poetics." Ginsberg, whom I was fortunate to learn from at writing and meditation workshops and retreats, spoke of his interest in taking pictures as "sacramental documentation," and came to recognize that the images he created were "valuable and historically interesting—maybe even art." What brings the reportage process most alive for an interviewer is when profound and sparkling material is offered by the interview subject spontaneously and in a way one hasn't expected—a form of transmission that can bring an extrasensory tingling, as if being asked directly by the subject, *have you got this?*

As readers will observe, I've had to be flexible in the way I reported the conversation in these seventeen selections. Depending on the editorial need of the publication that featured each at the time, the contents include both interviews and interview-based essays and reports.

Interestingly, the first essays with Gary Snyder and Nanao Sakaki led in each case to straight feature interviews some years later that addressed further topics. In itself this may be noteworthy, for an effective print interview requires a steady public diminishment of the questioner in order to focus maximum attention on the individual being interviewed. It may be that a veteran journalist is better equipped for this self-erasure. As the Buddha cautioned, the key lies in not becoming attached to one's own views. The skilled interviewer attends carefully to the subject, listening mindfully, remaining grateful for the opportunity, double-checking critical information on the spot for clarity and accuracy, and observing when moments of importance begin flashing on the radar. If one is able to solicit a further grace-note, or help develop a privileged point of information or idea for imparting to readers with special care, voilà, we have the angels' share.

These encounters engage some of the most influential popular figures of transpacific-infused counterculture in the United States over the last half-century—a magnetic field for Buddhists in North America and the West, and surely of interest to non-Buddhists also whose lives, arguably, have been impacted by the ideas of people in the book. This isn't news from the usual gang—it's the *unusual* gang. When viewed in hindsight it is apparent how significantly Asian spiritual teachings have resonated in the West, a cross-cultural awakening that has pollinated and hybridized with countercultural ideas from North America over several decades. Currently, for example, subtle manifestations of Buddhism can be recognized and understood through deep ecology's concept of living lightly and responsibly in stewardship with the Earth and here interviews with Gary Snyder, Nanao Sakaki, and Andrew Schelling among others bring light on this subject. In urban and community planning, dharmic-inspired thinking regarding design, reuse, and recycling has redefined what genuine sustainability might mean. Similarly, the widespread adoption of "mindfulness"—used as a friendly synonym for Buddhist attentiveness by publisher Arnold Kotler, Jon Kabat-Zinn, and others in presenting the writing and teaching of Thich Nhat Hanh to a large, mainstream audience—has percolated as a practice into everything from personal and social relationships to policing to organizational management theory, equating in a contemporary way with what Christendom once understood as the Benedictines' *ora et labora*: our prayer and work, intention and effort, are One.

These thinkers have helped change the shape of the world as we now view it. During a time of postmodern fragmentation in the arts, meditation practice is increasingly used as a way of teaching oneself and others how to pay fine attention, as William Blake reminds us, to minute particulars—first to breathing, and so to beauty. As the encounter with Thich Nhat Hanh clarifies, through *vipasyana*, deeper insight meditation, the reality of interconnectedness points us toward the true nature of objectivised phenomena: that the physical body as receptor becomes a vehicle for consciousness within a web-like series of networks, empty of separate individual existence within "the rise and fall of the ten thousand things"—an important view that now links Western physics with Buddho-Taoist metaphysics from Asia.

If this grouping of speakers and reports has a historical relevance, it may be in their more or less collective expression of how, in Buddhism, the work gets done and readers will find His Holiness the Dalai Lama, Robert Aitken-Roshi, and others speaking to this point. In North America's earlier post-WWII experience with Buddhism, teachers and even instructive books were comparatively rare. As Gary Snyder notes in "Wild Mind," early interpreters in the West generally came "with an educated background. So we tended to overemphasize the intellectual and spiritual sides of it, with the model at hand of Zen, without realizing that a big part of the flavour of Buddhism, traditionally and historically, is devotional." Nowadays, with the commodification of "virtual" popular culture and of what were once countercultural practices—"yoga" fashion apparel or "Zen" cafés—it is getting easier to forget what it means to be a part of the everyday, organic world. Identifying the authentic jewel in the lotus has gotten trickier. Hence, the value in having such living exemplars as Governor Jerry Brown, Diane di Prima, Joanne Kyger, or Sulak Sivaraksa to manifest the real deal.

Esthetically, this collection of voices draws on a shared sense of spiritual and philosophical practices and approaches by seekers, teachers, and leaders who are connected in some way within a web of discourses—from environmentalism to poetry and literature, politics, community activism, and religious mentorship. Their vision is broad and tested, encompassing a diverse range of contemplative and action strategies suitable for addressing the neuroses and suffering of the early twenty-first century. Typically their powers derive from patience, from kindliness, and from perseverance in a traditional wisdom path, or "mystery," as medieval Europe's guildhalls referred to acquiring mastery of their specific skill. The eminent translator Red Pine, America's master storyteller Maxine Hong Kinston, poet Allen Ginsberg, and jack of all trades wandering bard Nanao Sakaki demonstrate the ways of "walking the walk" that set the truly masterful apart from others who struggle in the old ruts simply "talking the talk."

Oddly, during the shepherding of this book I was obliged to return to India on a work project. As the departure date neared, news reports of political instability throughout South Asia cropped up frequently, and I grew apprehensive.

My wife brought home a bag of fortune cookies, however, and immediately I began receiving positive reinforcement from this unlikely source: "You are Heading in the Right Direction," "You and Your Partner Will Soon Experience Great Happiness," "You Are Heading for a Land of Sunshine and Fun." Each evening after dinner things felt more certain, yet some uneasiness remained. Shortly before leaving, an article by UCLA scholar Robert Buswell Jr. incited my attention. In "Korean Buddhist Journeys to Lands Worldly and Otherworldly," he writes:

> Travel for religious training, missionary propagation, and devotional pilgrimage has been an integral part of Buddhism since its very inception. Buddhism began as an offshoot of the indigenous Indian śramana tradition of itinerant wanderers (Jaini 1970), and the religion called its monastics bhiksu or bhiksuni, that is "wandering ascetics" (literally "beggars"). Initiation into that ascetic life was termed a "going forth" (pravrajita, Kor. chul'ga) from the indulgent life of a householder; we might today call this a "setting out" on a journey of personal discovery.

This came as an epiphany. My voyage now had a context, a kind of official purpose that made my heart feel solid. What had my anxieties been about?

I wondered if returning to the original source of what has proven a worthwhile, fulfilling life might not lead to disappointment. There was but one way to find out.

Happily, the sense of grace was still all there. In the small red and white temple by the lake the altar was as unchanged as I remembered it, and the great, weathered drum was there, the lettering on its skin like a magical incantation. We heard the mantra then, *Na-Mu Myo-Ho Ren-Ge Kyo*. . . . We joined in the prayer and the chant grew louder. Soon, another wave of devotees joined and we were chanting in unison, over and over, *Na-Mu Myo-Ho Ren-Ge Kyo*, as the dharma drum began like mountain thunder. For nearly forty years I have carried that heavy rhythm inside and again it all surged forth as the chanting came in wave on wave, all in it together, the Lotus Sutra, deep in the heart of the jewel that arises from the mud of the world, and the realization came like a shower of blossoms . . . unforgettably, the real deal.

Evam me sutam, "Thus have I heard."

In gratitude to all the many guides along the ancient way,

> Trevor Carolan
> University of the Fraser Valley,
> British Columbia

Notes

Buswell, Robert Jr. *Journal of Asian Studies*, 68, No. 4, 1055.

Ginsberg, Allen. *Snapshot Poetics*. Introductory Discussion. San Francisco: Chronicle, 1993, 8–16.

Thompson, William Irwin. *Pacific Shift*. San Francisco: Sierra Club, 1985, 76.

Chapter 1

Dancing with China's Old Masters

With Master Red Pine/Bill Porter

In the West all our major spiritual traditions have been based upon some authoritarian figure telling you what's what—the monotheistic religions, or a guru or someone. But suddenly here was this Tao that gave me a personal relationship with everything. In short, everything was up to me. The Tao says, "You're on the spot. We're not going to tell you anything; you're going to have to discover it." What a challenge. What an opportunity!

The January 1994 edition of Shambhala Sun *featured a brilliant excerpt from Bill Porter's book* Road to Heaven: Encounters with Chinese Hermits *that recounts his search for reclusive mountain Taoists and their practices. Burned out from freelance journalism I'd given up looking at magazines, but by next morning my own passion for telling stories was reignited by the possibility of writing on Buddho-Taoist subjects for a serious audience and I telephoned the editor, Melvin McLeod. "We were hoping you might call," he said. A year later, the phone rang for Nanao Sakaki who was visiting at our house, but who'd gone off wandering up the mountain out back, and I found myself talking to Bill Porter, aka Master Red Pine. He drove up from Washington that afternoon to meet Nanao and hours later the pair read to a packed audience at the Vancouver Dharmadhatu center. Next morning the three of us headed up the mountain trail together in search of the immortals. Under his pen name, Red Pine, Porter has quietly emerged as our generation's preeminent translator into English of classical Chinese spiritual and*

poetic texts. His unaffected "plain taste" translations include The Heart
Sutra, Poems of the Masters, The Diamond Sutra, In Such Hard
Times: The Poetry of Wei Ying-wu, Tao Te Ching, *and* The Collected
Songs of Cold Mountain. *Porter is candid in his views of China and its
contemporary existential condition. Under his own name he has also
authored* Zen Baggage, *a peerless account of his travels to Taoist,
Buddhist, and literary pilgrimage sites throughout China.* Finding
Them Gone, *a companion volume of his poetry research and Chinese
travels, will appear in 2015. On a camping journey down the Olympic
Peninsula in the early summer of 2011, my wife and I paid a call to his
home in Port Townsend, Washington and this comprehensive interview
with Master Red Pine unwound over pots of tea.*

TC: *Your readers know you as an old China-hand, but where were you
raised?*

BP: I was born in 1943 in Los Angeles to a father and mother who
respectively came from Arkansas and northern Michigan. My father
grew up on a cotton farm just outside Little Rock; my mother came
from Calumet, a copper-mining town. When I was eleven or twelve
we moved up to Idaho. So I think of myself as growing up outside of
Coeur d'Alene.

TC: *Can you tell us something about your growing-up years?*

BP: My father loved to hunt and fish. He was wealthy and had a chain
of hotels that he could operate out of an office anywhere, so we
bought Bing Crosby's house in Hayden Lake. Bing Crosby was from
Spokane, just across the border from Coeur d'Alene, and he was
recently divorced—he was Catholic and the Pope had granted him an
annulment. He'd bought another place across the lake in a secluded
area so the paparazzi would leave him alone. We moved north in '53
or '54, and I was sent down to boarding school in Los Angeles. My
father was alcoholic and used to beat my mother. Finally she got wise.
She got a divorce, but they hated each other so much that the divorce
and property settlement lasted fourteen years.

TC: *You intimate this in the last chapter of* Zen Baggage. *It's a bit like
Dickens'* Bleak House.

BP: Exactly. All the money disappeared. I learned early on that money
isn't so much evil as it is like flypaper; it just catches everybody. When
I was kid, the only people I had real human relationships with were

the people who worked for us—maids, gardeners, drivers. Not so much my father or mother, or the people who came around; they were mostly looking for my father's money.

TC: *You served in the army.*

BP: Yes, but first my father got one of his lawyers to arrange for me to go to college in Santa Barbara, in 1961. I studied art but flunked out; I had no talent. The next year I went to Palomar College near Escondido, studied psychology for one semester, and flunked out the next. Then I went to Pasadena City College and studied English literature for one semester, flunked out again and got my draft notice. I'd had a German girlfriend in Pasadena and she was thinking of home. In '64, the Vietnam War was getting into full swing. They had this deal in the army: you served your two years, but if you agreed to extend for three years, you'd get your choice of any training that the army offered, or any place where the army served. I extended and said "Germany, please!" They sent me to Fort Benning, Georgia to learn how to repair Jeeps. I remember never finishing [a class on how to fix] brake systems when we got orders saying, "Next week you guys graduate and we're sending the entire class to Vietnam. We need Jeep Mechanics." I said, "But wait, we've got a deal. . . ." They said, "This is the army, son."

TC: *So your first Asian cultural experience was in Vietnam?*

BP: No, when those orders came it was payday week. Me and another young guy said, "Screw this." We took a bus to the airport in Atlanta and flew as if we were being transferred to LA. We'd typed up orders—you learn to do a lot of crazy things in the army. I bought a '54 Chevy convertible and we drove out of LA up Highway 395.

TC: *It's '64, you're AWOL in a convertible headed exactly where?*

BP: Back to Coeur d'Alene where I'd had my first love affair, my first introduction to an intense physical relationship. Near Yosemite the other guy talked me into letting him drive. He didn't have much experience. Going down a mountain we hit some gravel and turned and rolled over twice down an embankment, ending up in a ravine near a tree. Nobody got hurt; just cut up a little. There were no police. Park rangers eventually came and towed the car. They didn't know we were AWOL, so we continued by hitchhiking. Next day we were in northern California or Oregon somewhere and this kid picks us up.

He was running away from home. We said, "Hey, we're AWOL from the army, so let's just do this together!" We drove all night and next morning a cop pulled us over. He had a bulletin on this kid's license plate. He talked to us separately, then said to me, "This guy says you're AWOL." You know how when you're young, you learn to think fast? I said, "No, it's a misunderstanding. We haven't been drafted yet." In those days you had thirty days to change the location of your draft board, where they then had to draft you again. The cop took us into town, tried to call the army, but it was Sunday. Nobody answered. He said, "I guess you guys are okay," and let us go. I eventually hooked up with the woman in Coeur d'Alene. After a week, we all realized we had to do something else.

TC: *What happened?*

BP: My young sidekick played saxophone and he had the idea of teaching me. He said, "We'll go to Massachusetts and form a jazz combo and support ourselves that way." It sounded like a perfectly good idea to me. We started hitchhiking and were down to our last five dollars. In Montana we got hit by a blizzard. I said to hell with it, walked into the nearest town and turned myself in to the police. They sent someone to bring me back to Fort Benning. I explained things to the sergeant major and he said, "You've got a point. You wash dishes for a month and I'll straighten this out for you." And he did. He sent me to clerk's school, then on to Germany. I did my time there.

TC: *And the German girl?*

BP: I went to her house outside the Black Forest and they said, "Oh, so sorry. She's married an Italian guy outside Los Angeles." Anyway, I spent my army time in Germany, loved it.

TC: *Where did you study your Chinese?*

BP: When I left the army in '67, I returned to Santa Barbara and chose anthropology as my major. Getting ready to graduate, I wanted to study for my PhD with Margaret Mead and Ruth Benedict at Columbia. They had financial aid you could apply for. One was a language fellowship. You had to specify the language, and it had to be a rare one. I'd just read *The Way of Zen* by Alan Watts and it made perfect sense, so I wrote "Chinese" and Columbia gave me a four-year fellowship. They only gave out two fellowships in the department that year, and one went to me. I had to study Chinese pretty much full time with a dragon of a teacher. Eventually I met a Buddhist monk in Chinatown and said, "This is for me—the practice, not the book-learning." So after two years I quit the fellowship.

TC: *You went AWOL from Columbia. . . .*

BP: Well, yeah . . . I had to formally renounce the fellowship. I went to Fo Kwan Shan—Buddha Light Mountain monastery in southern Taiwan, that someone at Columbia told me about. I lived there for a year in '72. Hundreds of tourists would show up every day. I stood out like a sore thumb and felt very uncomfortable. I felt that I didn't have the ability to focus, to practice by myself without the distraction of people staring at me all the time, so I decided to attend a College of Chinese Culture near Taipei to improve my Chinese. That's where I met my wife, Gu. She was studying for a degree in philosophy. We took a class together in the philosophy of Alfred North Whitehead. After a semester I felt my spoken Chinese was good enough, so I went to live in another monastery for about two and half years.

TC: *Were you also following monastic practice, as a lay monk?*

BP: Yes and no. I was never a monk. I was allowed to do whatever I desired, but they wouldn't let me do any manual work. I would meditate maybe four hours a day, and since I had all this other time on my hands I started reading. To improve my Chinese, I thought that I might begin translating it from books with a dictionary. The abbot just happened to publish the complete poems of Cold Mountain in a new edition, and he pirated Burton Watson's English translations of a hundred of the poems. He gave me a copy, so I said, "Oh, I'll start working from this." That's how I began translating Cold Mountain's poems. Around 1975/'76, I moved to a farming community where I got hepatitis so badly that I could hardly walk. My mother gave me a one-way ticket back to the States and on recovering I found work in the Forest Service for six months to build up my physical strength. That was in Springerville, where they had a huge burn on the New Mexico–Arizona border. Apache-Sitgreaves National Forest. In '77, I moved back to Taiwan where I'd still see Gu every weekend. It took seven years for her parents to finally agree to let us get married.

TC: *Why was that?*

BP: I didn't really have a job. I made $100 to $200 a month teaching English. Expenses were about the same. Gu and I figured it would take about $5,000 for us to get married. Her parents said I had to stop sleeping on the floor on *tatami* mats: I had to get furniture, start sitting down on chairs, I had to buy some gold, we had to have a banquet, I had to take her on a honeymoon. We figured $5,000. The only way I could get that kind of money was smuggling. So I started smuggling Rolex watches into Korea. Real ones. The duty was a hundred percent. In a bad week we'd do Omegas, but usually it was Rolex. There were three or four of us mules in the stable and we'd go about three times a month. Depending on the demand each trip, we'd carry about forty watches. We took twenty watches through customs in specially made suits and left another twenty in bond, which we picked up on the way out and then brought back the next day from Japan. I was an "antique dealer." That was my shtick. Anyway, it worked great. It took a little over a year and I got my money. We were getting married and the boss says, "How about taking your wife on a honeymoon to Japan, just half a trip? I'll get you both tickets." My wife said, "No, let's not do it." That trip, everybody got arrested. I had to go visit them all in jail in Seoul. They were finally released on a presidential amnesty. That's how I got married.

TC: *Somehow you began writing and translating.*

BP: About six months after all this a friend of mine who was a copy editor at *The China Post*, the large English language newspaper, headed home to Australia. He needed someone to take his place. I did that for about a year when a fellow I knew said, "Hey, the English language radio station here just got money from the Asia Foundation. They're looking for someone to do news, to translate stuff about China, Taiwan." They hired me and I became their local news editor. I'd come in at 5:30 a.m. and translate the top ten stories from the Chinese newspapers, summarize them, put them on the air. [I would] do interviews throughout the week, update stories. I did that for six years from the early 1980s until '89.

TC: *How did you begin publishing work in the U.S.?*

BP: I decided I wanted to go to China and find hermits. I applied to the Guggenheim Foundation to find hermits, thinking it was such a good idea they'd have to give me the money. At the time I was doing a weekly interview program meeting the power people in Taiwan, and I was interviewing the plastics king, Winston Wong. He's a billionaire, one of the world's biggest producers of plastics. Brilliant guy.

Perfect English. We were having our interview and I said, "Did you ever see the movie *The Graduate*?" He said yes. I asked, "Would you tell the son, 'Plastics, son, plastics'?" He says, "No, I would tell him 'Follow the *Tao*.'" I was so impressed with that. I told him that this was probably going to be my last interview because I'd applied to the Guggenheim Foundation to go to China to follow the Tao into China and find hermits in the mountains. He said, "That's a great idea. If they don't give you the money, I will." And, of course, they didn't, and he did. I quit my job at the radio station and went off to find hermits in China. Then I stayed home and wrote *Road to Heaven*.

TC: *That book arrived like a thunderbolt. Not so long ago, relatively few books were available in English on Taoism or Buddhism. And it was an industrialist who helped fund it?*

BP: Right, at the same time Gu and I were deciding what to do next. Could we bring our kids back to America to learn English? We had no money. I was so broke the news director paid my rent for four months. Then Li Ka-Shing, the richest man in Hong Kong, received the first private broadcasting license ever given there. He hired my radio station boss in Taiwan, an American, to come and run it, along with my news director friend. They asked if I'd go with them and do a program on Chinese culture. Could I give them two minutes of culture reporting a day? I thought that I could, and said I had an idea, too—a travel program.

TC: *This must the roving reporter work you mention in your books. . . .*

BP: That's it. I started at the mouth of the Yellow River and I traveled all the way to its source, reporting all along the way. Next, I followed the Silk Road all the way through to Islamabad. For two years I went everywhere in China: all the hill tribes in the southwest, all the Buddhist temples, all of the great poets' graves. I did 1,120 two-minute radio programs—240 per program series—and everybody in Hong Kong loved the program. I saved my money, the job paid well: Hong Kong does that. I was a celebrity there for two years. In 1993, I came to Port Townsend and bought the house I'm living in now. I've put on a second floor, fixed up the garage for friends to stay, and have lived here since, working on translations of other books, struggling like anybody does in America to try to stay alive and put food on the table. Thank god I've had food stamps. That allowed me to stay here. It took me a long time to figure out how to make money in America.

I tried waiting on tables, working in a bakery . . . that left me so tired I couldn't translate. I finally decided to go into credit card debt. My aunts, who are mentioned in *Zen Baggage*, died and left me able to pay off this debt, and I started over again. Within a couple of years I was in debt again. Around 1997, the Hong Kong government called up out of the blue and said, "Can you come back and give us some of the reporting like you used to put on the radio? How much would that be?" They wanted twenty two-minute spots. I said, "Enough to pay off my credit-card debt in the low-twenties." *Done!*

TC: *This was all in Chinese?*

BP: No, I'm known here for my Chinese. In Taiwan, Hong Kong, I'm known for my English. Then when I returned to Washington State, some local people asked if I'd lead them on a visit to China. They offered to pay me. Now, every year I take a small group of people over on a special cultural tour through China.

TC: *Can you recall what it was that incited your attention to Chinese culture?*

BP: Sure. In the West all our major spiritual traditions have been based upon some authoritarian figure telling you what's what—the monotheistic religions, or a guru or someone. But suddenly here was this Tao that gave me a personal relationship with everything. In short, everything was up to me. The Tao says, "You're on the spot. We're not going to tell you anything; you're going to have to discover it." What a challenge. What an opportunity! That's what I saw in Chinese culture; that it was all open to me, whether it was Confucianism, Taoism, or Buddhism. It was always that same openness. I had never experienced anything like it in the West. Here, everything was closed, a very narrow door: "You've got to believe this and act like this: if you agree with this concept, this ideology, you can pass through this door." Suddenly, it was amorphous in a very self-determining way about how you wanted to live. I love that. It was attractive to someone like me, although maybe not to others.

TC: *What makes translating and writing about classical Chinese poetry and culture special for you? Do you think about what it might have to teach Americans in what's starting to look like the late stages of an empire?*

BP: People ask this from time to time. The only thing I can tell them is what *I* get out of it. That's what I care about in all this. It's *my* awakening, the experience I have confronting these writers who have written these things. They have helped me open up my own mind, my own awareness, but it requires my participation, and that's the crucial thing. I think somebody who is open and willing to participate in a religious tradition can do just as well in Sufism, or any religion in the world, even Christianity for that matter. Chinese poetry was the environment that allowed me to actively participate. Chinese poetry doesn't do it by itself. For me, I have to find a way to live, to think. I find the beautiful moments in a person's life very touching. The Chinese can be so human, so honest. In English poetry I don't get honesty to the extent that I get it in Chinese poetry. There are loads of Chinese poets who are just as baroque, just as jaded and corrupt as anywhere else, but maybe because I've chosen certain poets in China who are really honest souls, I've been able to grow as a person by being their friend. That's what Chinese poetry means to me. It's so friendly. You feel like you can just sit down with this person, this poet, and have a cup of tea together. They lived 1,500 years ago—doesn't matter. You feel like you're best buddies.

TC: *What sort of impact or influence do you think Chinese poetry has had on North American arts and letters?*

BP: First of all, I think the Chinese poetry that has been translated and transmitted to the West, and that has been appreciated by the Chinese themselves, has a lack of intellectualism. It's not interested in ideas. It's interested in sitting down and having a cup of tea and looking up at the moon. It's about living in the world and appreciating the Tao of the moment. The impact of that insight has rippled in the West like a rock thrown on a pond. You now see it affecting other people in the West who may have no knowledge of China or Chinese poetry, but they've somehow picked up on that in their own writing. You see shorter lines in poetry, or notice the way that interest in the natural world and in simple, everyday events is being observed. I think a lot of that comes from Asia, as opposed to Europe.

TC: *You've collected and translated the Tang dynasty poets in* Poems of the Masters. *Do you see them aspiring at all to answer such questions as "What is poetry?"*

BP: You're viewing this as a reader. It's a little different for me and is hard to put into words. The only reason I'm interested in Chinese poetry is so that I can translate it. Translation for me is like a performance art. I have to become the personal dance companion of the person who I'm translating, which is a whole different experience than reading a Li Bai [Li Po] poem. I've somehow become captivated by the experience of trying to dance with Li Bai, with Wei Ying-wu. I "see" the Chinese poem not as an entity carved in stone, but as an idea of the real poem—as a manifestation behind which something is motivating Li Bai. There's an inspiration. I see the poem as nonlinguistic, as not having words but having been put into words because that's the only way it can be communicated to another human being in our civilizations. As a translator, I have to find that place where the poem is coming from.

TC: *Is there a borderline between translating and recreating? How far do you go in your own interpretation of the original text?*

BP: Every translation is a recreation, but so is the original poem. There is no original poem. The question is, when you tell a joke that made you laugh, do you make others laugh?

TC: *Through the occupation following WWII, Americans were introduced to Japan's Zen-inspired aesthetics. Similar qualities resonate through Wang Wei, Li Bai, and other Chinese poets—a slightly sad feeling that recognizes the lonely beauty, the impermanence of everything.*

BP: That's there all right. It's not specific to the Japanese; the Chinese share this. One thing I should note is that I don't read books *about* Chinese poetry. All I do is to translate. My point is that I'm working at a nonlinguistic, even a noncultural level with these people who felt deeply and who danced beautiful dances. As a translator, I try to share that beauty. I have to try and hear their music. It's my way of honoring that dancing. I never think about whether it evokes feelings that are about Zen or the Tao.

TC: *Wei Ying-wu, who you translate in* In Such Hard Times, *has themes that read like Roy Orbison or Ray Carver—life in small towns, career failures, the loss of his wife. His poems feel a lot like country music's "hurtin' songs." Tu Fu is like this, too.*

BP: There *are* some hurtin' songs in these poems! It's true. The Chinese share that love for hurtin' poems.

TC: *Could this be a helpful way for teachers to make Chinese poets more accessible to younger North American readers?*

BP: It comes down, I think, to their institutions. Confucius said, "You want to straighten out the world? Then straighten out your country. To straighten out your country, you've got to straighten out your state. To straighten out that, you need to straighten out your village. Then straighten out your family, and ultimately straighten out yourself. To do that, you have to be honest." That, to me, is the key to Chinese poetry: *honesty.* They've cultivated the openness of their own heart. A heart hurts; it's also open to the world. That's why the Chinese poem can be mystical, or rooted in mundane affairs, or in the poet's own personal agonies. It's all one thing. It's not that there are different kinds of poems. It's all this one heart. The original character meaning of the word poetry means "words from the heart."

TC: *In an interview, Andrew Schelling contrasted this uncomplicated, stripped-down view of poetry with postmodern approaches that he suggests are deliberately complex.*

BP: I don't know who this started with, but T.S. Eliot is a good example. If you don't have the notes, you don't know what the poem is about. Chinese officials classically were tested on four things. In ancient China—by this I mean up to 130 years ago—you couldn't be an official if you did not have a sound body, good calligraphy, the ability to write a good essay, and the ability to write a poem on the spot. Poetry, calligraphy, essay, physique. You were expected to qualify at a high level in these. So poetry has always been part of a gentleman's repertoire, his tool kit. Now you could build the Great Wall of China with some of the crappy poetry that was written, probably in honor of some minor visiting official, but that poetry hasn't been preserved.

TC: *After your years at this, have you a favorite poet?*

BP: Tao Yuan-ming [365–427]. He's the best for me—the language, the way he put words together. He was an official who served briefly, then went and spent the rest of life in a mud-house village. I visited the village where he lived. It was 1,700 years after he lived, and his last male descendent had just died. It's in *Zen Baggage.* He was half-hermit, half-elitist who decided the middle ground is to live in a small village and hang out with the farmers, have friends visit, go off and wander in the hills, and have a good bottle of wine whenever possible. He's not widely known here, but he's the best.

TC: *You've noted that 25 percent of Wei Ying-wu's poetic output was "poetic correspondence." Are we losing anything in the email age?*

BP: We're losing the ability to have depth, that's all. We're becoming more and more superficial. It's becoming apparent in many aspects of our culture. Superficiality. We accept that for speed. Things are speeding up.

TC: *Your translation of the* Diamond Sutra *has something of everyday simplicity about it.*

BP: It's the everyday sutra. It starts with the Buddha when he goes begging in town. There's no other sutra that you can find where the Buddha goes to town begging. The sutra makes that point from the beginning. That's what he does. Every day. That's the Diamond Sutra, about how the Buddha did it.

TC: *Isn't it also about reducing everything down?*

BP: Exactly—the formlessness. Hui-Neng in the Platform Sutra likes formlessness. It's his favorite term. He felt people were becoming too attached to forms, to ways of doing things—"I will meditate like this, I will bow like that, wear these clothes, say these words. Therefore, I am a bodhisattva." That was what he hit people over the head with—formlessness! Formlessness!

TC: *Looking at Buddhism's development in North America, it seems to want it all—the ritual practices, meditation, the salvation. Maybe it's like Detroit—the "fully-loaded vehicle"?*

BP: Americans are Americans. It's really hard for them to approach Buddhism as the Easterner does. We're stuck with the fact that we're coming out of a couple of thousand years of the development of a materialistic worldview. Our sense of the spirit is different. We want everything, and enlightenment is just another thing. When we first get interested in Buddhism, I expect a number of us may approach it that way. The key is whether there's a teacher to straighten you out about this, or whether it becomes just another acquisition.

TC: *You've also translated from Taoism—the Tao Te Ching. What's your understanding of this idea of there being "a Way," a higher, virtuous way to live?*

BP: In the Tao Te Ching I think that it's more a case of there being a slightly *lower* way. Lao-tzu has a different take. Every Taoist does. Lao-tzu says there's less, not more; it's better to be weak, not strong, dark and not light. In fact, the original meaning of Tao comes from where Lao was born. He came from a small state that was controlled by the state of Chu. The Chu were controlled by the Miao people. In the Miao language, the word "Tao" means dark moon. Lao-tzu's Tao is the Tao of the dark moon. For him, the advantage is to be dark because the light's going to shine. What we're going to do is cultivate more darkness. This is completely opposite to the *I Ching*, which cultivates the full moon—how to be successful in all things, in every situation. But Lao-tzu is about how to fail. By being dark, you're destined to grow into the brightness. I see Lao-tzu's Tao the way a surfer looks at a wave: you look at that lowest point, go for the trough, not the crest or you get crashed. Go for the lowest point in the wave and you can ride it forever. That's Lao-tzu's Tao, according to me—to find the weak spot, the dark spot and hang out there in anonymity.

TC: *Let's take a big swerve here. You're an incorrigible sports fan. Is there something in baseball especially that pumps your tires?*

BP: Yes, I love baseball because nothing happens. Then suddenly it does.

TC: *The dark moon!*

BP: Right. You can have a conversation at a baseball game. What other sport can you leave for a while, get a beer, come back and nothing has changed?

TC: *You've written a couple of the best travel books, if that's the right term, ever to come out of Asia—*Road to Heaven, Zen Baggage. . . . *What next?*

BP: My Guggenheim project is to write a book like *Zen Baggage* about poetry. The project is called *Mountains and Rivers in Chinese Poetry.* I've got twenty poets in China, and I've developed an itinerary based on the mountains and rivers in their lives, physically or emotionally. I'm going to go to those places where they lived those moments, days and weeks. I'll visit those places, translate the poems they wrote there, take photographs, meet some people, have some experiences on this trip—like *Zen Baggage.* It'll be a six- to eight-week trip. *National Geographic's* China edition will send a photographer. Like all my books, it'll take me a year to write it after that. It won't be out until the spring of 2014.

TC: *The Tang Dynasty is still regarded as China's Golden Age. Chang'an Avenue, the grand route through Beijing, is named for the old Tang capital. Any thoughts about modern China?*

BP: Absolutely. The Chinese have never been so interested in their past as they are today. They've been deprived for so long. They no longer have to bust their butts to feed themselves and put a roof over their heads. They're intensely interested in their own past. It's part of their tradition and it's what makes them proud. It's also part of the revived nationalism that's happening. And it's why someone like me can sell a hundred thousand copies of a book in the Chinese edition about their culture in less than a year, when it's hard to sell a fraction of that in America. It's not ironic that the people who are most interested in China today are in China.

TC: *Do you see anything coming out of China's rising global power?*

BP: Sure, rising global power. The West has indulged itself in the most absurd ways in terms of military and foreign adventures, in the way that nations run their economies, their politics; look what's happened. I'm sure the American empire has passed its high-water mark, and the Chinese are going to take advantage of that. They don't have the sense that their national security is being threatened in places like Iraq or Vietnam. They don't have to confront you. In fact, the Chinese and most Asians hate confrontation and will do anything to avoid it, yet they'll come out ahead because they don't confront you. They're patient and they'll outlast you. But the Chinese have their own problems—the terrible, brutal government. You can't say anything really good about it. I wouldn't want to live in China. Money is everything there. I meet Chinese people with money and they're all interested in trying to turn it into knowledge and into an appreciation for their own culture, although I fear in some ways it may be too late. The only way you'll see a real change is if the economy were to undergo a collapse. Right now the government delivers. The people appreciate that and stay out of politics. But there's always dissent in Chinese politics. Every day there's a demonstration somewhere in China.

TC: *What's your current project?*

BP: I have a small edition of *The Oxherding Pictures and Verses* from P'u Ming that has just come out. All I've been working on is translation. I don't have any other travel books on the go.

Next spring my translation of the *Lankavatara Sutra* comes out.

TC: *Didn't Jack Kerouac mention the* Lankavatara Sutra *in his early work?*

BP: These classic works have banged around at different times. Michael McClure told me that he tried in vain [to translate it], he and Gary Snyder both, but they gave up on it. A lot of people in the West have tried to work on it because it had such a huge impact on early Zen, but the only access was a translation done eighty years ago by D.T. Suzuk, which is very difficult to read. I've done the translation and tons of notes; it'll be like my other translations of the sutras. Hopefully, it'll be clear. When I return from my next China visit in November this fall, I'll begin work on the background to my *Poetry Baggage* [*Finding Them Gone*]. It'll take me about six months to find 120 poems, twenty poets. I figure about six poems per poet, beginning with Confucius and ending with Cold Mountain. That'll be a poetry, translation, and travel book. After that, about five years from now, I want to write a biography of Empty Cloud, the Zen master Xuyun. He died in 1958, I believe. An Italian woman doing her PhD on him in Paris says he lived to be 116.

TC: *Writing, translating . . . the way is endless, but it's a lean life. What keeps you going?*

BP: I love to translate. It's like being in love. I'm totally happy when I'm translating. It's hell too—it's a challenge. I'm driven to do what I do because I love it.

Port Townsend, WA

Chapter 2

The Wild Mind of Gary Snyder

We have ecology, there's the possibility of a sacred ecology; eventually we'll have a sacred economics. That will be when the insight of ecology, the spiritual obligations of ecology, and the real potentialities of economics are brought together.

The contributions of Pacific Northwest-raised poet, essayist, and generational sage Gary Snyder continue to inform the emotional, philosophical, and activist heart of our current ecological discourse. Snyder's language and commitment as a poet and notable teacher can be understood from a transpacific perspective as a rethinking of what citizenship might mean in the global age. In 1985, I attended a five-day workshop that Snyder led at Hollyhock Institute on Cortes Island, B.C. and the experience was instrumental in helping me clarify key issues in my own life. At the heart of Snyder's vision is a nondenominational renewal of reverence for the interconnected sacredness of creation, and from his Riprap (1959) *and* Cold Mountain Poems *onward, his work has spoken to the essential, life-sustaining relationship that he argues must exist between individual, "place," and community. Our paths intersect from time to time, along with those of the broad community of writers, teachers, leaders, and other regular folks—some who also appear in this book—who have found connection through the ethical mandala of his work. We met for this interview in 1995 at the old Vance Hotel in Seattle. Snyder's essay collection* A Place in Space *had just come out and his long-awaited poetry suite* Mountains and Rivers Without End *was due to arrive soon after.*

Asked if he grows tired of talking about ecological stewardship, digging in, and coalition-building, the poet Gary Snyder responds with candor: "Am I tired of talking about it? I'm tired of doing it!" he roars. "But hey, you've got to keep doing it. That's part of politics, and politics is more than winning and losing at the polls."

These days, there's an honest, conservative-sounding ring to the politics of the celebrated Beat rebel. Gary Snyder, though, has little in common with the right-wingers who currently prevail throughout the Western world.

"Conservatism has some very valid meanings," he says. "Of course, most of the people who call themselves conservative aren't that, because they're out to extract and use, to turn a profit. That's not respecting tradition; it's not respecting heritage, anything. Curiously, eco and artist people and those who work with dharma practice are conservatives in the best sense of the word—we're trying to save a few things!

"Care for the environment is like noblesse oblige," he maintains. "You don't do it because it has to be done. You do it because it's beautiful. That's the bodhisattva spirit. The bodhisattva is not anxious to do good, or feel obligation or anything like that. In Jodo-shin Buddhism, which my wife was raised in, the bodhisattva just says, 'I picked up the tab for everybody. Goodnight folks. . . . '"

In a prodigious collection of essays published in 1990 as *The Practice of the Wild*, Gary Snyder introduced a pair of distinctive ideas to our vocabulary of ecological inquiry. Grounded in a lifetime of nature and wilderness observation, Snyder offered the "etiquette of freedom" and "practice of the wild" as root prescriptions for the overarching global crisis of our time.

Informed by East-West poetics, land and wilderness issues, anthropology, benevolent Buddhism, and Snyder's long years of familiarity with the bush and high mountain places, these principles—previously developed in his modern classics *Turtle Island*, *Earth House Hold*, and his translations of Han Shan's *Cold Mountain Poems*—point to the essential and life-sustaining relationship between place and psyche.

Such ideas have been at the heart of Snyder's work for the past forty-five years. When Jack Kerouac wrote of a new breed of counterculture hero in *The Dharma Bums*, it was a thinly veiled account of his adventures with Snyder during the mid-1950s. And while Snyder has often reminded us since of the hazards in mistaking him for that

novel's fictionalized romantic hero Japhy Ryder, Kerouac's efferves-
cent reprise of a West Coast dharma-warrior's dedication to "soil
conservation, the Tennessee Valley Authority, astronomy, geology,
Hsuan Tsung's travels, Chinese painting theory, reforestation, Oceanic
ecology and food chains" remains emblematic of the terrain Snyder
has explored in the course of his life.

One of our most active and productive poets, Gary Snyder has also
been one of our most visible. Returning to California in 1969 after a
decade abroad, spent mostly as a lay Zen Buddhist monk in Japan, he
homesteaded in the Sierras and worked the lecture trail each spring
and fall for sixteen years while raising a young family. By his own
reckoning he saw "practically every university in the United States."

Snyder's work as poet-essayist has been uncannily well-timed,
contributing to his reputation as a farseeing and weather-wise inter-
preter of cultural change. His Pulitzer Prize–winning *Turtle Island*
arrived as an avatar of the environmental movement's blooming in
the early 1970s. *The Real Work*, a meaty compendium of interviews
and talks, came five years later as an antidote to the cultural and
political vacuity that stifled North America for a decade. And with
Axe Handles he brought his spare, down-home poetic line to a new
generation in the 1980s.

In between there have been other nuggets: a fine India journal, and
the collections of poetry mirroring a life of many flavors—including
his early years as a logger, seaman, and fire-lookout. *No Nature*, a
gathering of new and selected verse in 1992, presented evidence of
how thorough and resonant Snyder's poetic voice has been. With its
title distilled from Hakuin's "Song of Zazen," the book garnered him
a National Book Award nomination.

His 1995 collection of essays *A Place in Space* brought welcome
news of what he had been thinking about in recent years. Organized
around themes of "Ethics, Esthetics and Watersheds," it opens with a
discussion of Snyder's Beat generation experience, and evolves as a
kind of flow chart in the development of his creative vision.

"I'm a poet," he explains during a meeting about the book in
Seattle, a town he knows well, having been raised in the Pacific
Northwest. "I don't write prose as process; I write it under duress. The
watershed essays in *A Place in Space*, for example, were all written
after 1990 and constitute a kind of community exercise. Many were
actually written as talks relating to specific community-based issues,
or for benefit events, so I wanted to get them out and share them

more widely. At the same time, since I quit traveling in 1987 to concentrate on finishing up my projects—some of which I began in my twenties—I've been holding a number of other uncollected prose pieces in mind.

"Thinking about how these pieces related to each other," he continues, "I began to see connections in my own thinking, and I recognized that the watershed essays explore further some of the suggestions put forward in *The Practice of the Wild*. More interestingly, I noticed how even the most oblique and diversely directed sets of ideas still had a thread that held them together. So it was a gratifying creative exercise, and a kind of personal illumination to see these threads of thought running through the material, and then more or less declaring them into the three categories of Ethics, Esthetics and Watersheds."

One essay addresses the human and physical geography alike of the pivotal North Beach area, which provided community to San Francisco's "poetry renaissance" of the 1950s—a movement essential to what would come to be called "the Beats." The Beat generation itself is explored as a perennial incarnation of a historic, creative, community-minded Otherness, and the effulgence of America's poetry scene of the early 1960s is discussed in a helpful summary that was originally published in Japanese. Newcomers to Snyder or Beat culture will appreciate these firsthand accounts of that era, as well as the insight they offer into the literary, spiritual, and political traditions that informed the period. Roughly analogous to China's Tang Dynasty or Elizabethan England, the Beat generation, Snyder writes, was not "an intellectual movement, but a creative one."

"It was simply a different time in the American economy," he explains by way of detail. "It used to be that you came into a strange town, picked up work, found an apartment, stayed a while, then moved on. Effortless. All you had to have was a few basic skills and be willing to work. That's the kind of mobility you see celebrated by Kerouac in *On the Road*. For most Americans, and in Canada, too, it was taken for granted. It gave that insouciant quality to the young working men of North America who didn't have to go to college if they wanted to get a job.

"I know this because in 1952 I was able to hitchhike into San Francisco, stay at a friend's, and get a job within three days through the employment agency. With an entry-level job, on an entry-level wage, I found an apartment on Telegraph Hill that I could afford and

I lived in the city for a year. Imagine trying to live in San Francisco or New York—any major city—on an entry-level wage now. You can't do it. Furthermore, the jobs aren't that easy to get."

The freedom and openness of the booming post–World War II economy made it possible for people such as Snyder, Kerouac, Allen Ginsberg, Lew Welch, and others to consciously disaffiliate from mainstream American dreams of respectability. And as Snyder writes, these "proletarian bohemians" chose even further disaffiliation, refusing to write "the sort of thing that middle class Communist intellectuals think proletarian literature ought to be."

"In making choices like that, we were able to choose and learn other tricks for not being totally engaged with consumer culture," he clarifies. "We learned how to live simply and were very good at it in my generation. That was what probably helped shape our sense of community. We not only knew each other, we depended on each other. We shared with each other.

"And there is a new simple living movement coming back now, I understand," he notes, "where people are getting together, comparing notes about how to live on less money, how to share, living simply." When Gary Snyder points something out, it generally warrants attention: his thinking has consistently been years ahead of the cultural learning curve. Nowhere is his prescience more obvious than in "A Virus Runs Through It," a previously unpublished review of William Burroughs' 1962 *The Ticket That Exploded*.

Snyder regarded Burroughs' psycho-portrait of a society obsessed with addiction and consumerism, "whipped up by advertising," as an omen. Understanding that Burroughs has gravely telegraphed the anti-ecological culture taking shape in America, Snyder concludes eerily that Burroughs' "evocation of the politics of addiction, mass madness, and virus panic, is all too prophetic."

"We were very aware of heroin addiction at that time," Snyder explains. "Kerouac, Ginsberg, Burroughs, Holmes, and their circle in New York became fascinated with the metaphor of addiction in the light of heroin, smack. Marijuana was not an issue, but the intense addictive quality of heroin, and the good people who were getting drawn into it, and the romance some people had for it, was a useful framework for thinking about the nature of capitalist society and the addiction to fossil fuels in the industrial sector. It was obvious."

Many of original arguments addressing pollution and our addiction to consumption have by now become mainstream: reduced fossil fuel dependence, recycling, responsible resource harvesting. Others remain works-in-progress: effective soil conservation; economics becoming a "small subbranch of ecology"; learning as individuals and families to "break the habit of acquiring unnecessary possessions"; women being totally free and equal; "cultural and individual pluralism, unified by a type of world tribal council. Division by natural and cultural boundaries rather than arbitrary political boundaries."

Engaging the themes of transformation and responsible stewardship, he writes, "If humans are to remain on earth, they must transform the five-millennia-long urbanizing civilization tradition into a new ecologically sensitive harmony-oriented wild-minded scientific-spiritual culture."

Recognizing that the global pollution problem is in fact the over-population problem, Snyder articulates that significantly reduced world population must be accomplished before nature does the trick for us. He advocates "a vigorous stand against the policy of the right wing in the Catholic hierarchy and other institutions that exercise an irresponsible social force in regard to this question"; as well as legal and voluntary abortion, the encouraging of sterilization and vasectomy programs, correction of "traditional cultural attitudes that tend to force women into childbearing," removal of income tax deductions for more than two children above a specified income level, and appropriate scaling of these deductions for lower-income families to keep them equally attentive.

As an ecological philosopher, Snyder's role has been to point out first the problems, and then the hard medicine that must be swallowed. His upaya, or skillful means of galvanizing our attention and energies toward accomplishing the goals he envisions in *A Place in Space*, is storytelling. In this regard Gary Snyder has become synonymous with integrity—a good beginning place if your wilderness poetics honor "clean-running rivers; the presence of pelican and osprey and gray whale in our lives; salmon and trout in our streams; unmuddied language and good dreams."

"My sense of the West Coast," he says, "is that it runs from somewhere about the Big Sur River—the southernmost river that salmon run in—from there north to the Straits of Georgia and beyond, to Glacier Bay in southern Alaska. It is one territory in my mind. People all relate to each other across it; we share a lot of the same concerns and text and a lot of the same trees and birds."

Raised in the Pacific Northwest, Snyder grew up in close proximity to the anthropomorphic richness of the local Native American mythology, the rain-forest totems of eagle, bear, raven, and killer whale that continue to appear in school and community insignias here as important elements of regional consciousness. It is unsurprising that they—and roustabout cousins like Coyote—have long been found at the core of Snyder's expansive vision. Literal-minded rationalists have had difficulty with Snyder's Buddhist-oriented eco-philosophy and poetics. His embrace of Native Indian lore only further ruffled orthodox literary imagination, and in the past his poetry was criticized as being thin, loose, or scattered.

As Snyder readers know, the corrective to such interpretations of his work is more fresh air and exercise. Regarding Buddhism, his take is offered simply and efficiently. "The marks of Buddhist teaching," he writes in *A Place in Space*, "are impermanence, no-self, the inevitability of suffering and connectedness, emptiness, the vastness of mind, and a way to realization."

"It seems evident," he writes, offering insight into the dynamics of his admittedly complex worldview, "that there are throughout the world certain social and religious forces that have worked through history toward an ecologically and culturally enlightened state of affairs. Let these be encouraged: Gnostics, hip Marxists, Teilhard de Chardin Catholics, Druids, Taoists, Biologists, Witches, Yogins, Bhikkus, Quakers, Sufis, Tibetans, Zens, Shamans, Bushmen, American Indians, Polynesians, Anarchists, Alchemists . . . primitive cultures, communal and ashram movements, cooperative ventures."

"Idealistic, these?" he chuckles when asked about such alternative "Third Force" social movements. "In some cases the vision can be mystical; it can be Blake. It crops up historically with William Penn and the Quakers trying to make the Quaker communities in Pennsylvania a righteous place to live—treating the native peoples properly in the process. It crops up in the utopian and communal experience of Thoreau's friends in New England.

"As utopian and impractical as it might seem, it comes through history as a little dream of spiritual elegance and economic simplicity, and collaboration and cooperating communally—all of those things together. It may be that it was the early Christian vision. Certainly it was one part of the early Buddhist vision. It turns up as a reflection of the integrity of tribal culture, as a reflection of the kind of energy that would try to hold together the best lessons of tribal cultures even within the overwhelming power and dynamics of civilization."

Any paradigm for a truly healthy culture, Gary Snyder argues, must begin with surmounting narrow personal identity and finding a commitment to place. Characteristically, he finds a way of remaking the now tired concept of "sense of place" into something fresh and vital. The rural model of place, he emphasizes, is no longer the only model for the healing of our culture.

"Lately, I've been noticing how many more people who tend toward counterculture thinking are turning up at readings and book signings in the cities and the suburbs," he says. "They're everywhere. What I emphasize more and more is that a bioregional consciousness is equally powerful in a city or in the suburbs. Just as a watershed flows through each of these places, it also includes them.

"One of the models I use now is how an ecosystem resembles a *mandala*," he explains. "A big Tibetan mandala has many small figures as well as central figures, and each of them has a key role in the picture: they're all essential. The whole thing is an educational tool for understanding—that's where the ecosystem analogy comes in. Every creature, even the little worms and insects, has value. Everything is valuable—that's the measure of the system."

To Snyder, value also translates as responsibility. Within his approach to digging in and committing to a place is the acceptance of responsible stewardship. Snyder maintains that it is through this engaged sense of effort and practice—participating in what he salutes as "the tiresome but tangible work of school boards, county supervisors, local foresters, local politics"—that we find our real community, our real culture.

"Ultimately, values go back to our real interactions with others," he says. "That's where we live, in our communities."

"Living in place" then, is a process—one that redefines our personal stake in the community, for in the larger Buddhist sense, community includes all the beings—the "ten thousand things" of everyday, garden-variety existence. Our job then is to develop community networks that extend beyond the obvious political divisions of age, class, race, gender and employment—boundaries that keep us apart, and which Snyder believes are brought to us by the media.

"You know, I want to say something else, too," he continues. "In the past months and years Carole, my wife, has been amazing. I do my teaching and my work with the Yuba Watershed Institute, but she's incredible; she puts out so much energy. . . . One of the things that makes it possible for me, my neighbors, to do all this is that the husbands and wives really are partners; they help out and trade off. They develop different areas of expertise and they help keep each other from burning out. It's a great part of being a family and having a marriage—becoming fellow warriors, side to side."

Snyder's views on family once raised eyebrows. In an essay entitled "Passage to More Than India" published in the *Evergreen Review* in 1968, he stated flatly that "the modern American family is the smallest and most barren family that has ever existed . . . industrial society indeed appears to be finished." Through the years his recommendations concerning new cultural approaches to the idea of family and relationships have customarily had a pagan, tribal flavor. These days, he calls it community.

"I'm learning, as we all do, what it takes to have an ongoing relationship with our children," he relates. "I have two grown sons, two stepdaughters, a grown nephew, and all their friends whom I know. We're still helping each other out. There's a real cooperative spirit. There's a fatherly responsibility there, and a warm, cooperative sense of interaction, of family as extended family, one that moves imperceptibly toward community and a community-values sense.

"So, I'm urging people not to get stuck with that current American catchphrase 'family values,' and not to throw it away either, but to translate it into community values. Neighborhood values are ecosystem values, because they include all the beings.

"What I suspect may emerge in the political spectrum is a new kind of conservative, one which is socially liberal, in the specific sense that it will be free of racial or religious prejudice. The bugaboo, the one really bad flaw of the right-wing, except for the Libertarians, is its racist and anti-Semitic and antipersonal liberty tone.

"A political spectrum that has respect for traditions, and at the same time is nonracist, and is open and tolerant about different cultures, is an interesting development. I'd be willing to bet that it's in the process of emerging, similar in a way to the European Green Parties that say, 'We're neither on the left nor the right: we're in front.'"

"One of the things I'm trying to do, and I believe it's the right way to work," he says, "is to be nonadversarial—to go about it as tai chi, as ju-jitsu: to go with the direction of a local community issue, say, and change it slightly. We don't have to run head-on. We can say to the other party, 'You've got a lot of nice energy; let's see if we can run this way. . . . '"

Yet as anyone involved in community and regional activism learns from experience, amicable resolutions of this type are not always the result. "Sometimes you do have to go head to head on an issue," he nods reluctantly, "and that's kind of fun, too. 'Showing up' is good practice."

Snyder remembers a fight some four years ago over open-pit mining. "I was the lead person on this one, to get an initiative on the ballot that would ban open-pit mining, or at least put a buffer zone around any open-pit mine. The mining companies from out of town spent a lot of money and did some really intense, last minute, nasty style campaigning, so we lost at the polls.

"But not a single open-pit mine has been tried in our county since then. We understand from our interactions with these people that we won their respect. They were smart enough to see that they may have won at the polls, but we were ready to raise money and willing to fight. That's standing up."

With the growing importance of community coalition-building, Snyder says he is finding it increasingly useful to narrow his ideas concerning bioregionalism, or his notion of a practice of the wild, down to a shared neighborhood level.

"That's why I talk about watersheds," he explains. "Symbolically and literally they're the mandalas of our lives. They provide the very idea of the watershed's social enlargement, and quietly present an entry into the spiritual realm that nobody has to think of or recognize as being spiritual.

"The watershed is our only local Buddha mandala—one that gives us all, human and nonhuman, a territory to interact in. That is the beginning of dharma citizenship: not membership in a social or national sphere, but in a larger community citizenship. In other words, a *sangha*; a local dharma community. All of that is in there, like Dogen when he says, 'When you find your place, practice begins.'"

Thirteenth-century master Dogen Zenji is a classical Asian voice that Snyder has discussed frequently in recent years. "There are several levels of meaning in what Dogen says. There's the literal meaning, as in when you settle down somewhere. This means finding the right teaching, the right temple, the right village. Then you can get serious about your practice.

"Underneath, there's another level of implication: you have to understand that there are such things as places. That's where Americans have yet to get to. They don't understand that there are places. So I quote Dogen and people say, 'What do you mean, you have to find your place? Anywhere is okay for dharma practice because it's spiritual.' Well, yes, but not just any place. It has to be a place that you've found yourself. It's never abstract, always concrete."

If embracing the responsibility of the place and the moment is his prescription, a key principle in this creative stewardship lies in waking up to "wild mind." *A Place in Space* begins with a note to this effect, proposing that "art, beauty, and craft have always drawn on the self-organizing 'wild' side of language and mind."

"The practice of meditation," Snyder writes, "must have a little to do with getting beyond 'wild mind' in language. Spending quality time with your own mind is humbling and, like travel, broadening. You find that there's no one in charge, and are reminded that no thought lasts for long."

Laughing a little, he clarifies that "wild" in this context does not mean "chaotic, excessive or crazy. It means self-organizing. It means elegantly self-disciplined, self-regulating, self-maintained. That's what wilderness is. Nobody has to do the management plan for it. So I say to people, let's trust in the self-disciplined elegance of wild mind. Practically speaking, a life that is vowed to simplicity, appropriate boldness, good humor, gratitude, unstinting work and play, and lots of walking, brings us close to the actually existing world and its wholeness."

This is Gary Snyder's wild medicine. From the beginning it has been devotion to this quality that has served as his bedrock of practice, his way of carving out a place of freedom in the wall of American culture. In his omission of the personal in favor of the path, he exemplifies the basics of the Zen tradition in which he trained.

The influx of trained Asian teachers of the Buddhadharma to the West in recent years has raised questions about whether the first homespun blossoming of Beat-flavored Buddhism in the fifties actually included the notion of practice. As one who was there and has paid the dues in both East and West, Snyder's response is heartening.

"In Buddhism and Hinduism, there are two streams: the more practice-oriented, and the more devotional streams," he explains. "Technically speaking, the two tendencies are called *bhakta* and *jnana*. Bhakta means devotional; jnana means wisdom/practice. Contemporary Hinduism, for example, is almost entirely devotional— the bhakta tradition.

"Catholicism is a devotional religion, too, and Jack Kerouac's Buddhism had the flavor of a devotional Buddhism. In Buddhism, the idea that anybody can do practice is strongly present.

In Catholicism, practice is almost entirely thought of as entering an order or as becoming a lay novitiate of an order. So that explains Jack's devotional flavor. There's nothing wrong with devotional Buddhism. It is its own creative religious approach, and it's very much there in Tibetan Buddhism, too.

"Our Western Buddhism has been strongly shaped by late nineteenth- and early twentieth-century Asian intellectuals," he notes. "D.T. Suzuki was an intellectual strongly influenced by Western thought. And the same is true of other early interpreters of Buddhism to the West.

"We came as Westerners to Buddhism generally with an educated background," Snyder notes. "So we have tended to overemphasize the intellectual, and also the spiritual sides of it with the model of Zen at hand, without realizing that a big part of the flavor of Buddhism, traditionally and historically, is devotional. This is not necessarily tied to having a lot of practice, but is tied to having an altar in the house—putting flowers in front of it every day, burning incense in front of it every day, having the children bow and burn incense before it. The family may also observe certain Buddhist holy days such as the Buddha's birthday by visiting a temple together, and so forth.

"With that perspective in mind, it isn't so easy to say, 'Oh well, Jack Kerouac wasn't a real Buddhist.' He was a devotional Buddhist, and like many Asians do, he mixed up his Buddhism with several different religions. So it's okay; there's nothing wrong with that. You can be a perfectly good Buddhist without necessarily doing a lot of exercises and sitting and yoga; you can be equally a good Buddhist by keeping flowers on your altar, or in winter dry grass or cedar twigs. The mindfulness that goes into keeping your house like a Buddhist house is very important, very interesting.

"I know people who think they're Buddhist—you know, who do the sitting and that, but who forget to have an altar in their house because they think it's too much like religion. That's Western intellectualism. There's a big tendency right now in Western Buddhism to psychologize it—to try and take the superstition, the magic, the irrationality out of it and make it into a kind of therapy. You see that a lot," he says. "Part of my Buddhist teaching out in the world these days is to say to people, 'Are you, do you want to be, a Buddhist?' They say, 'Yeah.' And I say, 'Well, you really don't have to be, but if you do, then find out what it is to keep an altar in the house and to change the flowers and make that the first step in your practice: something that is obviously religious.

"Let me say that I'm grateful for the fact that I lived in Asia for so long, and hung out with Asian Buddhists," he summarizes. "I appreciate that Buddhism is a whole practice and isn't just limited to the lecture side of it, that it has stories and superstition and ritual and goofiness like that. I love that aspect of it more and more."

At age seventy-one, Gary Snyder works now from the zenith of his professional form. For many years he has taught creative writing at the University of California, leading workshops and participating in the interdisciplinary Nature and Culture program. Five years ago, his long-awaited volume *Mountains and Rivers Without End* was finally published. A sequence of forty-five poems, portions of it had appeared intermittently ever since Jack Kerouac first dropped word of it in *The Dharma Bums*.

Snyder acknowledges that he worked "like a demon" from 1987 onward to complete his late flurry of masterworks. "I realized I wasn't going to live forever and that I'd started a lot of parallel projects, with lots of interesting notes to each one, so it'd be a pity not to put all that information to good use. When the chance to teach at UC Davis came, it gave me control over the rest of my time and I used it to finish these books. [With] *Mountains and Rivers* done, I don't have to write anything further. Anything after it is for fun. Maybe I won't be a writer any more. Maybe I'll clean out my barn."

Aging and health, though, are not at issue with Snyder. He works at keeping in good condition and in 1995 still spent three weeks hiking in the Himalayas with a group of family and friends. "We trekked up to base camp at Everest; went over 18,000 feet three times, and were seven days above 16,000 feet," he says with obvious relish. "We went from Namche Bazaar to Tengboche, then up the Khumbu drainage and from there crossed over an 18,000-foot pass to the Imja drainage up to the base of a mountain called Island Peak. We were with Sherpas all the way. Everybody was in pretty good shape and I only lost four pounds in a month, so I'm not thinking a whole lot about aging. . . . It's not the kind of thing I'd start to give lectures on for the aging baby boom generation."

Snyder's journey provided him with insights into the questions of karma and reincarnation, which eco-philosopher Joanna Macy believes may hold special relevance for North Americans. Macy argues that deeply ingrained American frontier values such as individualism, personal mobility and independence may contribute to the idea that "[i]f this is our only one-time life, then we don't have to care about the planet."

"The concept of reincarnation in India can literally shape the way one lives in the world," Snyder notes, "and many Tibetans also believe in reincarnation quite literally. So in that frame of mind, the world becomes completely familiar. You sit down and realize that 'I've been men, women, animals: there are no forms that are alien to me.'

"That's why everyone in India looks like they're living in eternity. They walk along so relaxed, so confident, so unconcerned about their poverty or their illness, or whatever it is, even if they're beggars. It goes beyond just giving you a sense of concern for the planet; it goes so far as to say, 'Planets come and go. . . . ' It's pretty powerful stuff. It's also there in classical Buddhism where people say, 'I've had enough of experience.' That's where a lot of Buddhism in India starts—'I want out of the meat wheel of existence,' as Jack Kerouac says."

An ecosystem, too, Snyder concludes, can be seen as "just a big metabolic wheel of energies being passed around and around. You can see it as a great dance, a great ceremony; you can feel either really at home with it, or step out of the circle."

Somewhere, early on, Gary Snyder wrote that the great mercy of the West has been social revolution—its changes bringing greater freedom, choice, and mobility into individual life. The great mercy of the East, he noted, is its tradition of bringing individual insight into the self, nature and the void. In a warm account that closes *A Place In Space*, Snyder writes of the quarter-century he has spent at Kitkitdizze, his home-place in the Sierras, and of his attempt to integrate the best lineages of East and West into his life and work. The essay offers a rare, demystifying glimpse into what is important for Gary Snyder about the *mana* of this precious planet.

"We are all indigenous," he reminds us. So it is appropriate that in relearning the lessons of fox and blue-jay, or city crows and squirrels—"all members present at the assembly"—that we are promised neither too little, nor too much for our perseverance. This poet, who for so many now reads like an old friend, invites us to make only sense. After all, in recommitting to this continent place by place, he reckons, "We may not transform reality, but we may transform ourselves. And if we transform ourselves, we might just change the world a bit."

Seattle

Chapter 3

Grounded in Humanity

Gary Snyder on *Back on the Fire*

*W*ith *his essay collection entitled* Back on the Fire *(2007), Snyder again demonstrated why he is one of North America's most beloved literary elders. Written with wide-ranging insight that reveals Snyder's mature, but still-evolving approach to thinking about ecology, poetry, and citizenship, the essays include poignant autobiographical reflections on his Pacific Northwest origins, extensive anthropological travels, old friends from the poetry trade, and meditations on building sustainable community in the rugged landscapes of the West. Grounded in humanity, these searching—and sometimes provocative—writings also serve as a call to action, inviting us to make friends with imperma-nence and error while working to make a difference against the war on nature. We spoke in a small courtyard in Davis, California in the late spring of 2007 with Gary's son Gen, and my son Patrick attending the conversation, as well as contributing to the interview's generational ladder of awareness.*

TC: *Gary, about five major essays in* Back on the Fire *touch on forest fires, and you observe how attitudes have evolved toward fire suppres-sion in various types of land-use areas. You also propose the idea of using fire as a metaphor for looking at deeply held beliefs that we may be obliged to change in light of certain experiences. Was that a conscious part of your thinking in these essays?*

GS: Yes, that's definitely part of how my thinking along these lines evolved, although I was already considering things in this light years ago in terms of Buddhist thought, in which there is no radical black-and-white/good-and-evil dualism, and in which you are urged to look on even the most negative kinds of behavior and negative kinds of thinking in the light of "what can we learn from them?"—to think if it is possible to make them into allies. You know, at a talk someone once asked Thich Nhat Hanh, "What do I do with my anger?" He said, "Take it by the hand; think of it as your little brother. . . ." And then work with it. . . . The same is true, ultimately, about the way we think about death. We live in a society that demonizes death. We have a medical system that feels every time somebody has died, that it has failed. They can only think about keeping you alive, they can't think about helping you die. And if the question of death goes beyond that, they hand it over to religious people who don't know how to handle it very well, or who have a kind of ideology that they translate it into. So that's all part of the thinking here.

TC: *You were once a young lookout who was involved in fire suppression. You note how you believed then that it was the right thing. Certain assumptions we've had about forestry practice appear to be changing.*

GS: They're changing years later. Not suddenly. The essays talk about this, but from different sides, and not all in the same way. If you look at the last line of that one essay it talks about "Following the Dao."

TC: *In "The Ark of the Sierra" you note that the language used in fire-fighting parallels the old Cold War rhetoric.*

GS: That's interestingly true if you back into the literature, the practices, the protocols. In their fire suppression work, the U.S. Forest Service has one specific division of its budget and its personnel directed and trained for fighting fires. This has been true for years and they've got all the equipment. In the discussion, the planning, the approach, and in the seminars on handling a fire—the way you study how the fire is proceeding, what do you do during a fire, how you go about attacking it, how you distribute—it's all military language. For decades there was nothing in that language or in that line of thought that suggested there was anything we could learn from fire, or that there was anything about fire that had a positive place in the ecosystem. So that's part of the problem. In particular, with the Cold War going on for a number of years after WWII, the language of forest fire and of wildfire fighting almost exactly paralleled the language of the Cold War. The language of the war on drugs does the same—"we must oppose this enemy." There's a full-page ad that has recently been coming out in the *New York Times*, which says, "Say No To *No*." It's a coalition against the idea of having a war on drugs. This is a shift in thinking that's going on at several levels.

TC: *Currently in British Columbia and Alberta we have a serious pine beetle infestation.*

GS: We have beetles, too. Not too heavily. Just enough. Let me ask you, is that lodgepole pine or is it ponderosa pine?—because lodgepole pine beetle kills are as much a problem now up in Idaho, Montana, and Wyoming.

TC: *We don't seem to be getting the kind of winter cold snaps that help control the beetles.*

GS: Yes, maybe it's also partly climate change. It's hard to know what brings on a huge beetle infestation like that. With ponderosa pine we have western bark beetle and Ips beetle infestations periodically, but it's only really severe during drought periods when the water levels in the soil are lower. Then the sap pressure up in the bark in the tree is lower, so that the sap ooze can't push the beetles out. We know that ponderosa pine gets hit with more beetles during drought. There's also some consequences of air pollution caused by cars. It weakens the pine trees. Up in your area, the question of which species is involved is a serious question. It could be climate change. I don't see fire suppression per se causing that. They do say that in Yellowstone National Park, where they let a big forest fire go twenty years ago, that at the time there was quite an outcry from the public saying, "Whoa, we shouldn't let the fire burn like that." But it's coming back beautifully now—strong and young and green. There's the thought that it was simply overdue for a fire. And that maybe is the case where you are.

TC: *That's part of the debate.*

GS: We do know the answer for the Sierra type and southerly ponderosa pine forests. We don't need to wait for a total stand-destroying fire if we can get in there and start thinning and burning under it ourselves. We also know that it's the type of forest that can survive big fires. I don't know if any lodgepole pine forest can ever survive a big fire. They grow so close together. You see, the ponderosa pine will grow very far apart. What happens in west-side Douglas fir forests is another question altogether. They have stand-destroying fires, you know, like every thousand years. But it always comes back. What the future holds, we don't know.

TC: *It's a touchy one, but you've suggested tolerating small fires and reducing the undergrowth load in the mid-Sierras.*

GS: It's a complex issue. In the USA it boils down to this: national parks are where you totally maintain wilderness. That means whatever the natural process, you let it run through. So that could be a beetle infestation or it could be a forest fire: you don't try to stop it—whether it's insects or anything else. That's what they did in Yellowstone; they let it burn. That's what they do in Yosemite National Park. If a fire starts there from lightning or from any reason at all, they'll just let it burn. [It depends] on the type of forest you have—if it's a more variable forest, you'll never get a totally stand-destroying fire. What you'll get is a mosaic—green patches, yellow patches, black patches, brown patches. These are very healthy. Deer will come back throughout the whole thing. The mosaic is a healthy condition because it allows for a lot of different habitat for a lot of different species. And you get your green survivors. It's to the advantage of towns and communities and to the advantage of the long-term timber industry, and to the concept of sustainable forestry, to have small fires and to set small fires, and to let small fires burn, but to stop fires from burning that might get into a huge fire. Now, this is not *wilderness management*. True wilderness management is letting whatever happens happen. It's all contentious stuff when it comes right down to it. Most of what I've written in the book addresses California-type, Sierra-type forest issues that would also be replicated in the Rockies, and in parts of Mexico, and on the east side of Washington, Oregon, and British Columbia, but not on the west side.

TC: *A line in one of the essays goes, "and not second-guessing God." That's an interesting line to hear from Snyder.*

GS: That was a talk I gave to a diverse group that included county supervisors, timber industry people, Forest Service people, Bureau of Land Management people, California Division of Forestry, and small-business people in Nevada City, California. That whole metaphor was a Christian metaphor. If God didn't want—and I don't remember quite what I said—rattlesnakes, centipedes, poisonous lizards, cougars, grizzly bears, [and] weasels on the earth, he wouldn't have put them on the ark. That's what we have to think about—there's your Christian argument for biodiversity. If they're here, it means God put them on the ark, so I guess we'd better take care of them. That's why I say, "Maybe we'd better not second-guess God." I'm borrowing religious language for my own purposes.

TC: *It's a sidebar issue, but you note the irony of people who are from more urban or suburban areas moving into more edgy rural environments—folks "who are quick to love nature, but have little concern for the local resource economy."*

GS: That's a tough point. I'm speaking from both sides. [These are] suburban-type people who come into Nevada, El Dorado, or Placer County. They say, "We love nature, but we don't like the gravel industry"—getting gravel out of old riverbeds. Or, "We don't like any mining and we don't want logging anymore." Well, that's the old resource economy. There is a place for it. On the other side, the resource economy has to learn to modify itself, to calm down, to be quieter, to drive more slowly, not to log on a Sunday, all those things; to use quieter chainsaws.

TC: *So there's a way to make money and make sense, too.*

GS: There has to be. These trees are going to keep growing. People are going to keep using lumber. So we have to balance how we're going to take it out in a way that we can all live with. Some of the essays in *Back on the Fire* were written ten years ago and I took a lot of hits over them. But things are changing. A subject that people won't let you talk about one year, will be what everybody agrees is the right thing ten years later.

TC: *Your essay "Ecology, Literature and the New World Disorder" notes how the Greeks had a mythology that tied people to the natural world. Do you see this as part of a new meta-narrative for, say, the global future?*

GS: The environmental movement isn't standing still in terms of its idea systems. In terms of negotiating the troubled waters between religion and Darwinism, between spirituality and science, all of this is being worked on; people are living through it. At the moment, when people talk about global interconnection, there are probably two rather different meanings. One is economic interconnectedness, business interconnectedness, corporate interconnectedness, as a model for the twenty-first century. We're always going to be economically interconnected; that's the idea of globalization. Another suggestion is that traditional nation-state boundaries and nationalistic sentiments are outmoded, that the nation state is retro, and that the model for the future will be the city-state—the Singapore, the Hong Kong, the Venice or Athens or Amsterdam of old, where the city was a center of trade, finance, and learning, and when they didn't think in terms of nation-states and state boundaries. That's an interesting shift.

TC: *The nation-state idea has been around a while; since, what was it, the Treaty of Westphalia in 1648?*

GS: Yes, it drew up the principles of "how we should conduct war from now on." Sort of civilized it a bit.

TC: *The European Community is already working with the concept of "pooled sovereignty."*

GS: Right, so let's think of its equivalence in nature and ecology. Interconnectedness is, initially, the simple equality of the physical universe, and in particular the equality of the biological universe, which does not operate by any one single set of boundaries. Migrating tundra swans, cranes, ducks, and geese will go from Siberia, Alaska, or Canada to southern California; that's one of the larger models of bioregional transit. Then there are caribou migrations, salmon migrations—everybody is overlapping in very interesting ways. Through all that, one can chart out how energy is transferred from one organism to another, through food chains and energy pyramids. This is what people are trying to understand and visualize in terms of ecology. *Eco*-logy and *eco*-nomics have the Greek root, which is oikos, household. Years ago, one of my funny little dumb formulas was, "we have ecology; there's the possibility of a sacred ecology; eventually we'll have a sacred economics." That will be when the insight of ecology, the spiritual obligations of ecology, and the real potentialities of economics are brought together. But that's way off into the future. Meanwhile, globalization is kind of a disaster. This morning on NPR, there was a report on the vitamin industry. It said that what we don't realize is that right now, almost all the vitamins used in the western world come from China. And China has them all because they bid low on everything. They've lowered the price on everything. It started out with vitamin C at $10 a kilogram. Now from China it's $2 a kilo. The problem is that so many of their products are polluted. They have poisons in them, and nobody knows which is which, or how to get them out. The United States government has cut way back on its food investigation laboratories and is continuing to do so. So we've gotten ourselves into a jam. We can't even de-globalize that yet. We could have seen it coming if we'd paid attention to the inadequate Chinese system for evaluating itself. The Chinese don't put strict standards on how they make these things, and we don't look at them either. Now they're poisoning the world. That's globalization.

The paradox is that we have a society, a national polity that has certain values and standards, and people all believe in that. Then you have corporate philosophy and globalization, and they run exactly 180 degrees opposite to each other. The nature of corporations and globalization is to maximize profit at any cost; they have no concern for the integrity of their own country or its values. That is the contradiction that we're living right on top of. I was in North Carolina three weeks ago in a town called Hickory where they told me twenty thousand jobs had been lost in the last three years. I asked what kind of jobs these were. They said they were in the furniture industry; it's all gone to China and it's being sold out of Walmart. In many ways, that's what globalization has done. I don't think we should look at that as a positive variety of interconnection. It's not fairly weighted. Another principle that is coming into play more lately is "eat locally, buy locally"; there's an economic and ecological principle that's worth returning to. Especially when you figure if energy prices keep going up, it will add a great deal onto the cost of importing stuff from China. The costs of producing things locally, at least in the Western hemisphere, are going to be a lot more attractive.

TC: *You tell a wonderful little story in "Toward the Thousand Year Forest Plan" about an old pine tree in a Korean nunnery. Once a year they pour a gallon of rice liquor around the root perimeter to "cheer it up."*

GS: All of those East Asian Buddhists are also animists, you know. Naturally. It's true! And so are the Greeks.

TC: *A couple of literary items: Robert Duncan and Jack Spicer pop up a time or two in your new book. What sense did you have of these fellow poets?*

GS: I went to the Bay Area when I was twenty-one. I didn't know anybody there; I was interested in studying Asian languages, but I was also writing poetry, and I was a bohemian, and I lived in the bohemian quarter over in North Beach. I got an apartment there. Pretty soon I was meeting the literary crowd, and before I knew it I was at parties and bars where Duncan and Spicer were hanging out, and I got to know them all, and Kenneth Rexroth. They accepted me and read my poetry and we talked back and forth about it. It was a couple of years later that Allen Ginsberg and Jack Kerouac came to town, but we already had a lively poetic community. I gave a seminar on this a few years ago, and eventually maybe I'll write an essay on it. But those names come up because they were very familiar to me and I count them as real teachers.

TC: *Were you all poetry buddies or was there a sense of something larger?*

GS: There was a sense of community. After the *Six Gallery Reading* [in 1955] suddenly it all became extremely well-known, but there was a powerful movement there already. There's a book about this by Michael Davidson—*Poetry and Community in Mid-Twentieth Century San Francisco*. He gives credit to all of those guys. He especially gives credit to Philip Whalen and points out that Ginsberg was a great entrepreneur and a great publicist, as well as a fine poet.

TC: *In terms of activism, you observe that in difficult times what writers and artists can do is to simply "bear witness"—to not forget.*

GS: That's really true. We shouldn't forget that this is an old role of the artist throughout history.

TC: *Haiku is taught in every elementary school nowadays. You note Yves Bonnefoy's remark that "haiku is a necessary awareness that can only remain central to the West's poetic thought."*

GS: I think it's on its way, but I wouldn't say it's anywhere near there yet. This doesn't translate into consciousness and respect for that idea in the English department, or in the Comparative Literature department, or in the *New York Review of Books*, where they want to see more irony and intellect. The postmodern mental habit is anti-simplicity, among other things.

TC: *In one essay you bring up "eco-criticism." Does referring to eco-literature in terms of literary theory finally give it academic respectability?*

GS: Most modernists are circling around eco-criticism like vultures around a dead cow, looking to see, "Is there anything we can make use of in this?"

TC: *You have new editions out soon of your* Passage Through India *and your classic work on Haida mythology*—He Who Hunted Birds in His Father's Village. *Dealing with aboriginal material can be tricky. Our Canadian poet, Robert Bringhurst, received plenty of critical feedback over his acclaimed Haida translations, which Margaret Atwood champions as North American equivalents of* Beowulf.

GS: I know a little about Haida Gwaii [formerly the Queen Charlotte Islands] because I wrote my book on Haida mythology and I've got nothing but negative feedback about that—I even got it before Bringhurst, so now we both get it. He's written the foreword, the introduction, to the new reissue of my book, and I've talked to Jack Shoemaker, publisher of the new Counterpoint Books about publishing Bringhurst's latest book, *The Tree of Meaning.* It surprises me that he is still unknown south of the border. This'll be his first serious book appearance in the U.S. The new edition of *Passage Through India*, by the way, contains over sixty photographs that were previously unpublished.

TC: *This year marks the fortieth anniversary of San Francisco's "Summer of Love." Do you have any sense of the importance of that time?*

GS: I looked in on it. I was in the Bay Area, from Japan, for a while in the spring of '67 and was present at the Human Be-In at Golden Gate Park. I blew the conch to open and close it. And I chanted some dharanis in Sino-Japanese on the microphone, and Allen Ginsberg was doing something. So I got to see the way all those kids looked and they were a pretty sight. There was a lot of color in the clothing, a lot of invention and imagination in the way everyone was doing things. The girls were stunning; the guys looked great, too, and they were all friendly with each other. So I imagine they had a really great summer, but I was back in Japan by then!

TC: *Last point: part of your skill has been to discuss complex ecological issues and still manage to set them within a context that lay-readers can follow and absorb. Good back-catchers do this in baseball; they signal and backstop play for the whole field.*

GS: I use a few baseball expressions, but they're really common usage. One of the things I've been trying to do for a long time is to find a vocabulary, a way to talk and bring images out that will communicate from my rural, backcountry, out-in-the-woods upbringing and family culture to the intellectual and literary worlds that I've also lived in on the West Coast, with the intention of bringing the whole West Coast culture closer together. That's what I hope this book does for California. That it makes it possible for academics, businesspeople, loggers, Sierra miners, to realize they're together in the same place.

Davis, CA

Chapter 4

A Bloomsday Interview with Joanne Kyger

I don't think it was until I moved to Bolinas in 1969 that I really entered into a close relationship with the land around me in my writing. About the birds who live here, to this day the quail are probably my closest neighbors.

"*P*oetry has a lot to do with awakening," Joanne Kyger has noted. *I came to appreciate this while teaching a humanities seminar at Simon Fraser University in Vancouver. The readings included a constellation of writers associated with "San Francisco: the Athens of the American West," a large number of whom were Buddhist-influenced. I noticed how young male students gravitated to work by Jack Kerouac, Allen Ginsberg, Gary Snyder, Lawrence Ferlinghetti, or Kenneth Rexroth; by contrast, female students responded strongly to the poetry and poetics of Joanne Kyger and Diane di Prima. Accordingly, I began paying closer attention to the transpacific inflections that percolate through the work of other female writers like Maxine Hong Kingston, Amy Tan, Alice Walker, Jane Hirschfield, and bell hooks. In June 2008, Joanne Kyger was a featured speaker at The Beats In India, an Asia Centre symposium in New York. The event celebrated the journey made in 1962 by Kyger, her then-husband Snyder, and fellow American poets Ginsberg and Peter Orlovsky, and addressed "what drew the Beats to India and how they inspired successive generations of Americans to turn to the East for spiritual and creative wisdom." There was a sense of historical importance about the gathering. Two days later on Bloomsday, I spoke with Kyger at the loft home office of Vincent Katz, publisher of Kyger's poetry collection,* Not Veracruz *(Libellum Books).*

TC: *Joanne, you've recently come out with your "big" book—About Now: Collected Poems, at 800 pages. When Allen Ginsberg came out with his Collected Poems back in '84, it seemed monumental. Here you've been at it all the while, too, quietly, steadily plugging away. Any thoughts on the role of the "little books" that individually reflect a life in the craft and that cumulatively shape your masterwork?*

JK: Yes, the smaller books are the ones you can pick up and carry around. They have an intimate feel. I call my *Collected Poems* a "doorstop"—and there's Ted Berrigan's collected work and Philip Whalen's, as well. These books are useful; they're a kind of library work—you can refer to them, but they're not intimate in the way that you can easily handle them. I find that when I want to refer to a poem, I generally go back to the small press edition because I know where that poem is.

TC: *Your early San Francisco Bay Area involvement with the craft brought you into association with the Duncan-Spicer group. Several of those personalities would move on to Canada and become citizens— George Stanley, Robin Blaser, Stan Persky. Can you tell us something about the mood and flavor of those times?*

JK: Around '57 I moved to North Beach from Santa Barbara where I'd been a university student studying philosophy and literature. Paul Wienpahl, my philosophy professor, was teaching Wittgenstein, and Heidigger's thoughts about "being" and "nothingness." Then D.T. Suzuki's translations of Zen Buddhist texts became available, [and] it seemed the inevitable next step. It was through John Weiners and Joe Dunn that I met the rest of the people in an informal Sunday group, taught by Jack Spicer and Robert Duncan. Everyone hung out in a little bar called the Place. George Stanley was there, Dora Fitzgerald, who was married to Harold Dull, Ebbe Borregaard, and the others. After Black Mountain broke up in '56, a lot of poets followed Duncan out to San Francisco. Also painters like Tom Field and Paul Alexander. Spicer and Duncan started teaching these various poets informally and I guess that's when Spicer started the Magic workshop, of which I wasn't a part. There's a very readable book about this period by Lewis Ellingham and Kevin Killian called *Poet Be Like God*. It's a somewhat picaresque view of what was going on in the Duncan-Spicer group scene at that time.

TC: *What was it like to be young and hungry for poetry within such an artistic milieu?*

JK: It was totally exciting. It was like going to "actual" school. I had a small apartment obtained from a friend on Columbus Avenue, a few blocks away from City Lights bookstore in North Beach. I was working at Brentano's bookstore and the whole "Howl" trial had come down at that time. Before this, in Santa Barbara I'd associated with a young group of writers and with a sculptor named Mark DiSuvero, who became fairly well known. With a few others we started their first literary magazine. My writing hadn't really developed yet; actually, I wrote a column, humorous journalism, for the college newspaper. I still wasn't sure what poetry was.

TC: *You'd studied with Hugh Kenner at UC Santa Barbara though.*

JK: Yes, he was teaching freshman English, introducing Pound and W.C. Williams. At this time Pound wasn't even allowed to be taught at any of the U.S. schools. Kenner was Canadian, the campus was fairly new, and there were a few people from Germany who had come and who were specifically interested in studying Pound, so Kenner was something of an anomaly. I didn't know how to write. I wrote with a great deal of emotion, and I wrote for the school newspaper, but I didn't know how to spell, and I didn't write in real sentences. Nothing I wrote was polished and Kenner thought I wrote a column that parodied him—I was reading James Thurber and Robert Benchley, a lot of satirists—and he gave me a D in freshman English! When I came to San Francisco and read "Howl," that was such a different order of emotion and language—I was immediately thrilled by it. Then I began participating in this small group after being introduced by John Wieners and Joe Dunn, who had been students at Black Mountain College. Jack Spicer was encouraging Joe Dunn to print a small series of White Rabbit books, these little 25¢ books— they did Charles Olson, Jack Spicer's *After Lorca*, Borregaard, Stanley. . . . So these little books were coming around and they were easy to read. I was still thinking about what poetry was, and by reading some of my own pieces, which I had started to write, I found myself being accepted. I was on my way then.

TC: *Any reflections about the larger influence of that period on your own work, your own life and times?*

JK: Well, I went to Japan [in] January 1960, after I'd met Gary Snyder in '58. He'd come back over from Japan and read at one of the Sunday meetings and I was really taken by him and his poetry, his direction.

When I came to North Beach in '57, everyone said, "Oh, you should have been here last year; Kerouac was here, everyone was here then."

TC: Speaking of Kerouac and Snyder, there's a reference in one of your early poems from "Journal, Oct. 9, 1958" to the "Dharma Committee." What was that?

JK: I think that was when *The Dharma Bums* had come out. Spicer has this Dada surrealist sense, you know, having encounters in bars, totally nonacademic environments. He loved to set us up. The Dharma Committee was kind of a joke, like Spicer saying, "So you're interested in Snyder, are you—well, let's start a Dharma Committee." I didn't even know what dharma meant. Spicer really encouraged this surrealist humor to go on.

TC: It's surely one of the earlier references to dharma in American culture, but that's Kerouac for you.

JK: Jack had a very keen ear and was writing things down all the time in his pocket notebook. It's pretty clear if you read his letters that he was writing exact renditions of what was going on. He was one of the best typists I've ever seen. He was able to transcribe very quickly what was going on, to go with whatever he saw, and with such style. He and Ginsberg and Burroughs read a lot of James Joyce out loud and they went into improvisations; they'd make up characters and act out little scenes for each other. They had a flair for the dramatic, besides the open-ended sentence; I think Joyce gave Jack especially an open mind, an open consciousness in his writing.

TC: It's Bloomsday today, of course. Was Kerouac's French-Canadian/ Atlantic sensibility welcomed by the San Francisco lit community?

JK: The San Francisco Poetry Renaissance didn't have anything to do with the Beats at all. It had to do with the Berkeley Renaissance group that was basically Spicer and Duncan and the teachers they had there, along with Helen Adams, James Broughton, Landis Everson, Robin Blaser, and a few others, as well as William Everson. There were others who were interested in communal living. Rexroth, of course, was seminal in terms of a kind of socialist political stance, and his familiarity with the California landscape. Radio station KPFA had also started up in 1947. This energy moved across the bay to San Francisco—San Francisco always had its own culture, style, artists, politics. When I was there, the Beats were considered a New York City phenomenon, coming and causing a lot of Grey Line tourist bus trips that would go through North Beach and cause a hullabaloo. There was a certain amount of resentment against this much-publicized phenomenon of the Beats, the Beatniks.

TC: *At some point you encountered the Pacific Northwest poetry contingent—Lew Welch, Gary Snyder, and Philip Whalen. Is it possible to quantify what their influence brought to Bay Area arts and letters?*

JK: Perhaps in terms of work specific to location. The Six Gallery reading was a meeting, a collision of all the groups—the Pacific Northwest, San Francisco, Ginsberg, the Beats from New York. You had Michael McClure, Philip Lamantia, Rexroth as the emcee. Kerouac was there, [and] Gary Snyder and Philip Whalen. Spicer was going to be part of it, but he was stuck back east, and Duncan was in Majorca or teaching at Black Mountain. It wasn't only the San Francisco people who were blessed by the alchemy of that historic event.

TC: *Somewhere in all of this there's the East-West House that you were involved with.*

JK: Essentially, East-West House was modeled after the Institute for Asian Studies when Alan Watts, among others, taught other like-minded people in Asian Studies. It closed and a group of students decided that they would start a communal house in which people who were interested could study Buddhist texts, Japanese, and go to Japan. Snyder had already gone there on his own. Gia-fu Feng, a translator from Chinese whose edition of the *Tao Te Ching* is still circulating, was living there, too; also Claude Dahlenberg and Philip Whalen. Gai-fu went down to Big Sur and became part of the beginnings of the centre at Esalen. I was there at the East-West House in 1959 for a year and the house had been running for some years by then. They had sort of loosened their constraints and allowed women, and other non-Japan-directed people to live there. But by then I was planning to go to Japan. There was an overflow of people from East-West House and so they started something called Hyphen House, which was the hyphen between East and West. That was a few blocks away in what is now Japantown. Close by there was the Soto Buddhist temple where Shunryu Suzuki was invited to come and be the priest for the Japanese community in spring of 1959. He started zazen practice in the morning, open to everyone. He became the catalyst for beginning the Zen Center of San Francisco. I learned to sit there during the year I spent at the East-West House before going to Japan.

TC: *Before we head to Kyoto, can we get some sense of what the Pacific Northwest poets brought to arts and letters in San Francisco? A nature literacy? For example, attention to birdlife, to local flora, is persistent throughout your writing.*

JK: When Lew Welch came, he brought a particular kind of high energy. He also lived at East-West House for a while. Philip Whalen's observations were always his own, from his own original and quirky mind. Snyder was more formal, using Native American texts, his own work experiences, and explorations of the Pacific Northwest. I don't think it was until I moved to Bolinas in 1969 that I really entered into a close relationship with the land around me in my writing. About the birds who live here, to this day the quail are probably my closest neighbors. You get used to watching what's going on around you; you get to know what they're saying—the scrub jay announcing when someone is arriving. Bolinas is the location of the Point Reyes Bird Observatory, [which] started back around 1965 and is a very well-known organization. They started banding birds and studying them and received enough endowments and patrons that they've begun studying birds farther afield—like the penguins in Antarctica. This is a great location for birds here, with a lagoon for blue herons and American egrets, [and] many migrating ducks. Every year when the gold crown sparrows come down from the north with the white-crowns, they have the Gold-Crown Festival. The gold-crowns have a very singular song, three descending notes. And they usually arrive right on the autumnal equinox.

TC: *So you're readying for Japan. . . . What was the feel of things as you were gearing up to leave?*

JK: Don Allen edited the second edition of *Evergreen Review*, which was called "the San Francisco Scene," because by then the San Francisco Renaissance had already mixed with this Beat thing and it was a cultural phenomenon. Something was happening. It had become a way of dressing, of semi-dropping out, of music and jazz with poetry, smoking grass—a cultural attitude that was a gigantic contrast against what the mainstream '50s were all about. Music was certainly a part of the North Beach scene—there was the Modern Jazz

Quartet, Dave Brubeck, Paul Desmond. There were famous clubs to hear jazz. John Weiners gave me Olson's "Projective Verse" to read, and as a way of looking at writing and the page it was extremely important to me. Duncan had come to represent this attitude of the poet, of believing that you *lived* the life of the poet. Spicer was this cutting-edge sort of bullshit-detector all the time—whether a poem was *true* . . . you could tell if someone was faking it. "Poetry" poetry was out to lunch, so there was an *astute* sense of where you were coming from. These were valuable teachers.

TC: *And so Japan.*

JK: The four years I spent in Japan were spent more or less reading what was there in the British and American Cultural libraries. There was Cid Corman's *Origin* magazine, where I first read Lorine Niedecker. I was just practicing my own work—how to put words on the page, determining what's important, and when your emotion is going to take over, where to do your own internal editing before the work gets to the page. There were a number of figures writing or translating in the local community—Philip Yampolsky, Burton Watson, and the young poet Clayton Eshleman. Clayton was studying informally with Cid Corman—he was eager to find out things. And then I also practiced sitting. There were no books to read about Zen in English then, and I was encouraged just to pay attention to breathing.

TC: *You returned to California.*

JK: After four years away I came back. Don Allen had visited and he wanted to publish my first book, *The Tapestry and the Web*. I found out that I was okay as a writer, whereas before I wasn't sure. Stan Persky started publishing something called *Open Space* magazine in 1964, which was very important. He put it out every month and ran things by Robin Blaser, Ebbe Borregaard, Lew Ellingham, et cetera, and everyone kind of turned everyone else on. I wrote a series of poems for him; Stan was still working in North Beach, so that was the cultural center.

Then there was the 1965 Poetry Conference in Berkeley and that essentially established certain poetry-political lines. Spicer died after that. I believe that's when Warren Tallman invited Robin to come up to Vancouver and Stan went up with him; George Stanley, too, I think. Weren't they offered jobs? That made a big difference.

TC: *Did any other writers from that era have an influence on you?*

JK: Albert Saijo. He published a little book about hiking in the Sierras, and then more recently *Outspeaks*, from Bamboo Ridge Press. It's one of my favorite books of poetry. He's so direct about what he does and says. He was there at the beginning of the psychedelic revolution in San Francisco. Lived at the East-West House. Learned Zen meditation from Nyogen Senzaki in the late 1940s in Los Angeles. Very unaffected. He was a close friend of Lew Welch and Philip Whalen and Gary. A very modest fellow.

TC: *When you came back from Japan the Vietnam War was escalating. Did it affect the way you thought about your work?*

JK: Yes, but not overwhelmingly so. I lived in New York City, 1966 to '67, for a year and was part of a whole group there that became the Yippies. I worked doing some demonstrations with Keith Lampe (Ponderosa Pine), and "flower power" became one of our slogans. One of the Yippie group, Ed Sanders is responsible for trying to levitate the Pentagon, although Allen Ginsberg is often given credit for that. After the Be-In in San Francisco, we decided we should have something in Central Park and called it the "Spring Out." People smoked banana peels. But California was still more open about having a psychedelic revolution, dropping out, and generally being more politically confrontational.

TC: *During your years away you traveled India with Allen Ginsberg, Peter Orlovsky, and your then-husband, Gary Snyder. Regarding your experience there or in Japan, can you speak to how Buddhism or dharma practice might relate to your writing? You've mentioned at the symposium how one comes to pay attention to the moment, to details.*

JK: In India I became aware of this historical phenomena called Buddhism, which had 2,500 years of "moments." Seeing the origins of Buddhism in India, the Bodhi Tree, the Deer Park at Sarnath, Vulture's Peak, the great university of Nalanda, all in this cultural context of India, was an awakening. So world history became an awareness in my writing. In Japan, since I didn't have a teacher, I learned the patience of sitting—that there isn't really anywhere to "go," although your mind surely wants to move like a rabbit.

TC: *You've also mentioned from your experience in India how you observed that when the Tibetans brought their diaspora* *down to India's historical Buddhist sites, they also brought their devotionalism.*

JK: Buddhism had not been practiced for centuries in India, although all the historical places related to the Buddha had been carefully tended to by British archaeologists as part of a historical past. Then all of a sudden these places became full of the devotional energy of the Tibetans, with their friendly energy, and the power of the Vajrayana Himalayas with them.

TC: *You've been associated with Naropa University and its writing programs. Allen Ginsberg used to say, "Teach what you know—your own practice, own awareness." Anything recommended for writers who may be coming up now?*

JK: It depends on what you know. I guess there could be a certain number of Frisbee players teaching their practice. But you have to recognize what your awareness shows you, and what your practices can be. Travel is certainly a way to see the world and your place in it. Understanding that you are in, or a part of, a lineage of writers and teachers. That you didn't invent your "awareness," your practice—but are nonetheless individual in your own way and your understanding is unique.

TC: *Allen also used to say that the duty of the poet is to expand consciousness.*

JK: Yes, he said, after experiencing the power of yage [an Amazonian psychoactive used in divination ceremonies], expand your consciousness so it encompasses your own death. Good advice, if you can do it. But don't you think we are already a part of that "expanded consciousness," that it has already happened?

TC: *Have you any response to the idea that Allen Ginsberg "walked out" at a certain critical moment from the Beat celebrity that ultimately killed Jack Kerouac? In '62 Allen dropped off the radar and ended up traveling in India, part of it with you and your then-husband.*

JK: After reading *Kaddish* at the San Francisco Poetry Center, he traveled to South America for six months, by himself, initially to take part in a reading with Lawrence Ferlinghetti in Chile, and then went on to travel in South America on the yage trail. He took it eight times altogether, and then he decided he needed a teacher, which he thought he could find in India. He probably dropped out of sight from the heightened publicity surrounding the Beat generation at that time, but returned from his travels and helped facilitate the counterculture revolution in the early '60s. Also he never really drank alcohol, so he didn't have Kerouac's problems in that regard.

TC: *In the various individually published accounts of that journey there are points of subtle (and not sometimes not so subtle) discrimination between how some group experiences are reported by Allen, Gary, and yourself. Anything about your own personal approach in this?*

JK: My journals were written on the spot. Gary's were written after he returned, as a letter. And Allen's were edited. Being the sole woman on the trip, there were, of course, differences in the physicalities of travel. But that would be true of any trip.

TC: *After meeting with a youthful Dalai Lama, you come away and write in your journal that Allen "[a]ctually believes he knows it all, but just wishes he felt better about it."*

JK: A slightly sarcastic tone, but true, I think.

TC: *You've already got one other new collection of poetry out following your collected,* Not Veracruz (Libellum). *What's your sense of the poetic grounding in this mature work?*

JK: Grounding? Hopefully the simpler, the better.

New York

Chapter 5

And So Make Peace

Talking Story with Maxine Hong Kingston

There's this amazing faith that artists have, that somehow with art we can change the world and make peace. It's an incredible faith, I mean aren't there times when you don't believe it for one moment? . . . Look at the Dalai Lama. He practices nonviolence and he loses his country; his people are tortured and killed. The Chinese have totally taken over in a cruel way and are exploiting Tibet—they've taken its riches, cut down its forests. What satisfaction is there if you practice nonviolence? [Once,] Ted Saxauer looked at me in surprise and said "Yes, but the story isn't over." Of course! The story isn't over.

For more than thirty-five years, novelist Maxine Hong Kingston has written on the complicated chains of history, nostalgia, and spiritual yearning—on the soul of place and home, and her words have come to seem like having a wise older sister in the next bunk whispering stories to us late at night. At PEN International's 54th World Congress in Toronto in October 1989, she spoke to its theme of "The Writer: Freedom and Power." I hadn't heard her speak before, although her books The Woman Warrior and China Men rang with the weight and responsibilities of growing up with an enormous East Asian cultural heritage. Her socially engaged presence and commitment to the idea of peace as its own strategy stood out among the more than six hundred writers in attendance. In a short excerpt entitled Toward a Book of Peace that she later sent me for an anthology project, Hong Kingston observed how "the ancestors connect us *tribally and globally and guide our evolution toward becoming a humane species." In perhaps her least known work,* Hawai'i One Summer *(1998), Hong Kingston articulates an intercultural vision of what building community might mean in our emerging planetary age. It can be, she explained, its own "practice" or wisdom path, not built once and for all, but imagined, practiced, and re-created. A committed antiwar activist, since the early 1990s she has led writing-and-meditation workshops for veterans of America's wars and their families. Her anthology* Veterans of War, Veterans of Peace *(Koa Books), harvests their work in presenting a broad view of the power of story to help redeem and heal the wounds of torn history. In October 2008 while the U.S. was entangled in Iraq, we spoke at her home in Oakland, California during a spell of fine Mediterranean weather. The work on poetry she refers to has since been published as* To Be the Poet.

TC: *Maxine, how did you get involved with veterans and the veterans' writing workshop?*

MHK: The start of it was Thich Nhat Hanh. I had gone to a couple of retreats that he had led and there came a time when he said he wanted to hold a retreat for veterans of the Vietnam War. He called for veterans of the war to meet Vietnamese people, and also other Americans. So he had a ceremony with all these old soldiers and himself as a veteran of that war, and they had all kinds of ceremonies including hugging meditation. There's Vietnamese and Americans together, and Thich Nhat Hanh said when you hug one Vietnamese you hug them all. These soldiers who had been in the war were now embracing another person in their arms, and that leads to reconciliation. I was observing all of this and I thought, "They need one more thing; these veterans need to have artistic expression—like, ah, a spiritual life is not enough!" They needed an artistic life. I continued to participate in these retreats, and I brought a writing workshop. Actually, the writing workshop became the center of what veterans do in these retreats. Thich Nhat Hanh called it a retreat within the retreat. We did our own rituals and our own ceremonies, and the main practice was writing, to get their stories down. Once in a while we would break out into a larger group and listen to a dharma talk and we'd meditate with a larger group. But on the whole we would have our own room, our own separate table. Thich Nhat Hanh only came to America every other year, and

Therese Fitzgerald, Arnie Kotler, and I were thinking this isn't enough; so we held these retreats on our own, always emphasizing the writing, some artistic expression. Somewhere in this I got a Lila Wallace Award that said that I should use part of the money to do some community social work. I used it to carry on these writing workshops for veterans and their families. We met once a month for three years. At that point I tried to disband them; I didn't want it to be like therapy that goes on for a whole lifetime. It all seemed natural at the end of the grant.

TC: *Are these people working writers themselves?*

MHK: Most are just really veterans. Once they get in, some do become convinced that writing is the way they are going to come home from the war, to heal their wounds. What I tell them is, "You went to war, to a terrible place and you lived to tell the story; you need to tell us what you learned when you were out there. This is your gift; this is what you need to give to society and to your life." There's a sense of urgency; all these things are held in them, and when it just comes out it's so beautiful because they've been cooking it all these years, decades. It's been working in there. It amazes me how well[-written] their first drafts are. I can't do that. They can. It often comes out perfect, they don't need to rewrite, and I think it's because they've lived it and they've ruminated and saved it for twenty years. All I need to do is say, "Here's a piece of paper, a pencil, let it out."

TC: *Do they all let it out?*

MHK: There's another side that was sometimes a tough hump to get over with many of them, because their previous experience in communicating had been in therapeutic situations. A lot of them were repeating what they'd said in therapy groups for a long time. Some of the transition was us insisting that this isn't that same experience, it's not reaching an emotional high and then going back and climbing the same mountain again. The difference between shouting out your experience in a group and writing it down is that you can perfect it in writing, reach a kind of end with it. You process it and then it becomes art. You turn war and chaos into art. There was a small percentage of dedicated writers who came into the group—they knew that. Their knowledge path was to say, "It's not screaming out what happened to me in 1971, it's writing it down and perhaps changing it, perfecting it, molding it."

TC: *And turning it into a product?*

MHK: Well, as a Buddhist we don't think about a reward or a product. We're just supposed to appreciate what's happening right now. I never promised them that they were going to have a book or readings or money or anything. "You write this story for its own sake."

TC: *How did this book actually come into existence then?*

MHK: It must have been three or four years ago. People were seeing that we were accumulating a huge body of work—all kinds from everybody. Some people were getting impatient and they began publishing on their own. At a certain point I saw that we had lot of work, and I thought, "Is it possible that we could pull this together?" It happened that Arnie Kotler who had previously established Parallax Press began Koa Books as a new company, so it all fit. His first book was Cindy Sheehan's story. Arnie was present at the beginning of the first veterans' meditations and now he had a publishing company. The whole universe fit and this book could come out.

TC: *Was there any turning point that galvanized for you the urgency of working on this project to promote peace?*

MHK: Not a crucial point. It all seemed like a steady, ongoing project. The longer we worked at it, the more we began to feel like a sangha, a community. When the Lila Wallace Award was over I tried to disband the group but they refused to leave! I tried to change it a little bit by suggesting that we disband the big group and begin many little sanghas. But nobody left. Then I simply said, "Well, we're just going to meet for the rest of our lives," and that's what we have now.

Perhaps one galvanizing point though was the fire that swept through here in 1991. It burned 3,200 houses, including this one where we lived, as well as *The Book of Peace* that I was working on. Afterward I was thinking, "How do you create again after something has been destroyed, after you have experienced destruction? How do you get going again, and how do I write again because my book has burned?" I didn't want to just go by memory. An idea came up that I mustn't write alone, that I should have a community. All this was happening at the same time as the veterans' retreats. I thought, "Because I want to write a book of peace, the people I want in this community are veterans, people who've experienced war and know what that is."

TC: *Michael Wong, one of your book's contributors who once fled to Canada, writes of the Vietnam War, "Our honor died at My Lai." Can I ask what you feel may have similarly died at Abu Ghraib in Iraq, or Guantanamo?*

MHK: Oh goodness, I don't know if I can answer that, because we're always doing such things. We go into these terrible places and we come out of them again and again. Bush and everybody is saying "We don't torture." Well, obviously we do torture and then we deny it. I would hope the idea that we are the good guys has died. In these workshops what I want is for us to write stories. When we write them we can understand them, become aware. If we could just understand the truth of what happened, then maybe we can change what happens in lives. About the idea of changing history, when an occurrence first happens it's just chaos. Nobody understands what it means, it's an explosion. But if we can get it into words then we change things from chaos to order, because it's through order that we understand human events. There's this amazing faith that artists have, that somehow with art, we can change the world and make peace. It's an incredible faith; I mean, aren't there times when you don't believe it for one moment? There are times when it doesn't do any good; you work as hard as you can and here comes Abu Ghraib and more people killed.

TC: *Even Confucius faced this long ago. Doesn't he say, "The wise person does his duty even though all along he knows it's hopeless"? Yet don't we have to do it anyway? It's like the old belief out west that "cowboys do the right thing, even when nobody's looking."*

MHK: That's right—we do it anyway. If your premise is that guns, bombs, bayonets are not right, and that we will not use that power, then you have your brush, your pen, and that's all you allow yourself. W.S. Merwin is building a rain forest on Maui. He says that with global warming it's not going to do any good for him to plant trees, but he does it anyway.

TC: *Your writers' group motto is "Tell the Truth." Many of their stories reflect how commonly violence in the home begins long before any front-line combat.*

MHK: Yes, by the time it gets to war, violence is already way down the line. But in the same way love can also start right here, in the home, in each one of us. We need to learn ways of expressing the pure energy of our feelings—anger and hate feelings especially—in a healthier direction that's beneficial to the world.

TC: *In your introduction you mention Odysseus and his post–Trojan War saga. Like every wandering mariner, he constantly talks about his story as he travels, yet it's only when he finally returns home that he can discuss it fully. A lot of your book's contributors talk about returning "home."*

MHK: We're all existentialists. We create that home wherever we are, and the most important aspect of our writers' home is the sangha we make around us. I am very interested in the idea of return. The Buddhists talk about how with every breath we return to our body, but you know we also have to return to our consciousness. . . . When you go to war, you become a raging killer beast. Odysseus goes to war, but it takes him twenty years to return. In telling his story all along, he's changing back from a killer beast into a human being. Now, Aristotle says that the greatest joy in art is recognition. When Odysseus finally gets home, people don't recognize him. We have one writer in the book, John Mulligan: he went to war, came home, and his own mother didn't recognize him. His own mother. At least we can speak.

TC: *Speaking of language, you've published a collection of poetry with Harvard University Press,* To Be the Poet. *Have you rededicated your-self as a poet? Are long books too energy-depleting, or are you plowing a new field, rotating the crops?*

MHK: It's all of that. It also tells of my desires that I should have some fun, write something short, and not have all these cares. I admire poetry so much and I want to be able to write in that heightened form.

TC: *Is this something new or an old affection? Ursula LeGuin also made a recursive move to poetry, although this might alarm her agent.*

MHK: Right, agents don't like that! I began as a poet when I was a child. I was constantly uttering and singing and writing poems. What's coming to me now is a long poem. I'm thinking, "What is it that I want to be at the end of my life?" I want to concentrate all of life and look forward to age, to the end. So what's coming is a long poem, five strong beats to every line, softer beats in between; many, many lines. This is the right form for me. I had about a hundred pages and then went back and did it again. Poetry is a perfect form for an older person because I don't need to tell everything; I can jump around in time. I can skip a whole lot. It's not as detailed and as descriptive as prose; it's more impressionistic, less plotted. I think that's the big difference between poetry and a prose work—plot. And I never liked plot anyway; plots just contain everything. We don't want to be constrained, we want to be able to fly all over the place—that's what poetry does.

TC: *Simone Weil says that the purpose of art and words is to testify—the way the trees blossom and the stars come out at night. Do you think Buddhists might conceive of art and literature as works of* metta *or* karuna—*kindness or compassion?*

MHK: Aristotle says pity and terror are what drama brings forward in order for us get the catharsis of art. Because I have a narrator in there, I did think that I was writing in the way of karuna, compassion, with *Tripmaster Monkey*. I wanted to be invisible so that everybody else could go about their drama and their plots. I began to see the narrator as Avalokitesvara, Kuan Yin [the Goddess of Mercy]; the narrator is very close to myself and I didn't want anything bad to happen to any of my characters. I wanted to give them gifts; I wanted to correct them; I had a sense of being their creator and the person who gives them blessings. That attitude of being the kind narrator began in *Tripmaster Monkey* and when I went on to other works I felt very clearly that I could even manipulate situations and atmospheres, so that we could see what kindness and compassion are like. The idea is, "How do we make peace?" Peace is actually created and that means creating a good relationship, creating a good sangha, and writing stories. Technically, writing and telling stories is traditional in all cultures: it's probably built into our DNA that they have rising action that leads to a violent climax. We all love that sense of drama, that frightening climax. Well, I got thinking, "Can we write a story in which this climax is nonviolent and still be exciting?" That is against everything our culture is teaching us. Television, movies . . . there's that violent climax. Can I write counter to this? Will people buy these stories? What will all the critics say?

TC: *The Burmese monks and other protesters were recently chanting "metta" when confronting the military dictatorship. They want a better social and economic situation for people. Can Gandhian methods prevail in any other context than that of a British-style empire?*

MHK: You're talking about a big stage—Burma, India, China. But the ways of peace are constantly taking place on small stages every moment, everywhere, right now, each and every one of us, every single moment. We have the opportunity to make peace all the time. With the root of these small practices, I'm sure they result in many scenes of love and being together. This Burma situation is at a stage where it's too late; it comes after many acts of failing to show compassion. So we end up with this horrible situation and we think, "Now let's practice our compassion." Well, it's too late. It's very hard for compassion to win out in such a situation.

TC: *Burma, where the democratic movement is struggling and which is Buddhist, is a thrall of China's military dictatorship. Next door in southern Thailand, Buddhist monks are being assassinated by Islamic terrorists who are basically warlords. With all this realpolitik coming at us, what can a nonfiction style encompass if it's only peace-speak? Can it be a language of political method and effective action?*

MHK: I was talking with Ted Sexauer from the book, who's a Buddhist practitioner himself, and was complaining, questioning all these ways of nonviolence—do they really work? Look at the Dalai Lama. He practices nonviolence and he loses his country; his people are tortured and killed. The Chinese have totally taken over in a cruel way and are exploiting Tibet—they've taken its riches, cut down its forests. What satisfaction is there if you practice nonviolence? Ted looked at me in surprise and said, "Yes, but the story isn't over." Of course! *The story isn't over.* The Dalai Lama gets pressured. There are those who say, "C'mon now, be a leader. We're going to have a revolution. We'll fight back." But he says, "I'm for nonviolence." *The story isn't over.*

TC: *Marshall McLuhan reckoned that words without action are only a cool medium, impractical. What about your simple, and, for many, deeply moving strategy in* The Fifth Book of Peace? . . . *"Children, everybody, here's what to do during war: In a time of destruction, create something. A poem. A parade. A community. A school. A vow. A moral principle. One peaceful moment."*

MHK: Right, it doesn't mean you have get arrested in front of the White House. Just create *one* peaceful moment. Amitav Ghosh says we need to find a way of writing in which nonviolence is dramatic. He tells about the riots involving Hindus and Muslims. There's a group of neighbors who say that the rioters are not going to force them to remain hidden in their houses, so they all set out together to walk on their street. Then they see a group of thugs and we all know what's about to happen, you get beaten up, right? But silently, the women take their scarves and hold them in a circle around their men. The bad guys don't move at the sight and the crisis passes—can that work as a dramatic moment? It's so brief! How can we write more? As Virginia Woolf said, we leave it to the poets to write these short pieces.

TC: *Is there something here about "the Other"?*

MHK: In the writing workshops there's usually a dislike of officers. Occasionally, though, someone of officer material will attend. After meditation and getting to know one another, telling their stories, over time they become less and less officer-like. Another guy in there, Scott Morrison, he wanted to be a writer all along. He came to our group because he wanted to play his own mind and thinking against some really hard, right-wing patriots. Wanted to spar with them in putting out his peace[ful], liberal thoughts. He said, "I just can't meet any. They keep disappearing." They've come in, officers, right-wing patriots, then they change. Being quiet with oneself, these ways of meditation . . . maybe it does change people. But I don't know if these are the ones we have to change. The people who believe in the [Iraqi] War and romanticize the idea of America coming to the rescue are very difficult to convince otherwise. They are easily led. These are patriots who I think put the religion of the country above their own religion— we've become a warrior society, and if you simply say "freedom" and "America" people will react to it.

TC: *When your country becomes your religion, that's nationalism . . . it's dangerous.*

MHK: Yes, but the real danger is the separation developing between the people and their sense of being able to do anything about it. Support for Iraq is down to around twenty-eight percent. That's a profound disconnect between the people and their sense of what elected government is. In place of action it all becomes irony, something bitter to laugh at. This is what is dangerous.

TC: *Being an activist is fashionable nowadays, but people can mistake talking about action for actually doing something and really taking action.*

MHK: There's a story from Ted Sexauer in the book. He goes to Fort Benning and makes up his mind to confront a general. It's such a hard situation. Of course, he tries to meet the general on a human level. But as the Quakers say, "How do you speak truth to power?" Many of us have had a chance to meet these powerful people, at the White House or elsewhere. It's so easy to be struck speechless. We care about etiquette, about not being rude. If you're vulgar, you can be so easily dismissed. And if you're nice you can also be dismissed.

TC: *In the popular media—most of which rolled over like spaniels with their legs in the air during the invasion of Iraq—there's an assumption that the '60s generation ideals of peace, love, freedom, equality, and happiness were naive and just died out. Do you feel that's the case, or have these ideas mainstreamed, even percolated underground?*

MHK: All of us old '60s people, we're still here. A lot have been involved with organizations all through the past forty years. They're reemerging: that's why when the Iraq war started the demonstrations were put together so quickly.

TC: *Growing up, were you exposed to Buddhist teachings?*

MHK: When I was a child we had all the rituals and holidays. My parents didn't call it anything but Confucianism. And even then, we didn't really call it that. In China they take it all—Taoism, Confucius, and call it "Chinese religion."

TC: *The missionary mind never quite understood that syncretic "three-in-one" tradition—Tao, Buddha, Confucius.*

MHK: Yes, or they call it "ancestor worship," which is very dismissive. That is so weird. We had the altars, the ancestors, and I feel I had some aspects of Buddhism. So coming across Buddhism as an adult felt natural, familiar. Growing up, we had several buildings—the Confucius Church, the Benevolent Association, also the Chinese Methodist Church. They were the institutions. You also had *home*. To this day, Chinese people still talk about the "home religion." So you don't have to have another place; you can have it wherever you put your altar.

TC: *Have you ever taken the jukai ceremony, anything like that?*

MHK: Yes, several ceremonies. The first was in Hawaii at the big Honpa Hongwanji Buddhist Temple, Japanese. They have a ceremony that they've made Hawaiian in which they declare people living treasures of Hawaii. Out of nowhere, they tapped me and I went there. All the wonderful robes, bells, incense, the drums, chanting. . . . It was really great. I thought everybody was a living treasure, but they recognized me. Another one was being at these retreats with Thich Nhat Hanh and he offered the Five Wonderful Precepts. We took the vows.

TC: *Were there any books or texts that had a major impact on your relationship with peace, dharma, activism?* The Spirit of Zen, *Alan Watts, and so on?*

MHK: I read those, but what really got me was reading the Beats. Jack Kerouac and Gary Snyder. It just seemed like so much fun to be a Buddhist. Be a dharma bum!

TC: *David Miller, a Honolulu writer, suggests the key in coming success-fully to a new country or place is "assimilation and creativity." How do you feel about multicultural affiliations, Asian-American, et cetera? Elizabeth Bishop, for instance, declined to appear in anthologies of women's poetry, preferring to be just "a poet."*

MHK: Ethnic studies is all around now. I would feel badly if I was pigeonholed into one category. I've seen my work in black studies, women's studies, Asian-American history, American and British literature—I don't feel bad about it because I'm in so many catego-ries. There's a linguistic concept known as "et cetera," where after every noun you put "et cetera." Then you say, "I am an American, et cetera." But I like that phrase, "assimilation *and* creativity": you inte-grate everything *and* you make more. You don't lose yourself; that's what some are afraid of. Political correctness often seems tied to a lack of humor.

TC: *To conclude with* Veterans of War, Veterans of Peace, *what are the chances of similar encounters coming out of the current Middle Eastern–Asian conflicts?*

MHK: The reason I think our first veterans' workshops worked is that Thich Nhat Hanh is a Vietnamese Buddhist. Most of these veterans were from the Vietnam War where they had seen the temples, the monks, nuns, the Buddhas, and there was curiosity about that. They would meet the Montagnards, the hill people, who would go to war with a small Buddhist statue in their mouths. So they were interested to get together—there was a chance of reconciliation with real Vietnamese. And they've been coming together all these years and have worked out their war stuff and their post-traumatic disorders. Now, will there ever come a day when some of the people coming back from Iraq and Afghanistan can meet with an imam and clerics together—Muslims and veterans, and come together and have these kinds of ceremonies that we have? Will it work better? We've met some of these young veterans at a bookstore in New York and that city seems the perfect place for it.

TC: *Maybe it'll be necessary.*

MHK: What's amazing to me is that after a war—with Japan, in Korea, Vietnam—we get all kinds of loving things: we have "war brides," we have families adopting Chinese and Vietnamese orphan girls, we have new family situations. First there's exotic countries, and then we have the war, then we have marriages. . . . I wonder, "Can't we just skip the middle part, the war, and get on with the loving family and wonderful new foods and restaurants part? Isn't that more compassionate?"

Oakland, CA

Chapter 6

The Bedrock of Practice

With Sulak Sivaraksa in Bangkok

Buddhadhassa said we should all be united, including those of faith, agnostics, and those without faith, because we're all spiritual beings and should unite against greed, hatred, and delusion. He was also the one who said that Buddhism is not only spiritual; it is also social and political. One of his books is called *Dhammic Socialism*.

The term *"Buddhist activist"* doesn't begin to cover the range of Sulak Sivaraksa's tireless work from his base in Thailand, which he adamantly refers to by its historic name of Siam. I'd read extracts from his writings in the Parallax Press dharma anthologies shepherded by Arnie Kotler in the 1990s; however, my real introduction to Sulak came through our mutual friend Ivan Kats at the Obor Foundation in Connecticut, who with Sivaraksa and other prominent Asian intellectuals was dedicated to promoting democratic ideas through cheap student editions in Asian languages of important world texts. Publishing projects have often brought Sivaraksa into trouble with various governments. Not long prior to our meeting in the cool interior of his old Siamese home in Bangkok early in 2007, Ajahn Sulak, as he is affectionately known using the honorific for teacher, had again been charged with lèse-majesté for allegedly defaming the king. It was a precarious moment. Twelve days previous the army had taken over the government in a coup. Fortunately, after another international campaign in his defense, Sivaraksa was relieved *of the grave charge against him. Canadian philosopher John Ralston Saul has written "whenever I ask myself a basic question of public ethics and public action, I end up wondering what Sulak would think. He has that great virtue of being true to himself and to the standards which somehow link all great moral philosophies." A co-founder of the Buddhist Peace Fellowship and a regular visitor to North America, noteworthy among Ajahn Sulak's prolific output is his most recent book* The Wisdom of Sustainability: Buddhist Economics for the 21st Century *(2009).*

For decades Sulak Sivaraksa has been his nation's leading social critic. A still vigorous champion of the urban and rural poor, as a lay Buddhist leader he has also led popular resistance to the excesses of the international economic development, which is rapidly transforming this Buddhist kingdom. Educated at Our Lady of the Assumption cathedral school along the banks of the Chao Praya River, which aided him in gaining command of English, he continues to live not far off in a traditional teak house of the kind seldom seen in Bangkok anymore. He remains a longtime director of the Santi Pracha Dhamma Institute, was founder of the International Network of Engaged Buddhists (INEB), is past chair of the Asian Cultural Forum on Development, and has been visiting professor at Berkeley, Hawaii, McMaster, Cornell, and Swathmore.

Following Thai custom, Pali-based reference is made throughout to "dhamma," rather than the more familiar Sanskrit-inflected spelling "dharma," seen commonly in the West.

TC: *Ajahn, in your essay "Buddhism in a World of Change," you write, "Buddhism enters the life of society through the presence of individuals who practice and bear witness to the Way, through their thought, speech and actions. . . ." As one of the co-founders of the Buddhist Peace Fellowship along with Thich Nhat Hanh, Robert Aitken Roshi, Gary Snyder, and others, how are you feeling about the success of the whole socially engaged Buddhist initiative?*

SS: I think the BPF is doing wonderful work. Regarding Iraq issues, recently Aitken Roshi wanted people to take action and they did. They went to Washington, DC and marched, didn't they? Tremendous. And before that, just before the Iraq war they also went there with Christians as meditators. So, I'm very proud of the BPF. On my recommendation they've now even elected a Thai woman to be president. Before this, the fellowship organization tended to be rather ethnically white, and I told them that they should make an effort get Asian Buddhists involved; otherwise Asian Buddhists tend to stick together, rather narrow.

TC: *What about the continuing relevance of Buddhism itself? With Buddhism growing in the West, currently it has a certain trendiness. That can lead to misunderstanding, as if it can be anything you want it to be.*

33. In a way that's right, because as you know, Buddhism has no dogma. You are not required to believe. So an agnostic can be a Buddhist; anybody can be a Buddhist. The idea is that you must practice, obviously. You must sit down. You must know how to breathe properly and so on. Again, you don't even have to recite the word "Buddha" if you don't want to. The idea is, mainly, "how to become awakened"; and how to transform greed into generosity, to transform hatred into loving kindness, to transform delusion into understanding. I think that's the hard core of practicing. Other things may help or hinder, you know, such as Tibetan *thangkas* [Tibetan religious paintings on cloth]: a thangka can be a great help, but it can also become a hindrance.

TC: *What about developments within Buddhism here in Asia, its original home?*

SS: I'm happy to note the situation of the Ambedkarite Buddhists—those taking after Dr. Ambedkar of India, who was converted in 1956. An untouchable, he was the most educated of Indians with a doctorate from Columbia, a doctorate from London School of Economics, admitted to the Bar: a Hindu and untouchable. But he said he would not die a Hindu. This made a clash between him and the ideas of Gandhi. Gandhi said you can be reborn better in the next life; Ambedkar said, "No, I'm going to change in this life; to become a Buddhist." And then, you know, thousands and thousands of untouchables—half a million—joined him. Yet, unfortunately, they have still had a hatred of the Brahmins, the upper class. I'm happy to say they are now changing. Last year, at the international meeting of INEB, we had a meeting at the place where Dr. Ambedkar was converted, at Nagpur. In this heart of the converted untouchables I told them that to be Buddhist alone is not enough; they must learn to transform.

So I invited the Dalai Lama to be with them. At first, a lot of people said to His Holiness, "No, you shouldn't go." They feared there might be violence because he is accepted by the upper-class Indians and so on, but he replied, "No, I'm a Buddhist, I must go." And it worked. Last year the Ambedkarite Buddhists were ready. At first, they didn't want any Tibetans, any foreigners, or their ceremonies; but now the Tibetans go to teach them and they're willing to learn meditation, and to learn the sutras in Sanskrit. In one year that's tremendous transformation.

TC: *Taoists say that even the status quo changes slowly. How do you feel about the nature of changes within contemporary Buddhism?*

SS: Things have to change with skillful means. For example, sometimes Western Buddhists can unfortunately feel they are superior to native Buddhists. You know, "We are intellectual, we are scientific, we are not superstitious." Yet at times they are even more superstitious in their own ways. This must change. And, of course, traditional Buddhist cultures themselves are also changing. Unfortunately, in this country, in Thailand, the sangha is becoming more and more consumerist. And in Sri Lanka the sangha is becoming more and more nationalistic. In Japan, Buddhism used to be nationalistic; now it's turned capitalistic and consumerist. Luckily, as international engaged Buddhists we can keep making small inroads, with some of us concerned for society and social justice, or others concerned with environmental alliances.

TC: *Perhaps something about the nature of Thai Buddhism, which so many foreign travelers here become exposed to. . . . It's Indic in origin and outwardly the Wats, the temples, appear highly ornate. But what about the animism that seems so prevalent—the amulets that are worn everywhere, the spirit houses you see outside homes and buildings?*

SS: To tell you the truth, Thai Buddhism is more Singhala-influenced from Ceylon. One of the routes where it landed from Sri Lanka led northward from near Nakhon Sri Thammarat in the south. About this animism, the fashion for amulets especially is new and tied to the rise of capitalism. They've made a lot of money on this. In the old days, amulets and so on were given only to a few people. Buddhism in this country has been diluted for around the past hundred years. And much more so since we have become part and parcel of the American Empire. The first dilution was that of King Rama V and his father. Most Thais regard him as the greatest king, the modern king. His father, Rama IV, was a monk for twenty-seven years, and he was the one who spoke English and appears in *The King and I*. In one sense, he was a very wise man in not allowing this country to be colonized. But then he tried to prove that Buddhism is scientific. So anything not scientific was not Buddhism. That means you can't talk about *samsara* anymore, you can't talk about Deva and all the mystery of life anymore. You can't talk about next life, past life. It should be the other way around! Science embraces the material part of life, but Buddhism—the spiritual—goes beyond this. That's number one. Since Rama IV, Thai Buddhism has become more Protestant, more westernized. He's the one who wanted to reform the sangha. He had a new reform movement, which I would call a Protestant movement. Secondly, his son became king; Rama V placed the sangha beneath the king, which was never heard of. You see, in a traditional Buddhist country you have the two wheels theory: a vehicle needs two wheels to move. So in any state you have one wheel of power upheld by the king and his ministers, but you also need the sangha: to be a force for righteousness, to be the voice of conscience, to tell the king not to be too aggressive. Unfortunately, the king took control of the sangha and now the sangha just worships the king.

TC: *That brings me to the case of Father Joey Maier, the Catholic priest who works in Bangkok's notorious Klong Tuey slum. How is it that in a Buddhist country, which you'd expect to be mindful of compassion, a Catholic Christian has come in and has to do the clean-up work?*

SS: Father Maier and I are friends. He's marvelous. He does wonderful work and he helps the young people in Klong Tuey to become ordained in the Buddhist tradition. With this kind of Catholic the idea is not about conversion; it's to serve God, and you serve God any way that enriches people. If it enriches them through the Buddhist tradition, then why not? So he helps them. He's very perceptive.

TC: *Can we consider for a moment how a profoundly Buddhist country like Thailand is responding to the pressures of globalization? Outside observers often feel that the Thai have a wonderful capacity to be impacted by events, to absorb them, and resume being Thai. Do you agree with this?*

SS: Up to a point. Particularly among the poor. This is what I feel good about in this country. The poor have been oppressed so much. Now, at last, they have empowered themselves. They have organized themselves, calling themselves the Assembly of the Poor. At least half a million membership, and they are now questioning globalization, questioning development. They are against dam-building, gas pipelines; this includes Buddhists and Muslims working together from the grassroots, and now the middle class is joining them. So the middle class in this country in the last five to ten years is also becoming more enlightened. They used to look down upon the poor, but now they feel they can learn from them because the poor are still very much in touch with nature, and in touch with themselves, whereas the middle class have lost that. They are controlled by computers, television, mass media. Now [they] are beginning to feel they need nature again. I feel sorry that the people in power don't realize this.

TC: *Does this Assembly organize electorally by backing certain candidates, or is it more along the lines of "people power" as we've seen, say, in the Philippines?*

SS: It's people power. Yes. They don't trust parliament because it's always being bought. It's controlled by entrepreneurs, by money.

TC: *How are they expressing their authority?*

SS: Sometimes they demonstrate and camp in front of government house for weeks; and they also march from one village to another to inform people, because they don't know each other, and since the media only portrays the upper class. So they want to get to know each other. And they walk—it's marvelous action. Dhammayatra— dhamma, and yatra—it means walk in the dhamma.

TC: *Like Maha Ghosananda, the late-patriarch in Cambodia—"Step by step . . ."—the title of his book.*

SS: Exactly! Same word. Ghosananda started his walk from our ashram outside Bangkok.

TC: *You've been proposed as a Nobel Peace Prize winner. This seems to entitle you to some form of public address. As a world citizen, what's your take on how things are looking internationally?*

SS: In my view, the world is now controlled by American imperialism, although they call it "globalization": the American way. It means that money talks, that weapons control, that a very few transnational corporations control everything—food, medicines, oil, weapons. And these naturally end up in crisis—not simply politically, but environmentally. Speaking as a Buddhist, I see things changing; in Buddhism, everything is changing. Although they control all the means, this imperialism has no moral legitimacy. That's why the 9/11 incident took place. We have to look for something much more alternative than that though, than an eye for an eye, tooth for a tooth. What we need is spiritual commitment, moral courage, and we need to resist the empire nonviolently. I think that is possible even in America itself. More and more people are growing aware of this; and in this regard I'm very proud of the Buddhist Peace Fellowship also. American Buddhists used to be goody-goody; they've tended to be upper class, middle class; they've wanted to be peaceful and have thought about their own soul—but without questioning their lifestyle from the point of view of there being so much suffering: "Why does this family have two cars; why so much waste?"

TC: *You really feel this is the case?*

SS: Well, as I say, things are changing. Colleges and schools are turning against having Coca-Cola, Pepsi-Cola, some of these things on school grounds. Students are against buying some cheap sweatshirts made in China. Now, I hope that these Buddhists and activists can have more time for meditation—and more of them *are* making time for this. The link that we need is for those who meditate to become more activist, and for activists to also have meditation. This, I feel, would be a new spiritual force, the answer for overcoming such things as the poverty crisis. I see this coming.

TC: *Not to get too far away from this theme, have you any thoughts on how exploitation may be occurring within the spread of Buddhism in the West? I'm thinking of films like* Samsara. *Films can attract a very large audience, however, women are drawing attention to this work for its graphic sex scenes and asking if this is necessary in what's purportedly a Buddhist work.*

SS: Hmmm . . . I've heard of this. You have to sell, I suppose. How you take a stand on consumerism and contemporary nature requires skillful means. I belong to the southern school of Buddhism where we believe that sex is not to be played up. But there are schools in

Tibetan Buddhism that believe sex is a wonderful thing. Look at Trungpa Rinpoche. He's still a great guru. They call him a *mahasiddha*. There's a great book out now about *Mahasiddha* and his crazy servants: who he copulated with and so on . . . I find that a little bit too extreme.

TC: *There's some talk of a Peace City developing in Laos to the north of Thailand. Laos is emerging as a new visitor center along the international backpackers' dharma trail. Any thoughts on this? Can it survive?*

SS: You mean the old capital, Luang Prabang? Good idea. It's lovely. Luang Prabang is now recognized as a UNESCO world heritage site. If they're not careful though, it will be spoiled like Khao San Road [in Bangkok]. But if they make an effort, they can do it. The Laotian sangha in my opinion is much better than the Thai sangha. As engaged Buddhists we collaborate very closely with them, and the chief monk of the Lao sangha has told me that he will never send Lao monks to be educated in this country anymore because they either come here and disrobe, or return to Laos and become very arrogant. He wants to train his own monks in meditation, with the sutras, and he has asked us to help with matters there such as dealing with sexual violence, globalization, and understanding structural violence—and through the international Buddhist network we have done. For four years now we have helped and it's very constructive. I'm very hopeful. We also work with the Burmese sangha, with a Burmese organization in Yangon. We work there with both Christians and with the Buddhist sangha, as well as the various ethnic groups—Kachin, Mon, Shan. And we do likewise with Cambodia. I've mentioned that we are involved with the Ambedkarites in India and now are beginning to work with Bhutan. We are hoping to have the third international gathering on Gross International Happiness here by the end of this year. Two years ago we had it in Halifax. Your Canadian author John Ralston Saul came to give the closing address to the gathering. I hope he will come again, too.

TC: *That's an easy idea for everyone to feel good about. A small country can give such a useful idea to the big world.*

SS: Yes, even the Thai government is using these words now! When we hear them we only think of Bhutan, but I think the idea originally came from the Dalai Lama. You know, the king of Bhutan recently abdicated in favor of democracy; however, I feel not so happy because they only look to the Western model rather than to the sangha model, the Tibetan model that is still practiced outside areas of control from China. Have you heard of Helena Norberg-Hodge? She has spent half her life in Ladakh and speaks Ladakhi. Her famous book is *Ancient Futures: Learning from Ladakh.* She says we have a lot to learn from traditional Tibetan culture in Ladakh; that the future is not in London, not in New York, but in Ladakh.

TC: *During a visit with Robert Aitken Roshi in Hawaii this past summer, we were able to chat a little regarding the roots of social engagement, of helping from a Buddhist perspective, and he recommended reading the work of Buddhadhassa, the Thai monk-philosopher. I believe you worked together. What was the essence of his teaching?*

SS: Before he died, he said that he had three points he wanted all his disciples to commit toward. Point number one—he said if you are a Buddhist, you must learn to practice basic Buddhism. That is, how to be altruistic; how to transform greed into generosity; how to transform hatred into loving kindness; how to transform delusion into understanding. He said these, of course, are available in other religions, also—not exclusively Buddhism. So point number two is that we must respect all the religions. Not simply tolerate, but respect. They may use different terms, different beliefs, but he said we must understand both worldly language and spiritual language. If you read [the Book of] Genesis, you read in worldly language that God created the world in six days. This is worldly language. But if you read the spiritual language, it means that the world had been transformed by a very spiritual being. Thirdly, Buddhadhassa said we should all be united, including those of faith, agnostics, those without faith, because we're all spiritual beings and should unite against greed, hatred, and delusion. He was also the one who said that Buddhism is not only spiritual; it is also *social* and *political.* One of his books is called *Dhammic Socialism.*

TC: *That sounds like what the Burmese military calls its system, one that's gone right off the rails.*

SS: Ah, that's why he didn't use the word "Buddhist"—because the Burmese use that. He specifically called it "Dhammic." Dhamma is not only Buddhist; it is open to any way, it's neutral.

TC: *Ajahn Sulak, many thanks. I think you're due to receive other visitors.*

Note: At the conclusion of this interview, Sivaraksa met with a delegation of poor senior citizens who had been evicted from their dwelling at an urban Buddhist temple. Bangkok newspaper accounts related that senior monks had decided to approve a major real estate development plan for their site.

Bangkok

Chapter 7

A Heart Free to Listen

The Awareness Practice of Thich Nhat Hanh

Where there is suffering, mindfulness responds with the energy of compassion.

*T*hich Nhat Hanh became known during the 1960s for his friendship with Dr. Martin Luther King Jr. Both opposed the Indochina Wars. During the War in Vietnam, Thich Nhat Hanh did important peace work that made it necessary for him to seek exile and he established a home community called Plum Village in France, where for more than forty years this Vietnamese monk has taught and offered concise explications of the deeper roots of Buddhist spirituality and practice. Thich Nhat Hanh customarily expounds on the fuller meaning of "looking deeply," which in its original Buddhist sense probes to the core of notions such as matter, self, and the inner nature of being. Looking deeply can also be viewed as an intuitive rendering of vipasyana, a term encountered these days in health and insight meditation programs. Through the notable influence of his early American supporters, "Thay" is widely associated with the popularization of mindfulness in North American culture, an idea that one is as likely to hear these days from a police superintendent as a yoga instructor. In reading some of his early texts in English—Being Peace, Cultivating the Mind of Love, and especially Living Buddha, Living Christ, one of his paramount concerns is with bodhichitta, the "mind of love" or even "enlightenment"; its flowering is very much for our time. In the early fall of 1995, I was invited to write *the following account of Thich Nhat Hanh and his teaching practice during a five-day visit he made to the San Francisco Bay Area. It was my first real opportunity to witness the appeal of a major international Buddhist teacher in the United States—from an audience of thousands at a civic auditorium, to a mindfulness walk with hundreds of others at Spirit Rock Center, to a private forum with business, spiritual, and celebrity film-star supporters. I only had one real question for him— "What happens when we die?" and having traveled a thousand miles to ask it, in the end I had to blurt it out in desperation above an audience as he walked away at the St. Francis Hotel. Thankfully, he turned, sat down, and expounded some of what unfolds here. In his answer he summarized more simply and directly the fuller nature of what interconnectedness means than any other religious teacher I have heard before or since.*

Somewhere during most climactic undertakings, there occurs a moment in which all that has gone before, and will come after, becomes transfixed in mind. For whatever reasons this defining, epiphany moment survives, thrives, and lingers in our psyche as a kind of touchstone, and again and again we return to it in search of a familiar, perhaps unknowable, magic.

I am reminded of this following a recent astonishing gathering in San Francisco. A global brain trust was lately convened there by the Mikhail Gorbachev Foundation. This "State of the World Forum" drew one hundred distinguished Fellows from the worlds of science, statecraft, economics, and the humanities. Their purpose was to search for, and articulate answers, to certain fundamental challenges as humanity prepares to enter its next historic phase of development on this precious planet: challenges such as the crisis of economic- and technological-centered models of human progress; the deepening global crisis of moral and spiritual deterioration; impending ecological chaos; and the uncertain architectures of international security.

The colloquium's luminaries were many: Nobel Peace Laureate Rigoberta Menchu, South African Vice-President Thabo Mbeki, Jane Goodall, Fritjof Capra, nuclear arms negotiator Max Kampelman, media boss Ted Turner, futurist John Naisbitt, Joan Halifax, Richard Leakey, Amory Lovins, Zbigniew Brzezinski, and, among scores of others, such Hollywood stars-with-conscience as Dennis Weaver and Shirley MacLaine. Joining the deliberations were two hundred and fifty global hitters in finance, resource extraction, information technology, national government, philanthropy, development aid, what have you. Riding herd on all this were ace moderators Hazel Henderson, Sam Keen, President Oscar Arias of Costa Rica, Dutch Prime Minister Ruud Lubbers, and the remarkable Mr. Gorbachev himself.

An obvious case of Beatnik genius at the controls, the breakthrough pow-wow linked up the Esalen Institute with the Pentagon, MIT, Wall Street's Fortune 500, and a grab-bag of stray cosmic tracers like the Patriarchs of Buddhist Cambodia, Mongolia, and Nestorian Christianity from Assyria and Iraq.

On the third day of Forum heaviosity, though, a little man appeared as magically as Rumplestiltskin. He arrived late at a midmorning dialogue addressing the topic of "Expanding the Boundaries of Humanness." The guest panel was diverse: Rupert Sheldrake, Deepak Chopra, Esalen Institute founder Michael Murphy, Episcopalian Dean Alan Jones. The late arrival was a Vietnamese Buddhist monk named Thich Nhat Hanh.

Discussion was free-ranging: how Descartes' three-hundred-year-old notions of mechanistic science still impact the Western worldview of Self, place, and spiritual relevance; how pilgrimage became tourism; how telepathic communication with other star worlds is worth a shot. Michael Murphy discoursed on golf and Sri Aurobindo; Deepak Chopra expressed the idea of the rational mind proving inadequate to comprehend nonlinear intelligence. Whew.

Somewhere between Dr. Chopra's bringing mysticism into the world of science, and someone or other's view of Celtic pre-Christian pagan consciousness, I became aware of an increasing buzzy muddification of my frontal lobes.

Dean Alan Jones then introduced the final presenter. Garbed in the drab brown robes of his order, Thich Nhat Hanh (pronounced Tick-Not-Han) is a small man. Most everything about him is prefigured by calmness, a soft yin-ness that goes beyond simple stillness. When he speaks, it is with great mindfulness—a word, an action, to which he is especially devoted.

He speaks quietly in good English with occasional French inflections. His words and speech are restful, easy on the ears and conscience like a balm. Members of the communities that have formed in response to his vision and teachings call him *Thay* (pronounced "Tie"). Born in 1926, he has been a monk for fifty-three years, dedicating himself to the practice and transmission of "engaged

Buddhism," a root insight-tradition melding meditation, awareness of the moment, and compassionate action as a means of taking care of, and improving, our lives and society.

In 1967 he was nominated by Dr. Martin Luther King Jr. for the Nobel Peace Prize, and has taught Buddhism at Columbia University. He is the author of seventy-five books.

Thich Nhat Hanh began with a story. "One day, I was practicing mindful movement in a wood with the people of our community," he said softly. "Every day we practice this, walking slowly, mindfully, to enjoy every step; then we sit down. One day, I suddenly realized that the tree standing in front of me allowed my movement to be possible. I saw very clearly that I was able to breathe in because of its presence in front of me. It was standing there for me, and I was breathing in and out for the tree. I saw this connection very profoundly.

"In my tradition we speak of *interbeing*. We cannot 'be' by [ourselves] alone; we must be with everything else," he continued. "So, for example, we 'inter-are' with a tree: if it is not there, we are not there either. In the *Diamond Sutra* the Buddha advises us to consider four notions: the notions of self, of humanity, of living beings, and of life span. He also advises that the practice of removing these notions from mind is not difficult; anyone can do it."

It was not mere brain fatigue, but what Thich Nhat Hanh had to say, and how he said it—without pyrotechnics or bombast; without jeweled elephants or eight-nectared realms—was like a glass of hot tea on a raw day. "If we observe things mindfully and profoundly," he explained, "we find out that Self is made up only of non-Self elements. If we look deeply into a flower, what do we see? We also see sunshine, a cloud, the earth, minerals, the gardener, the complete cosmos. . . . Why? Because the flower is composed of these nonflower elements: that's what we find out. And like this flower, our body, too, is made up of everything else—except for one element: a separate self or existence. This is the teaching of non-Self in Buddhism.

"In order to just be our Self, we must also take care of the non-Self elements. We all know this, that we cannot be without other people, other species, but very often we forget that 'being' is really inter-being; that living beings are made only of nonliving elements. This is why we have to practice meditation—to keep alive this vision. The *shamatha* practice in my tradition is to nourish and keep alive this kind of insight twenty-four hours a day with the whole of our being."

About then, a nearby Washington radio correspondent leaned over to whisper inquiringly, "What exactly is his tradition anyway? Is it Zen he's talking about, or is all of Buddhism like this?" The hard-boiled Capitol Hill reporter had apparently been told that to under-stand what the environmental lobby was fueled by these days, she ought to check out what the Buddhist monk from Vietnam had to say. I had queries of mine, however, because, to rework a line from Andrei Codrescu, as a teacher Thich Nhat Hanh appears to cultivate anonymity the way others crave publicity

Arnie Kotler seemed like a good source of answers. I knew his name from visits to San Francisco's Page Street Zen Center twenty years ago. Originally ordained in the lineage of beloved *Zen Mind, Beginner's Mind* teacher Shunryu Suzuki-roshi, Kotler is a board member, teacher, and publisher within the Community of Mindful Living—a loose-knit umbrella organization that supports more than one hundred smaller sanghas practicing in Thich Nhat Hanh's tradi-tion of living mindfully, daily, in the moment.

"Thay is a Zen teacher," Kotler related. "He's lived in Plum Village, a contemplative community near Bordeaux, France since 1966. Originally he's from Vietnam—Indo-China—so there may be an assumption that he's from a Theravada tradition. Thay likes to remind people, though, that Indo-China has influence from both India and China, and that Indian Buddhism especially means a lot to him. Vietnam's Unified Buddhist Church, which is suppressed there by the government, is a combination of Mahayana and Theravada tradi-tions with some cross-fertilization among them."

Placing Thich Nhat Hanh's background in context is useful, Kotler notes, "because we tend to think of Zen mostly as Japanese; yet that's only one manifestation—the one best known in the West. Thay is Zen, but he's not Japanese. He practices in the forty-second genera-tion of Lin-Chi's (in Japanese, Rinzai's) Chan/Zen Buddhism. The particular Vietnamese offshoot of this original Tang Chinese lineage is known as the Bamboo Forest School. Thay is in its eighth or ninth generation and he's very much embedded in the fullness of these tra-ditions. During the 1960s when his Vietnam Peace activism was at its height, he also founded a lay order called *Tiep Hien*, or 'inter-being.' It's in this mindfulness tradition that he's empowered fifty of his stu-dents to teach."

This helps explain the formidable association of teachers, scholars, and activists who, in various capacities, are affiliated with the booming growth of Thich Nhat Hanh–inspired "socially engaged" Buddhism in North America—Joan Halifax, Joanna Macy, Deena Metzger, Wendy Johnson, Maxine Hong-Kingston, Kotler, and others. The San Francisco component of Thich Nhat Hanh's recent U.S. visit also brought together distinguished teachers like Jack Kornfeld, Sylvia Boorstein, Ed Brown, and Ram Dass.

Several days earlier at Spirit Rock, the Marin County dharma center inspired by Kornfeld and other teachers, Thich Nhat Hanh led a "Day of Mindfulness" that drew more than two thousand people to the former nature conservancy's natural amphitheater. The daylong outdoor program included meditation, mindful walking, dharma-flavored music and song, silent eating, an offbeat organic "apple" meditation by Ed Espe Brown, and a lengthy, absorbing dharma talk by Master Hanh that became a sermon in the vale.

Happily, a mindfulness carpool scheme introduced me to new friends, so I was not alone in the large crowd. The landscape was beautiful—flowing ridges, woodland, and moor. The caw of scrub-jays and the chatter of small mammals carried on the coastal air, and vultures thermaled above the *lambun* prayer-flags along the trail. The event was an example of North American Buddhism par excellence.

"Today, communication has expanded greatly throughout the world," Master Hanh remarked. "Email, fax, voice pager—you can contact New York from Tokyo in half a minute so easily. Yet in families and in neighborhoods, between husbands and wives, between friends and each other, real communication is still difficult. Suffering continues, pain increases. In our time, many young people also do not feel connected with anything, so they look for something to get relief—alcohol, drugs, money—or they turn on the television set absorbing violence and insecurity.

"How then can the dharma help dysfunctional, emotionally hurt individuals?" he asked.

In response he advised, "Bodhisattva Avalokitesvara is a very good listener, a compassionate listener. We need to rediscover a way to talk and listen to each other as in a loving family. But what technology can help with this? I feel the need is for practice, for mindful listening. A heart free to listen is a flower that blooms on the tree of practice."

Listening to Thich Nhat Hanh one gradually attunes to the meditation bell, which is much a part of his practice path. The mindfulness bell is the voice of our spiritual ancestors, he instructs: "Its sounds call us back to our true home in the present moment—to emptiness. When we inter-are, we find peace, stability, freedom—the root of our happiness. With non-Self we discover the nature of emptiness."

Thich Nhat Hanh recommends study and chanting of the Heart Sutra as a means of understanding how everything can be empty of separate Self, while at the same time being full of everything else in the cosmos. In this dharma realm, he says, "birth, death, being and nonbeing do not truly exist." They are simply notions, he observes; and the practice of the Heart Sutra is the practice of removing all ideas—discovering the nature of nonbirth and nondeath. It is practice of transcending fear and all other kinds of thought perceptions.

What becomes increasingly clear is that what Thich Nhat Hanh instructs is not so much "Buddhism" as steady perseverance in meditative practice. "Deep listening," "deep touching," "deep seeing"—his own interpretations of the concept of *vipasyana*—are as applicable to Christian, Jewish, Taoist, or other spiritual traditions as they are to Buddhism, whatever sect you fancy. In keeping notes on the nine days in which I had opportunity to follow, listen, and sit in his presence, I realized how seldom he discourses on Buddhist theology—a point known to raise eyebrows among purists.

"That's correct. Thay doesn't talk about Buddhism much," agrees Arnie Kotler. "He talks about *practice*. As Trungpa Rinpoche informed us in *Meditation in Action*, his first book in English, meditation is Buddhism's core practice. That's very much what Thich Nhat Hanh is offering: meditation in activity. And I have a hunch that if you asked, say, Naropa people what they mean by 'action,' they'd say it's meditation in complete daily activity."

Inexorably, the meaning of what Thich Nhat Hanh is about waxes clear and ineffable as the call of the mindfulness bell. It is the *vipasyana* training, which beats at the heart of every Buddhist practice, and that, as Trungpa Rinpoche taught, is a jewel possessing two aspects: *shamatha*—stopping, calming, developing tranquillity and inner peace; and *vipasyana* itself—the cultivation of deep insight.

"Is he charismatic?" an old friend grown wise, but in weakened health inquired one afternoon in Golden Gate park.

"No," I answered her, surprised a little by my response. "Not in the usual sense. But he's the real thing. And he's a poet. My Vietnamese friends call him a living Buddha."

As a martial artist of long years, I share a taste for masters like Diogenes the Dog and Chuang-tzu, who on meeting emperors, and in their own unique fashion, brought notice to the world. So it was when Thich Nhat Hanh spoke at the State of the World Forum, first at the Humanness seminar, then later to Mr. Gorbachev and the eminences arrayed.

"Intellect alone is not enough to guide us," Master Hanh declared to them humbly. "To shape the future of the twenty-first century we need something else. Without peace and happiness we cannot take care of ourselves, we cannot take care of other species, and we cannot take care of the world.

"That is why it is important for us to live in such a way that, every moment, we are there deeply with our true presence, always alive and nourishing the insight of interbeing."

Interspersed in his dialogue were observations from *Living Buddha, Living Christ*. A brilliant articulation of the belief in a living holiness shared by both East and West's Buddho-Taoist and Judeo-Christian traditions, this new book effectively establishes a basis for the "New World Dharma" pointed to in such landmark texts of recent years as William Irwin Thompson's *Pacific Shift*, Gary Snyder's *Practice of the Wild*, and Alan Badiner Hunt's eco-Buddhist compendium *Dharma Gaia*.

"To me, mindfulness is very much like the Holy Spirit," he explained. "All of us have the seed of the Holy Spirit in us—the capacity of healing, transforming, and loving. Where there is suffering, mindfulness responds with the energy of compassion and understanding. Compassion is where the rivers of Christianity and Buddhism meet.

"In the Christian and Jewish traditions, we learn to live in the presence of God," he affirmed. "Our Buddhist equivalent is the practice of cultivating mindfulness, of living deeply every moment with the energy of the Holy Spirit. If we change our daily lives—the way we think, speak, and act—we begin to change the world. This is what I discussed with Dr. Martin Luther King many years ago: that the practice of mindfulness is not just for hours of silent meditation, but for every moment of the day. Other teachers like St. Basil have said it is possible to pray as we work, and in Vietnam we invented 'engaged Buddhism' so we could continue our contemplative life in the midst of helping the victims of war. We worked to relieve the suffering while trying to maintain our own mindfulness.

"So to conclude, the practice of looking deeply does not mean being *inactive*. We become very active with our understanding.

Nonviolence does not mean nonaction. It means we act with love and compassion, living in such a way that a future will be possible for our children and their children. Thank you."

It happened then. The temporality of language and power was reduced for a prolonged still moment to reverberant silence, to presentness. There was nothing left to say. The monk gathered himself, rose and departed as anonymously as he'd arrived. I'd remember this.

Somewhere during the days I'd asked him about the mystery of death. What happens when we die? Thich Nhat Hanh knows how to laugh. "Nothing is born. Nothing dies. That is a statement made by Lavoisier—not a Buddhist," he responded with something like a smile. "But as we know, Buddhists too are made up only of non-Buddhist elements."

The sound of women singing—nuns in his order—drifted up from a place nearby. "Breathing in . . . breathing out," they sang. "Breathing in . . . breathing out." Then an echo up the halls of the noble old hotel. "I am free, I am free, I am free." I thought for a moment of St. Francis of Assisi, then, looking about the room at my speechless companions, I could have sworn I saw the universe smile.

San Francisco – Vancouver

Chapter 8

Embracing the Responsibility of the Moment

The Zen Politics of Jerry Brown

> Spirituality has to entail an awakeness, an awareness and respect for other people. A politics based on that respect would have to exhibit compassion and concern whenever there's disproportionate suffering that could be avoided. So from either a Christian or a Buddhist perspective there is a basis for justice, mercy, compassion, it's true.

Visiting China as an elected official at a ports conference in 1998, I met Charles Foster, Executive Director of the Port of Oakland. While on an evening cruise from the city of Dalian, the ship's propeller snagged in a labyrinth of aquaculture nets and without power we drifted all night toward North Korean waters. Our Chinese hosts grew concerned and nervous guests needed to talk. From Mr. Foster I heard that former California Governor Jerry Brown planned to run for mayor in his city. Brown had been governor during my Humboldt State University student years and his unconventional leadership style had made a deep impression on me—one that I'd tried to emulate during my own local political career. Since then, he had run unsuccessfully for the U.S. presidency and the state senate; in contrast, he'd also hosted "We The People," a syndicated radio interview program with prominent thinkers concerned with social justice reform, globalization, the arts, environmentalism, and spirituality. Meanwhile, in the Bohai Sea at dawn we were rescued by a Chinese naval vessel. In the spring of 2000, having lost a reelection bid of my own six months before, I was keen to inquire how

Brown had coped with pain of public defeat. Could I learn from him again? In person, he was informal, straightforward, and visionary; a realistic man who understood what politics is all about. When he spoke, his Jesuit training came through, as did a fundamental concern for humanity, and while not widely regarded as a "Buddhist" he was comfortable and knowledgeable in discussing Buddhist concepts and insights. By then he'd been elected mayor and was a genuinely popular figure among working folks of all stripes in Oakland. When I asked about a good local place to eat, he directed me toward a barbecue joint near the waterfront with photos of two regular customers in the window—bluesman John Lee Hooker and former Raiders football coach John Madden. Instantly, I knew it was the right place. At that time, Al Gore and George W. Bush were campaigning for the U.S. presidency, but my gut told me that I'd just left a man who deserved to have the job. In 2011 Jerry Brown was reelected for his third term as Governor of California and has continued with his progressive leadership vision of "Not Right, Not Left, but Ahead."

In politics, an enterprise that in America has become more notable for hair dye, zippers, and spin doctors, and in which obvious intelligence has long been held suspect, Jerry Brown remains a maverick original. The son of former California Governor, Edmund "Pat" Brown, and now aged sixty-two, Brown studied three years for the Catholic priesthood at Sacred Heart Novitiate before leaving to major in Latin and Greek at U.C. Berkeley. He graduated in law from Yale, and in 1969 was first elected to a seat on the Los Angeles Community College board of trustees. A year later, campaigning as a Democrat reformer he was elected California's Secretary of State. In 1975 he was elected as the youngest Governor in California state history, serving until 1983.

As governor, Brown declined the state mansion and chauffeured limos. He lived a simple lifestyle, dated a popular singer, and occasionally repaired on Zen retreats with Buddhist friends. He personally spearheaded progressive legislation and the appointment of women and minorities to high office, initiatives in which he was not always widely supported.

In June 1998 Brown reentered politics. Elected as mayor of Oakland he embraced the daunting task of leading this needy, workaday city of 380,000 across the bay from his hometown San Francisco toward cosmopolitan rejuvenation. More than 28 percent African American in makeup, and with a legacy of urban blight Oaklanders have seen their social and political agendas brought to prime time by Brown. Amplifying the changes set in motion by his predecessor and aided by a voter-approved "strong mayor" city charter that he championed, Brown sharply addressed the city's longtime patterns of cronyism, reformed the school board, made sweeping changes in the police department and city hall staff, and worked at rehumanizing a weary downtown core in a fashion similar to Seattle's successful model to the north. Unsurprisingly, Mayor Jerry Brown ruffled plenty of institutional feathers. He enjoyed a communitarian lifestyle in an unpretentious, multipurpose warehouse adjacent to Jack London Square on the downtown waterfront. I met Mayor Brown at his office in Oakland City Hall. On his desk one notices a *mala*—prayer beads— and a sign reading "The Buck Stops Here."

TC: *Mayor Brown, Andrei Sakharov observed that we always prefer dead heroes to living men and women who may have made a few mistakes. What do you make of this?*

JB: When someone's dead, it's easy to look at their memory in a more positive light and minimize the flaws that most human beings have. There's a tendency that I think is pervasive to transmit a history that is more favorable than not. In Japan they don't like to talk about the rape of Nanking, or the germ experiments in Harbin, China, or the Bataan Death March. In America the history books don't like to talk about the massacre of the Indians, or really get into the slavery issue, or the war against the Filipinos. There's a rosy glow in all countries that conditions the history books, and this conditions our view of dead heroes.

TC: *What about guys like Jerry Brown who've been, and still are, in politics? In your Buddhist-inflected inaugural speech to the people of Oakland, you acknowledged that as a person you have flaws and have made your share of human mistakes.*

JB: Today, with the press doing the debunking that it does, the criticizing, the flaw-finding that generates news stories, there's a skeptical environment, which is the current way to frame people. That's just where we are at. By the way, there *are* flaws, at least from our more idealistic and naive ways of looking at things. People who are in politics are dealing with power. They are possessed of ambition. They are maneuvering, they're competing, and that process will generate plenty of less-than-ideal Mother Teresa–type behavioral traits.

Okay, that's inherent. We're in a world here where we have an idea that people are always flawed—Eisenhower, all the big heroes, whoever it is. It doesn't look at all like the hagiographies I read about when I was at the Jesuit monastery where the saints were all perfect, no venial sins even. Of course, we're in a world that is not a monastery. But I don't even know if there were perfect people in the monasteries before. I doubt it. In that environment there are plenty of flaws to talk about, and plenty of vices along with whatever virtues you can find.

TC: *What are some of the influences you recall from your growing up?*

JB: My grandmother used to read Bible stories to me from a picture book, all the different Bible stories—Moses, Delilah, and Samson. . . . Later, at school in the '50s, G.K. Chesterton was very much in vogue. And we read the essays of Newman—the idea of the university. There was an essay, I think it was called "Quality," about a shoemaker and how he was being displaced by the modern machine industry. I remember the ironic stories of Saki like "The Gift of the Magi," where the woman cuts off her hair to buy her man a watch-fob and, unbeknown, the man sells his watch to buy a comb for his wife. There was an environment growing up within the Catholic educational framework that there was a right and a wrong; that there was a higher path that one should be following. And obviously, when I went to the seminary that is precisely what propelled me forward.

At the seminary we read the lives of the Jesuit saints, Thomas à Kempis and the New Testament. After that, coming out of Berkeley and going to law school, there was a whole other set of influences—Nietzsche, Paul Goodman's book *Compulsory Miseducation*, which really critiqued education as a conformity-building structure—that really had an influence on me.

TC: *Somewhere or other you encountered Buddhist ideas.*

JB: I heard a speech once in the '60s in San Francisco at a symposium on the mind. Aldous Huxley spoke about a different kind of education. He said that our education system was cognitive, hyper-rational, and that it was leaving out the most important part of the human being. I remember going up afterward and asking him what he was talking about. He said, "Read *Zen Flesh, Zen Bones*." I'd maybe heard about Zen before then, but with Aldous Huxley's saying so, I definitely looked into it and it certainly had an influence on me.

TC: *That's a beloved little book by Paul Reps and Ngoyen Senzaki-roshi. What attracted you to it?*

JB: Just hearing those koan stories—they had a flavor that rang true. There was a zest to them that I appreciated.

TC: *You've been a friend of the Buddhist community for a long time. How would you describe your own engagement, how serious is it?*

JB: I'd say that when I went to Japan it was very serious because I practiced every day for six months and did four sesshins. It was at Kamakura. I did two sesshins under Yamada-roshi, and two under Father LaSalle, a Jesuit at a Jesuit retreat house there.

TC: *How about these days, is it a flavor that comes into your life or is there more?*

JB: I haven't been sitting lately. Not like I should be. I have a cushion right in the middle of my room. It's sitting there, but I've sat infrequently. It's an intention, but not a strong enough intention! But definitely an intention.

TC: *What circumstances prompted your decision to journey to Japan and study Buddhism?*

JB: I'd been interested in Zen previously and had visited Tassajara. I knew Baker Roshi and Gary Snyder. I'd read different things. Then in 1986 an opportunity arose when I could go somewhere for six months. It's not easy to do that. I'd been governor before and I had some time, although it was still difficult to get away; I'm embedded in my ordinary day-to-day life.

What happened is that I went on a trip to China with a nonprofit foundation and a group of people. We passed through Tokyo, so I just called up Sophia College and went into where a group of Jesuit priests lived. I asked, "Anybody here know anything about Zen? Who knows it?" There were two people interested, Fathers LaSalle and Heinrich Dumoulins, both elderly people. I had a conversation with Father LaSalle and took notes that I still have. He said, "Philosophy is dead; theology as we've known it is dead. What people want is experience—*experiencing* God." Then he suggested I talk with Yamada-roshi. So I went to see him at his hospital [where] he was a hospital administrator. Yamada-roshi said, "Well, come and practice." He invited me and I said, "Okay, I'll do it." I returned home, caught a plane back to Japan and found a place to live in Kamakura.

Every night I'd go and join the loose community of practitioners under Yamada-roshi. Father LaSalle would come by sometimes, too. In *dokusan* Yamada-roshi would always say, "You yourself are totally empty," and his saying that during *teishos* had an authority. He was speaking as someone who evidently had had a *kensho*. He had that clarity.

TC: *So you encountered emptiness. Does that awareness still resonate for you in some way amid political life?*

JB: What interested me was emptiness as a practice as opposed to an idea. The principle foundation for the Jesuit order—in fact, it's right in the Spiritual Exercises—is detachment, and the evil in Jesuit spirituality is inordinate attachment. Ignatius in his Foundations uses the word "indifference": you have to make yourself indifferent, whether your life is long or short, of wealth or poverty, honor or dishonor—it should all be a matter of indifference in order that you can follow the will of God. That's something I always found difficult; it sounded cold. The Buddhist notion and practice of emptiness seemed to explain this nonattachment, whereas in the Jesuits we were told to fight self: *adere contra*. It means go against oneself: *immolatio sui*—immolate the self—war against the self and all its attachments. Buddhism offered another type of insight.

TC: *In a broader sense, does your experience suggest that a dynamic is possible by which the spiritual might be bridged with the political?*

JB: Spirituality is one of those words that feel good, but what is it really pointing at?

TC: *Some sense of recognition, belief, commitment? A sense of the sacred? For instance, in Taoism there is a "way." How do you try and keep your politics consonant with the idea of there being a higher way, a virtuous way?*

JB: I don't think politics is distinct from other activities that involve a lot of people. It's as if you're running a store, or a movie theater, a dot-com business, a park, or being the mayor—there's simply a lot of activity. So a spiritual path to me is about being very clear in what you're doing: being clear in asking, "What is it I'm engaged in now?" From that clarity I make whatever decisions I have to make. So for me the spirituality, the path, would be the clarity. I went to hear

Krishnamurti several times and he would simply say, "Just observe." That's very much like sitting.

TC: *And it's a close cousin to the practice of mindfulness. You discuss this with Thich Nhat Hanh in your book* Dialogues.

JB: Yes, as a matter of fact he visited Oakland last year and we had a Day of Mindfulness. I issued a Proclamation as the mayor on the Eightfold Path. It's worth looking at.

TC: *Let's get specific: what's your evaluation of the usefulness of religious influence in politics? The argument being that some on the liberal side say they too should bring a spiritual perspective to bear on political questions, that they shouldn't cede the field entirely to the right.*

JB: Religious identity groups are a part of the business that politics engages in to build together enough loyalty and appeal that will create the fifty-one percent. Given the diversity of America, this can involve minorities, ethnic groups, and different regions. It's part of the mundane process of coalition-building and putting together a successful political marketing plan. If you think about the Right, the fundamentalist Christians are a certain group of people, twenty percent maybe, who are grouped around certain ideas and practices, and there is power there. They are in opposition to some of the practices of contemporary society like pornography, homosexuality, abortion— although not in opposition to others like capitalism, markets, technology, genetic engineering, and nuclear power. They're a group and there is authority there.

Now you can take the liberal side; they're not generally characterized by overt religious activity—although with the nuns, the sojourners, [and] the Protestant political activists there's certainly a tradition, from Martin Luther King Jr. to the Jesuits, [of] opposing the School of the Americas and expressing solidarity with Central America. There was a lot of religious involvement in those activities, and there's a Left religious commitment that's there. Some religious groups like the Catholic Worker Movement are not political; they don't want to get involved. Like Jehovah's Witnesses, they don't want to vote. They don't see the Kingdom as being of this world.

TC: *Do you think it possible, or even desirable, that there is a philosophical basis for good government from a spiritual point of view?*

JB: Spirituality has to entail an awakeness, an awareness and respect for other people. A politics based on that respect would have to exhibit compassion and concern whenever there's disproportionate suffering that could be avoided. So from either a Christian or a Buddhist perspective there is a basis for justice, mercy, compassion, it's true. The difficulty we see is in cases like Sri Lanka where Hindus and Buddhists are fighting; or elsewhere when Muslims and Christians or others are in conflict. There's a history here where religion hasn't been the peacemaker that it theoretically should be. Nevertheless, I believe [in] the practice of zazen, or the practice of remembering, of being more aware of good works; all this should call politics to a higher vocation.

TC: *Regarding higher calling, you went to visit Mother Teresa in Calcutta. How long were you there and what effect did this experience have on you?*

JB: I spent about three weeks working there in 1987, mostly at her home for the dying—the Kalighat. I was very impressed and moved by the volunteers who came every day. These were people who were spending six months there—Irish, Australians, Germans. I was very impressed by their presence, by their serving attitude because it was so out of phase with the commercial, with the political. People just showed up and helped bathe people, shaved and fed them, sprayed down the floors. It was a very good feeling to be involved in that—the human spirit. I'm attracted to that.

About Mother Teresa, I experienced her as a person of real clear authority, something I hardly ever encounter—someone who spoke in such a way that I was inclined to listen, to follow. I felt this woman was speaking out of some enlightenment, some clarity in her way of seeing. So that when she says, *that* is Jesus—that person lying on the floor from the streets of Calcutta who speaks a foreign language— and what you do for him, with him, *that* is Jesus. Well, this is not only supremely Christian, it is also supremely *compassionate*. I was in the presence of a woman who without hesitation would touch these people, would *be* there. She manifested her being and was grounded in a way that I've seen in very few people.

TC: *Mikhail Gorbachev has said that the importance of politics in our time has devolved to the local municipal or regional level. What do you make of this assessment?*

JB: In some part, yes. We have trading regimes, international alliances, global environmental treaties or protocols, too, and these are very important. You cannot solve global warming, or destruction of the oceans or Arctic glaciers, or protection of the ozone layer just by local action—even though everything always seems local because we're in a body, standing on our own two feet somewhere. So there is a role for the international work, there's a role for the national work, for all these different levels of organization.

Having said that, we need to recognize there is a difference, a vitality in a city. There are neighborhoods; there's West Oakland, there's Thirty-First and Martin Luther King Boulevard. There's a school. These are concrete images—you can see the people and encounter them and their issues. It's different than being governor, which is a more derivative position. The governor talks about a law that increases the penalties for crime, such as, "You will serve three more years in prison for robbing a house at night." That's what governors do, and then make speeches about it. As a mayor you can take action in a far more immediate way. You look at the number of commercial burglaries in the last three weeks in an area of Oakland, compare the statistics from three weeks before, and talk to the police chief about what we're going to do. So I get specific: I think about more police, more jobs, the schools. You can think about housing blight, all the different issues.

TC: *It's a new millennium. What can citizens do as individuals to get better involved? How can they bring themselves to the political process to get action?*

JB: In Oakland we get action through community policing, through parent involvement in the schools. We have community involvement in development proposals; all the immediate neighbors are asked their point of view on the project, say on whether a building should be demolished or a new business permitted. Then, of course, there are elections to City Council, to [the] school board, and there are bond proposals. That is a lot of participation at the local political level. People can join political organizations or neighborhood committees that do a lot more even at the nonpolitical level, because they also have their houses, their jobs, their spouses and children, their aches and pains, their television and movies, and their elixirs of one kind or another. Most people are involved in managing the private family environment that they have. The politicians have another domain that they function in and they carry on their activities.

TC: What about growing public concern regarding how appropriate local allocation of diminishing public resources can be ensured when special interests play such a large role in the fray?

JB: Special interest is a term that obscures the fact that the political realm is where decisions are made by many people regarding outcomes about money, taxes, buildings, or criminal prohibitions. In a capitalist society, money has an impact. It's about money. And if that isn't the most important thing, it's right up there. Therefore, anyone with a lot of money is going to have an impact, and usually his or her request is to be able to make more money. Now, if more money is added, theoretically that's generally a good thing. However, other people who don't have exactly the same personal interests may fight and say, you'd better give me some money; they're a union, or a homeowner group, so there's a struggle for decisions. As an example, there's a building that was constructed seventy years ago and some people said don't tear it down. The Gap store came along and said, we want to tear it down and put up a new ten-thousand-square-foot store. Now most people wanted that, but some people didn't. So you get these contests, and I find that at the local level citizens have a lot of clout.

TC: When you were campaigning for mayor you spoke of "America's unfinished agenda." What do you mean by that?

JB: Fostering conditions so that people of different ethnic and racial situations can live in harmony, as well as alleviating the harsh consequences of market capitalism and setting the framework for an economy that works within the environment explicitly, thereby becoming increasingly more sustainable.

TC: You've made Oakland's schools a key focus of your reformist work. Why?

JB: We've never had so many hours of organized educational instruction in the United States before, maybe even in the world; yet if you look at television and the number of hours people spend in front of it, and if you look at the way people are allocating their resources, you have to raise the serious question: What is this education for? Is it just to make happy hyper-consumers, or is it to teach people to think, to express themselves? Education today generally means getting a job and making the most money you can. I'd like to see some special schools here, like a performing arts academy and a vocational school teaching airplane engine and technical repair skills. I'd also like to see a college prep military academy—and I say this because of the discipline involved and the Pentagon money that could be brought into Oakland. And I'd like to see effective reading programs, but I also understand that education is another one of those terms that people invoke very easily to cover a multitude of questions. Not that long ago, when I was in college, it meant a liberal education to teach the whole man and it was based on time and eternity, which were Catholic ways of talking about the material and the spiritual.

TC: *Here's a materialist question: You've enjoyed success in your long career and you've hung out with celebrities. John Updike has expressed the view that celebrity itself has a peculiarly corrosive quality. What's your take on this?*

JB: Well, celebrity is certainly distracting. It offers an opportunity to make yourself feel good, which I might add can be very deleterious to the path of enlightenment!

TC: *Here's an Andy Warhol koan for you: You started out as a young, left-of-center liberal, and nowadays you're called a "nonideological centrist." You've also been called the Guiliani of the West, which seems to boil down to a pragmatic, infrastructure-building, local-issues-first position—what Warhol used to call "bringing home the bacon." Where are you at now?*

JB: Bringing home the bacon, exactly! That's what people in the city want—lower crime, a vital downtown center with exciting opportunities that are nice, not toxic. They want more shops instead of one major store, which is all Oakland has today. They want better schools where their kids can get ahead. So you've got to deliver that. And in a capitalist society, you get a flow of capital entering because there's a return equal to or better than other opportunities elsewhere. We are in that framework and I'm working with it. If you read the book I've done with people whose ideas have impressed me, you won't find a "left" ideology in many of the people you encounter in it. They're activists: Gregory Bateson, Ivan Illich, some of the impressive people I've met and worked with—these people and their ideas cannot be pigeonholed.

TC: You have a sense of yourself, then, as a kind of cultural transmitter for these theorists and their ideas?

JB: Somewhat. I like to try and understand them, which is a continuing effort. I can still read Bateson's *Steps Toward an Ecology of Mind* and be learning from it. There's still plenty to understand. This is part of my pursuit: I study these people to understand my own life, to understand the world that I live in and my role in it.

TC: What keeps you going? Why endure in politics when it can bring such pain?

JB: It engages me. It's here. It's like asking, why does the stock market take off? There's a certain zest in political life. I've also been around the political since my father first ran for office the year after I was born, so there's a skill, a practice, there's this knowledge. If I were to go and do my lawyer work, I'd be nowhere near the professional or the practitioner that I am of the political. So what is political? It's being able to see, to listen to different points of view. It's being able to articulate in a way that can marshal action. That's what I'm doing and it's frustrating at times. My work in radio was different: intellectually it was satisfying, but at the end of every day then what? I was able to draw good people who were really talking about the problems, but just talking sometimes isn't enough.

TC: Locally, there are bus drivers and folks you meet in stores who say they supported you for mayor in part because of your radio show—that you sounded like a man who was honestly searching for answers.

JB: That's good. As mayor, though, I feel there's more action. I can actually engage developers, police chiefs, neighborhood activists; I can help get a swimming pool built, increase recycling, create a charter school, bring a new restaurant to downtown as we're going to do next door to City Hall—a pleasant place to go after work where you can have a glass of wine and talk to people. That's energizing. It is a pleasure to be engaged in that as opposed to just talking, or whatever.

TC: Last question: you've had victory in public life and also experienced defeat. What can you tell us about the experience of defeat?

JB: I would say that in some campaigns where the stories aren't that pleasant and you're losing, defeat can almost be a relief. Maybe it's like death: you get sick, you suffer and suffer and you say, I'm ready to die now. Losing can be very unpleasant, but after a few years you forget about whatever the pain was and say, "I'm back fighting." I came back. I wasn't quite sure what [being] mayor was going to be like, but I find I'm very happy to be here. The old metaphors of Oakland as a city of crime, danger, they're pretty overrated now. We're strategically located and, increasingly, a fairly exciting place to be. The flow of money has now directed itself into Oakland. It's coming, and to that extent we may be able to attract more people of talent because the housing is a little cheaper, the weather is a little better, the openings are more abundant, and Oakland will continue to transform itself. I feel very grateful for the opportunity.

Oakland, California

Chapter 9

Avanti! The Dharma Poetics of Diane di Prima

When the time came for me, I went out on the streets and said what I had to say.

Walking past City Lights Books on Columbus Avenue in San Francisco in 2008, my wife and I saw a sign advertising "Tonight, Reading with Diane di Prima." We could hardly believe our luck. Like Joanne Kyger, di Prima was a favorite author among my students, and her street-wise language, imagery, and long record of political and social engagement have made her a distinctive voice in American literature. Buddhist imagery and influence permeate much of her mature work and this is evident throughout her memorable Revolutionary Letters with its signature motto, "The Only War That Matters Is The War Against The Imagination." Di Prima read from her Letters that evening. We had met before in Vancouver and she had generously contributed a cover comment for a Taoist co-translation I had published: she'd understood the work with penetrating clarity. During her mature career di Prima has taught regularly at Naropa University's Jack Kerouac School for Disembodied Poetics in Boulder, Colorado.

Thursday, October 11 was a good night to be in San Francisco. All around, the city's annual LitQuake Festival was in full bloom and at City Lights Books in North Beach, Diane di Prima's reading from her new edition of *Revolutionary Letters* demonstrated her working at the top of her poetic form. Warm, wry, compassionate, di Prima read from her politically charged work-in-progress that has endured through five published incarnations and over forty years. The current edition with twenty-one new letter-poems is published by Last Gasp Press.

Di Prima began with an explanation, noting that she first read her revolutionary poems in New York from the back of a truck driven by Sam Abrams. These early poems, she said, were structured using "street form"—quick, one-shot takes that could be read on street corners before heading off to the next location. "Rant From A Cool Place" (1967) is archetypal: *We are in the middle of a bloody, heart-rending revolution / Called America, called the Protestant reformation, called / Western man / Called individual consciousness, meaning I need a refrigerator / and a car / And milk and meat for the kids.*

Given the violent and vengeful nature of those stormy times, mobility and poetic shape-shifting were no small things. As di Prima reminds us in Letter #8, *Every time you pick the spot for a be-in / a demonstration, a march, a rally, you are choosing the ground / for a potential battle.* Plenty of the names who made political waves during the stormy '60s and who ended up dead are honored in this collection. Di Prima was no lightweight activist herself and *Revolutionary Letters* still kicks ass, hard. These are the rants, incantations, and prophetic warnings of a bard-seer on the run, ducking and dodging her way as esthete, mother, creative artist, and all-around dissenting American citizen who's been pissed off with the high-level hooliganism of the U.S. ruling elite since she was old enough to absorb her Italian grandfather's own revolutionary teaching.

The book's opening offers useful perspective: di Prima dedicates it to Bob Dylan and to her grandfather, a *"friend of the great anarchist dreamers of his time,"* who she says read Dante to her as a little girl, and named her mother after Emma Goldman. It gets saltier. Precise instructions for basic revolutionary activity: how to respond to martial force from the authorities, how to hide, set up neighborhood action plans, what foods and provisions are needed during a siege, fundamental strategies of every underground liberation force. Given the way things have been drifting, maybe it's timely advice.

The image on this latest cover of *Revolutionary Letters* shows that memorable in-your-face Italian beauty known to the world through her eternally hip *Memoirs of a Beatnik*. But as some poems age, so do poets. Di Prima's reputation as a beloved elder of North America's literary community is secure, but with an experiential wisdom shared by comparatively few other ranking American poets, she now projects the subdued aura and physicality of an eternally hip Queen Victoria, a poetic nobility earned through fire and *having been there.* Her later revolutionary poems may not be as volatile as earlier works, but they possess rich spiritual depth, reflecting a long evolving concern with ecological issues that entwine with even deeper yearnings for peace: *The dance of the I Ching is the dance of the star tide / Mathematics of the Zend Avesta / Geometries of Ife / The golden ikon of the Black Virgin / stands at the stone gateway of Tashkent / The flowering valleys of Shambhala / haunt our dreaming / What skeletons stalk there?* (Letter #77).

What we get is a poet who's walked the walk. There's no airy-fairy, self-conscious art-making fluff in this gutsy book, yet there is a constant sense of awareness, of poetic intent. Di Prima explains that while the poems in the series were hastily composed in the moment, "[a]fter the first three or four I saw that the poems were being written for performance." And indeed there is a sense of dialogue with her audience here, like words from a wise old friend we suddenly realize we need to hear from. "You can see in 'Canticle of St. Joan' that it is not a street poem," she says. Dedicated to Robert Duncan, the alchemical four-part mystic exploration of the ecstasy of St. Joan of Arc is anything but street poetics.

Regarding her optimism and ability as an activist poet to face up to grim U.S. politics, di Prima speaks with the candor of a neighborhood big sister: "I'm hopeful because every one of us, in a Buddhist sense, is intrinsically already past all the bullshit . . . the wars, Iraq—I'm hopeful."

Has she ever been afraid to say anything? "Of course! Why? Because I'm afraid. Why else do you think I'd want to say these things! But as a poet you have to speak out. What have you got to lose anyway? At this point in my life I try not to get other people arrested. . . . I'm working now on the second volume of my autobiography and I wish there were—there ought to be—a statute of limitations regarding what you can say about some things, some incidents, and some people who've affected your life."

Readers of di Prima become familiar with the Buddha dharma that runs throughout her poetry. The question of finding reconciliation, however, between the demands of the compassionate views it encourages and the anger that frequently accompanies political action is a central point of tension in her work.

"Most of the poems in *Revolutionary Poems* aren't written from anger," she clarifies. "The beauty and the joy and the possibilities of living and of celebrating life are enormous. In the same breath, you have to remember the Buddhist idea of wrathfulness—that whatever opposes compassion is a demonic form and an incitement to become mindfully wrathful. The difference here is that when you take it all *personally*, when you invest ego in it, then anger can arise. I remember Allen Ginsberg in the '60s getting worked up about the antiwar situation—and there was a lot to get worked up about in those times. He shouted one time, '*I will personally stop the war in Vietnam!*' When you take it to that level it gets pretty intense.

"You know, I was asked once after making an appearance in another city—I think it was for the Liberation News Service that used to provide news to hundreds of alternative publications throughout North America—I was asked, 'What is your plan for the city of San Francisco?' I was absolutely stopped in my tracks. My plan for *what*? I thought, 'Well, I can tell you what my plan is for the immediate week ahead, or maybe what the elderly Italian lady down the hall might think about prices in the bakery or the market, and if we talked to the black lady nearby we could probably come up with a plan, like, for the block,' but that just isn't how I was thinking—that big. Maybe that's what men do. Women are different because we're mothers—we deal with issues right here in front of us, on the ground. Maybe all of us old grannies ought to get together and just rip the world apart and change it. Pain or death don't matter to us anymore."

If defiance runs through the early revolutionary poems, it gives way to the long view of compassion even in the face of war in the more recent works. Fear, though, di Prima relates, was a motivating factor in the earlier pieces.

"The generation of today feels that it is scared, but we were the most scared people in the universe during the writing of these early poems. Coming out of the 1950s, the Cold War, we were *scared*. We didn't talk but to the twenty people we trusted. With the neocons I see that scaredness coming back, but it ain't worth it. There's plenty to be scared of because there are maniacs running the universe, but I tell young people especially, *it isn't worth it.* When the time came for me, I went out on the streets and said what I had to say. Before that, we holed up and just talked about it among ourselves. Remember, in the late '50s there were maybe hundreds of us that could network across the nation; that's all, hundreds. Yet, we could make things happen and it changed the world. With the Internet, with all the new technologies that younger people have at their disposal, the opportunities for networking and sharing information and ideas, there's so much more that can happen now. So we've got to be hopeful. I'm optimistic."

City Lights, San Francisco

Chapter 10

On Forgiveness and Compassion

H. H. the Dalai Lama

The essence of forgiveness is in not harboring hatred against others. Forgiveness does not mean that we forget the act committed against us. But, if in remembering the harmful act done against us we can remain aware of its wrongfulness and restrain from having hatred for the other person, we can have forgiveness.

In a confused, immoral age, His Holiness the 14th Dalai Lama of Tibet—scholar, exiled monarch, spiritual minister par excellence—like the late Nelson Mandela has become a world-respected moral leader. A warm and humble communicator, His Holiness speaks English with a fractured, musical cadence. He enjoys laughing at himself and when he's itchy, he stops to scratch. As a Buddhist logician he invites us to question crucial suppositions, including his own, emphasizing the importance of right effort in all our endeavors. "I am not so special," he explains. "I have no special powers—can't heal. So, you may not hear something new, but you may learn something new." His teaching is frequently rooted in the basic nature of cause and effect, of the interdependency of people, their actions, and outcomes: in his close presence you get a feeling of what it is like to encounter the Buddha. For many, the Dalai Lama's teachings also constitute a set of marching orders—right speech, right thought, right action, right livelihood—the basic Buddhist path of mindful living that can be pursued within the context of whatever individual spiritual tradition we may ascribe to, and that offers individuals the opportunity to become part of a larger community of belief. These days he fills stadiums. For years I've had a quote from His Holiness on my work desk reminding me "Anger serves no purpose: it's only function is to make one miserable." Another, by the door, came as a gift from my teenage daughter: "Not getting what you want, can sometimes be a wonderful stroke of luck." In May 2001 I was contacted by the Tibetan community in Portland, Oregon to ask if I could help find lodging for a dozen monks from Drepung Loseling Monastery. They would accompany His Holiness at a number of functions during his teaching visit to the city, including a talk to 8,000 high-school students whom he addressed as "Younger Brothers and Sisters" in discussing how to respond constructively to violence. Oddly, I was able to help the monks. The Tibetan community invited me to attend events there as a visiting dharma journalist, so I was able to present these questions for consideration by His Holiness during sessions over two days in his presence. Something significant begins to happen whenever this revered spiritual minister arrives in the West. Whole cities just feel better when he comes to town. In Portland, more than 40,000 people attended his public talks on compassion, developing warm-heartedness and nonviolent conflict resolution in a citywide festive atmosphere.

TC: *Ethically speaking, Your Holiness, how can ideas derived from Buddhist practice be incorporated in a practical way in everyday personal or community decision making?*

H.H: We must, I think, cultivate basic human good qualities such as tolerance, compassion, kindness, caring, and sharing. Cultivating this *bodhicitta*, or warm heart—compassion—for the sake of oneself and for others is a mental disposition or awareness I usually call secular ethics. We can also speak about this warm heart as a basis of faith, because even without religious faith you can be a good or happy person. If you have religious faith, that's very good, but without these basic values you will not have a happy family life. All human beings want happiness. True happiness comes not from a limited concern for one's own well-being, or for those one feels close to, but from developing love and compassion for all sentient beings. Here, love means wishing that all sentient beings should find happiness, and compassion means wishing that they should all be free of suffering. In order to build a happy family and society our work must start from one individual. We are all citizens of humanity, so our existence should be that of not causing pain to others. The development of this attitude gives rise to a sense of openness and trust that provides the basis for peace.

Peace, I think, is a manifestation of human compassion. All the teachings of the Buddha are rooted in the practice of compassion, in not harming. So, special emphasis is laid on the cultivation of compassion as a state of mind that takes the condition of sentient beings and wishes it to be free of suffering. In order to generate compassion, it is necessary to understand something of the nature of suffering: to have a sense of connectedness, closeness to that which we wish to be free of suffering. World peace must develop from inner peace. Inner disarmament, external disarmament: these must go together, you see. Peace is not just mere absence of violence—genuine peace must start in each individual heart.

TC: *You've said previously that the present is created from the past. What do you feel our chances are of genuine peacemaking in our new century?*

H.H: The twentieth century was the century of ideology, also of science and technology—an important century of human history. It was also a century of bloodshed. Many destructive wars took place. The destructive power of the technologies made many more people suffer. More pain, more suffering. By the end of this century every human being felt fed up with violence. The twenty-first century should be one of dialogue. I believe humanity is becoming more and more mature. From present reality, the concept of war is out of date. Our world is becoming heavily interdependent. Your future is your neighbor, so destruction of your neighbor is destruction of yourself. Therefore, our long-term goal is to demilitarize the world. It's a step-by-step goal. But some kind of conflict will always be there. If war is out of date, what resolution is there? Compromise. Respect. In modern times you cannot defeat the other side one hundred percent. So, we need to develop an attitude that there is no alternative to peace. Internal dialogue, inner disarmament. Whether it can be a happy, friendly, peaceful century or a violent, destructive one entirely depends on us. Truth, honesty, and optimism are very crucial factors, not just to have a happy day, but in making a happy world. Each of us has a responsibility to think, and to act. We also have a responsibility for the environment, to the planet. Similar with human rights, rights of self-determination. In the latter part of the twentieth century these things became universal. So, to help the world, I think we have a responsibility to act. We have the motivation, the power of vision. Therefore, it is entirely up to us.

TC: *These days we hear more about "mindfulness." How might we apply this particular practice?*

H.H: Through self-discipline. By engaging in ethical conduct, by abstaining from negative actions. Therefore, one ensures the means of actualizing the cessation of suffering from negative acts and their implications. What the Buddha taught was the practice of the Four Mindfulnesses—body, feelings, mind, phenomena. This is crucial for a more contented life. Drugs and alcohol, for example, may bring a sense of short-term peace but will ruin the body. Like sex—beyond limitation, you get in more and more trouble!

Where the primary focus is in understanding the ethical norms of adopting a spiritual practice, we can consider what is to be avoided, what is to be practiced, and so on. The way of doing this is by following a moral path, the path of virtue—abstention from negative acts. One needs enthusiasm and courage to observe such a practice of morality, and what's needed is a deeper understanding of negative actions and their consequences. This cannot be achieved by external discipline; it can only come from within by voluntary adoption of a spiritual discipline. For some one-month periods in Buddhist tradition we practice special mindfulness and try not to lose our temper, to familiarize ourselves toward compassion.

If we look at the life of the historical Buddha, he attained enlightenment through a long process of spiritual ascetics and hardship. If you look at the life of Jesus Christ, it is similar also. Not one of leisure. If you look at the commonality of the lives of the leaders of various great faiths, there is a message. It is this: that if we wish to make spiritual progress, hardship is necessary for spiritual realization. In this, one of the predominant attachments is toward the body, toward certain characteristics of the body. One other dominant attachment is the experience of pain and pleasure. Therefore, one analyzes these feelings and loosens the grip of pain and pleasure. Where do these attachments arise? As a kind of recognition: therefore, in mind. So, we analyze mind. The essential nature of mind is clear light: all defilements can be eventually removed from this clear light. The procedure for grounding the mind is rooted in the Three Practices: in morality, concentration, and wisdom. If we were to examine our thought processes underlying a negative action—strong-headedness, jealousy—the underlying motive or state of mind that motivates a negative act is really attachment, or what the Buddha calls desire. What becomes important is to cultivate antidotes, to counteract attachment.

TC: *In your new book* Stages of Meditation *you observe that this involves the method of "exchanging and equalizing oneself with others."*

H.H: The most important antidote is the "wisdom-realizing emptiness." The realization of emptiness acts as the direct antidote to the causes, which give rise to suffering. In Buddhist literature we find an explanation for cosmological evolution. There is a perpetual cycle of empty space that leads to a new cycle of evolution and so on. This is the world of cause and effect—of conventional reality, conventional truth.

All things come into being through mutual interdependence—all phenomena, whether of created concepts or conditions, come into existence through other factors. Since all things and events come into being dependent on other concepts and conditions, nothing possesses independent or intrinsic existence. There are different constructs that the mind creates. What they are, and how we perceive them is the illusion. The way of appreciating the nature of illusion is through understanding that all events are devoid of independent reality. This is what is meant by the term "school of emptiness." This nature of reality is known as ultimate truth, ultimate reality. By looking at ultimate reality, gradually one is able to eliminate, or root out negative actions, emotions. Emptiness—*Atman*—acts as a direct action to eliminating distraction.

So, two truths, and as Nagarjuna points out in his *Fundamental Treatise of the Middle Way*, or Madhayamika school, all the Buddha's teachings arrive through both conventional and ultimate truth. The first characteristic of suffering that the Buddha taught is that of transience—of change on the gross level, change on the subtle level: impermanence. The Buddha says that the very cause that brings a thing into existence is also the seed of its destruction. This suggests that in order for things to come into being or cease to exist, they are transient, impermanent on a moment-to-moment basis. Because all things are devoid of independent reality, then *karma*—an intentional act committed by an individual—can lead to other events.

Transformation must be affected in one's attitudes. This is the antidote to various mental afflictions, including the most confused state that perceives the nature of reality in a cognitive way. Certain categories of mental afflictions are intuitive; others are cognitive, such as grasping and extreme views. More impulsive poisons of mind arise as strong reaction. One of the ways of exchanging the individual's sense of commitment and purpose is the *Tonglen* visualization technique, or "giving" and "taking"—breathing in all the defilements or others, exhaling all our kindnesses. There could be a direct benefit of karma.

TC: *When another person has hurt us, or when violence is directed against us, one of the hardest things for us to do is to forgive. How do we overcome the pain of injury?*

H.H: If an act of violence is committed against you, even shooting, how do you forgive this? First, I try to develop a precautionary atmosphere, a willingness to develop positive emotion. Use self-defense. If you can, run away! Use reason and, eventually, your affection: there is a chance the other side becomes your friend. I usually suggest that the reason we should follow the nonviolent way is because as soon as we ourselves go against something, we become involved; it's just more violence, negative emotion. The essence of forgiveness is in not harboring hatred against others. Forgiveness does not mean that we forget the act committed against us. But, if in remembering the harmful act done against us we can remain aware of its wrongfulness and restrain from having hatred for the other person, we can have forgiveness. Delusion, hostility, anger—these are the Three Poisons of [the] mind. We need a powerful sense of self and of self-confidence in combating these mental afflictions, these negative processes. We can't be free completely from anger, jealousy, emotions—but try to minimize them, then the positive emotion, forgiveness, increases. The real destroyer of peace of mind, of our own happiness and fortune, is not necessarily an external enemy, but our own negative emotions. In Tibet, we lost our country but it brought positive possibilities to meet with people from other traditions.

TC: *Perhaps some thoughts on your idea of an ethics for the new millennium?*

H.H: The important thing is humanity. We are all the same. In the past, we've paid attention mainly to progress in the material field. But materialism gives us satisfaction on a mainly sensory level. Mental happiness is superior. Mentally, more inner peace, and verbally more calm—through family and the community. Material development alone cannot prevent human suffering. What is lacking is human affection: [in] this country, [there is] too much greed. You have all the facilities, but you are not necessarily very happy. Compassion is the source of all lasting happiness and joy. But recently in America and the West, more and more people are beginning to realize the limits of materialism. I think this is a very good thing. We need growth development in our sense of sharing, caring, patience, and tolerance. Eventually we have to adopt a new, more contented simple lifestyle—it's essential.

Another unfortunate thing in capitalism is the gap between rich and poor. Morally it is wrong, but also practically as well. Wrongsightedness leads to insecurity. The modern economy and our environment have grown heavily interdependent; the concept of "we" and "they" is obsolete. From a religious point of view, we are all created equal, so discrimination on basis of color, for example, is also senseless: it's a lack of compassion. Everything is interdependent. Therefore, taking care of others is actually taking care of oneself. I try my best to be something useful to others. I tell businessmen, "If your company wants a good image, you should show more compassion for your workers." After all, we are social animals. Our happiness is dependent on someone else. Positive thought, compassion, sense of caring—these are positives for good health.

From the selfish viewpoint, if you want good health, look deeper into your emotional world. People pay so much importance to physical beauty, but even more important is mental beauty. In education, we spend much attention on knowledge but not much on [a] warm heart. In order to make a contribution to humanity you need real education, so I think, please [pay] more attention to inner values. I believe this is the real preparation to build a better century.

A Grace Note Regarding Tibet's Political Situation

Tibet is one of the ancient cultures of the world. Today, there is every danger that this civilization will be eliminated, entirely. I would like to express my deep thanks to those people who take such an interest in our Tibetan culture, including Tibetan Buddhism, and who show such sympathy for the Tibetan cause. I appreciate this very much.

—H. H. the Dalai Lama

Portland, Oregon

Chapter 11

On the Trail with Nanao Sakaki

Oriental people say two ways to escape and be happy. Downtown—very busy, crowded place. Just be lost among many people, stay in a slum. Another is in high places. Live in a mountain cave. I've tried both. . . . Try walking mountainsides, the north. I love walking these places. That's me personally. Probably there is no solution. It's a good idea: no solution! Much wider perspective. If you have a solution, you're trapped in solution network.

During a reading in 1985, Gary Snyder read an unforgettable poem entitled "Break the Mirror" by his friend Nanao Sakaki (1923–2008). Five years on, I wrote Nanao and asked if I could include the poem in an anthology—the same in which a short piece by Maxine Hong Kingston appears. He replied, full of esprit, and said that one day he hoped to see British Columbia's wilderness. In 1995, I was standing in an Albuquerque airport queue when a lively looking Japanese elder approached and inquired about my gnarly walking-stick. His long white hair and beard looked familiar: "Nanao?" En route to Phoenix we compared mythologies: he was heading to Tucson to go desert walking; I'd just been doing the same thing near Santa Fe. He told great stories all the way. Those familiar with his work find it reminiscent at times of Charlie Chaplin, Basho, and the anonymous masters in Ngoyen Senzaki's and Paul Reps' Zen Flesh, Zen Bones. A few months later, Nanao landed in Vancouver with a backpack filled with outdoor gear: ice crampons, all-weather clothing, the lot. Ten memorable days followed, filled with snow-country hiking, herb picking, rascally *dharma talks, singing and chanting, joking with the kids, and living well. Nanao lived the dharma without talking about it much. Alas, even vagabond dharma bards need dental work, so Nanao and I collaborated on this piece to pay some bills. Joseph Roberts at* Common Ground *magazine kindly published it quickly and all was well.* How to Live on the Planet Earth, *Nanao's collected poems, has since been published in 2014 (Blackberry).*

In 1945, Nanao Sakaki was a young radar officer in Japan's Imperial Navy and tracked an American bombing raid headed successfully for Nagasaki. A short time later it was feared an earthquake or even a volcanic eruption had struck. Within days of this historic cataclysm Japan lay in unthinkable defeat. The nation's samurai code demanded mass military suicide but, at American command, the emperor intervened to reverse the order. Radarman Sakaki was spared his life. Demobbed from service, he viewed atomic bombsites where human beings had been vaporized into shadows on cement. In revulsion at anything remotely connected to militarism, Sakaki abandoned mainstream society; since then, with but a brief war-end stint in publishing that introduced him to many writers, he has led a life in the tradition of Japan's wandering poet-storytellers. For five decades he has walked the length and breadth of the Japanese islands, writing poems and speaking out against nuclear technology and industrial degradation of the environment. In doing so, Sakaki emerged long ago as the underground leader of his nation's anti-establishment culture—no small thing in Japan's ultraconservative society.

During the early 1960s, Sakaki also befriended American writers Gary Snyder and Allen Ginsberg in Tokyo's Shinjuku district and the three became lifelong friends. Snyder himself joined Sakaki in building a loose, ecologically attuned agricultural community on a volcanic island in the East China Sea, and his account of this "Banyan Ashram" in *Earth House Hold* became a critical text in North America's cultural revolution of the late '60s.

A vivid, weather-bronzed figure of seventy-two, Sakaki is an outstanding naturalist and a seasoned raconteur. A careful listener, he responds in good, musical English. His renowned humor is offbeat and infectious, yet there is no escaping his essential commitment to retooling the engines of modern culture, east and west.

Clear as creekwater and rich in nature wisdom, Sakaki's poetry reads like medicine. His sense of presence is palpable and, almost unconsciously, people around him become more mindful of small communal responsibilities. It is difficult to describe precisely why this happens, but as Kolin Lymworth of Vancouver's Banyen Books put it after an informal meeting, "Maybe Nanao just reminds us of that wonderful, wise older person we all seem to want, or need, to know."

A recent hike in southwestern British Columbia's Cascade Range offered Nanao an opportunity both to study the local vegetation and to elaborate further on what his work has to say to contemporary readers. En route, Sakaki relates that his passion for the wild began after reading Sir Laurens Van der Post's classic *Sands of the Kalahari*. "I was so excited after reading it in the British Council Library that I couldn't sleep for almost three days," he says. "It was so new, so different. Here's this hostile desert environment of lions and poisonous snakes. But Van der Post wants to understand the bushmen so much he finally comes to comprehend their philosophy, which is, 'There is a dream that is dreaming us.' That's *very* interesting to me! It's also a little similar to Chuang Tzu's butterfly dream in Taoism. So, as a young man, I had to think, what's real?—because the evolution of this idea is that we must go with the dream; there is no other choice.

"In my work later on," he continues, "I came in contact with Aboriginal people from Australia and Tasmania, and with Navajo people from the American Southwest who share almost this same idea. They live in timeless landscapes. That's good for me, you see, because I'm crazy for wild landscape; always I wish to see the desert or volcanoes, or Alaska—big space, pure like [the] empty mind of Buddha. But Japanese business[es], for example, they are cutting down Tasmania's forests for toilet paper. Terrible!"

Sakaki is uncompromising in his defense of nature and has worked for decades at heightening awareness in Japan of his nation's environmental policies. Few things have been as effective as his campaigns in the United States when literary friends such as Snyder and, formerly, Ginsberg have rallied other prominent writers and artists to spotlight events needling Japan's hypersensitive government. The external media pressure gets results.

"Our work for the twenty-first century will be reversing dams and big energy projects, replanting forests and cleaning water," Sakaki says. "Already in Japan we are seeing legal cases where representatives of endangered species are suing the government. Japan, remember, still has rich wild spaces and two thousand black and grizzly bears, where in an island ecology like Britain's they have disappeared."

The critical shortsightedness typical of commercial planning leaves Sakaki at a loss. Remote Banyan Ashram, for example, which drew visitors from around the world, is no more. Its low-tech success tempted Yamaha Corporation to offer local islanders the promise of jobs, enabling Yamaha to buy up the commune site for a glitzy tourist resort. Beauty is relative, however; what worked for remote islanders and back-to-the-land longhairs didn't translate quite as well when visiting Tokyo honeymooners found themselves subject to periodic showers of volcanic ash. Now, both projects lie defunct.

Here, the inevitable question seems to be, "What does this say, then, of our Western myth about Oriental societies taking a longer, shrewder, generational view of things?"

"About Asia, I'm not so sure," replies Sakaki. "The one example I have seen of this is among the Hopi people. They believe you shouldn't make an important decision unless you think through its effects for seven generations. This means we have to imagine how we, and the consequence[s] of our actions, fit in the scale of things. If you think of trees, they usually live longer than humans: harvesting a tree can be like meeting your own great-grandfather. So rightly, we should think, what's the appropriate thing to do here?"

Discussion of right practice and livelihood leads inevitably to the consideration of what role Buddhism, or Japan's Zen path, may have for modern Western culture. Sakaki's response is enlightening.

"Most Japanese Zen is uninteresting to me," he says. "It's too linked to samurai tradition—to militarism. This is where Alan Watts and I disagreed: he didn't fully understand how the samurai class with whom he associated Zen were in fact deeply Confucian; they were concerned with *power*. The Zen I'm interested in is China's Tang dynasty kind with its great teachers like Lin Chi. This was nonintellectual. It came from farmers—*so* simple. Someone became enlightened, others talked to him, learned and were told, 'Now you go there and teach; you go here, etc.' When Japan tried to study this, it was hopeless. The emperor sent scholars, but with their high-flown language and ideas they couldn't understand.

"Today," he adds, "many young people have lost their way. They're looking for salvation, checking many gates. They read Zen anecdotes, see Zen pictures—it seems perfect! Then they think about achieving enlightenment, but it's not so easy. . . . About enlightenment I always say, just forget about it. Everybody's already enlightened: people work at their jobs, the traffic moves along, so things are okay. A mother looks after her children, she makes their lunch, does her job well. That's enlightenment: just doing a good job."

For Sakaki, this version of right-mindedness extends without compromise to the last inning. "Once, hitchhiking in Southern Japan," he says, "I met my cousin who told me my father was very sick. Okay, we went to the hospital where I saw my father. He was surprised to see me.

"I said, 'So you are going to become Buddha!' You see, in [the] Amida sect of my family we say that when you die, you're becoming Buddha. My father, he kind of half-smiled. His face brightened. He said, 'Yes, I'm going to become Buddha, looks like!'

"So when my friends tell me, 'My father is sick, my mother is dying,' I say, congratulations! They are becoming Buddha!

"That's it," he concludes. "When it's time to sleep, just sleep; when you're sick, just be sick; when you're going to die, just die! Enlightenment!"

About the specific values that Buddhism may offer the contemporary West, Sakaki answers in terms of compassion.

"This is a big subject," he responds. "Tibetan, Zen, Pure Land— there are many good gates in Buddhism to the empty space within. You see, in original Buddhism there is no competition, but Western society is strongly rooted in just this thing; it moves aggressively onward. Real compassion goes beyond human society—to animal life, trees, water, rock. It's easy to relate to the environmental movement. Buddhism says we are all the same and the West, I think, is missing this. There is an Indian Sutra teaching—*Paticca Samupadda*— that discusses the perfect wholeness of all things and how they are joined. The Dalai Lama, Thich Nhat Hanh, the Diamond Sutra, they all talk about this."

And the way to compassion?

"Slow down," Sakaki smiles. "Slow down the metabolism, the whole mental image. Compassion is like a shadow—like the Hopi thinking seven generations on.

"After all, how we work out our difficulties is a social question, not spiritual or mental," he explains. "As a society, if we have no vision, all we're left with is bureaucratic process. That's too sad! Artists, poets have a responsibility for landscape, for wild nature. As a poet I feel my poems are also Sutra, in the way that a painter's good work is also drawing Sutra. And as listeners, if we meet a good poem, or discover a new landscape, we must have a good answer. In the end it becomes spontaneous, like question and answer. It's like hearing good music, really; it calls to me, I start humming, moving—I find I'm dancing! That's Zen: not thinking, not stopping halfway, not copying landscape but finally *becoming* the landscape."

Deep Cove, BC

Back on the Trail with Nanao

Nanao co-founded the Bum Academy, a renegade *troupe grotesque* that dropped out of conventional society to form Japan's authentic postwar counterculture. His crazy wisdom was unique and this interview during his second visit to British Columbia in 2004 allows his colorful English to run *au naturel*.

TC: *Nanao, you're best known for your love of desert landscapes. At the moment, you're visiting Vancouver on your way from a journey to Alaska. What draws you to the north?*

NS: It's a good place to think about history and the future. Alaska has so many wild places—glaciers, bears, many foxes. Not so much human culture. San Francisco, Tokyo, New York—too much terrible places! I love glaciers and being in desert.

TC: *Why exactly do you love these wild places so much?*

NS: No civilization. You can think clearly—who we are, where we are going. So, get away sometime. All your history—bye-bye! Already we are thinking new millennium must be something important for human beings. But that's all wrong. We must think another way about history: where we come from—not just two thousand, five thousand years, but thousands and millions years back to amoeba time; to place we come from. Why? This is our home, like family, so take better care.

TC: *We're meeting here in Deep Cove where it's still pretty wild, but Vancouver isn't far away. What's your take on city life?*

NS: People think too much in cities. Everyone has to move faster: watch that car! So much noise inside, confusion—like cancer!

TC: *You mention cancer. It seems to be everywhere around us these days, especially in cities. We all know people who've been stricken.*

NS: About cancer, I wonder: is it God's present, or not?

TC: *That's a very searching question, Nanao. In what way might it be a present?*

NS: Well, I also said "or not"? Does it come from God or from us? It's a good question: Where does cancer come from? Today it seems like we can fix so much—all kinds of disease, but the one thing we can't touch is our own spirit; so hard to fix!

TC: *Yet so many people are suffering.*

NS: Of course. Many good friends of mine have already died from cancer. All different kinds of people. Some of them fasted, were very healthy; others big eaters. Some were too much nervous; another quiet in nature. One was even young, a strong, healthy farmer. He had stomach cancer and died so quickly, two months! It's hard to believe. We understand so much now about science, but we can't understand this one. Why?

TC: *What do we do about it?*

NS: I listen to all my friends' stories and try to find a connection, an answer: What is wrong? So many questions!

TC: *Some people say cancer touches people who aren't peaceful inside, who are maybe too fussy about even little things. What do you make of this?*

NS: Stress!

TC: *What about this idea of perfectionism though? Is there a Buddhist or Asian perspective that might be helpful dealing with this particular— maybe Western—aspect of stress?*

NS: Well, seems to me that idiotic guys never go to cancer. And in mental hospitals maybe not too many people go to cancer either. But that's too dark a place, like medieval world. Not cheerful!

TC: *If it's about cheerfulness, where's the best place to just be happy?*

NS: Oriental people say two ways to escape and be happy. Downtown very busy, crowded place. Just be lost among many people, stay in a slum. Another is in high places. Live in a mountain cave. I've tried both.

TC: *But what about living happy-go-lucky everyday life here—a kind of suburban life?*

NS: Sure! Why not? Not everyone can be caveman.

TC: *You did live in a cave in New Mexico near Taos. But city life is probably the one that people are more familiar with these days. Do you know Tokyo pretty well?*

NS: Yes, I've lived there. No mosquitoes there. No wild places. Even no flies! It's a miserable feeling. After the war, I worked as secretary to a big publisher in Tokyo. It was good life—many interesting circles. I met many famous writers and artists; even I received a Christmas card from Albert Einstein. But soon I had to leave. Too many people there. So much activity, like living in beehive! I wanted to become a bum, like hobo. So I thought, try mountains. Now Tokyo is even worse shape! Another bad point is social reasons, like diesel smoke; it's terrible! Smoke coming out all over the world—Beijing, Seoul, Bangkok, even Katmandu. Too much! I can't understand it. So terrible for drivers themselves, and other people. I don't want to go to such places now. Why City Hall and Congress doesn't do something about this?

TC: *What's your alternative to such notions of progress?*

NS: Try walking mountainsides, the north. I love walking these places. That's me personally. Probably there is no solution. It's a good idea: no solution! Much wider perspective. If you have a solution, you're trapped in solution network.

TC: *So "no solution" is the best answer?*

NS: You must think for yourself. You must carry your own package, your own rucksack. It's a good way. Everybody wants to live long, but in India for centuries, after fifty years old people went to forest to die. Live quietly, in meditation; eat a little food, beg something from village, take water, then die peacefully. Look at me: already I'm seventy-seven. I'm ready!

TC: *With a proverbial eye to the future, however, you've said in the past that our collective human work for the future is to reverse the kinds of mega-projects you continue to oppose in Japan—the damming of rivers and the like.*

NS: Sure. I still feel that way. In the twenty-first century, our job is to reverse the big constructions that have wiped out the fish runs in our rivers and polluted soils and air, water. Why need more? In Japan, why the government builds a dam? To keep construction company busy! So many fish, mammals die—even wetlands are disappearing for birds. Who's left? Only people. It's very unnatural: crazy! China is doing this now with Yangtze Three Gorges dam—lots of environmental problems there: deforestation, pollution. . . . Time to reverse.

TC: *Any practical alternatives?*

NS: One answer may be no more big cities. Why everybody want to live in big city anyway? Maybe smaller cities for people to live in, like Bolinas outside San Francisco. Environmentally healthy. Everybody has small place, small gardens, small beach close by. It's okay.

TC: *Some of us in the Vancouver area have championed ideas like that politically. Property developers, and the politicians they have in their pockets, have other ideas though. And on the down side, Bolinas and the Marin area are very costly to live in.*

NS: I say to young people in Japan, go to mountain farm areas. Since the war, so many people go to city, now many village areas are abandoned. You can live almost for no rent. It's possible to grow food and live quietly. You can pick plants for medicine, and no need to use toilet paper. True. But to buy land in Japan is so expensive. I never own land myself—too complicated. In Canada or Alaska, I think younger people could still buy land. It's a good idea to make community.

TC: *You yourself founded an influential commune in southern Japan during the late '60s.*

NS: That was Suwa-no-se Island. Very far south. Village people there gave me land, so with friends from Tokyo, Kyoto, yes—we had commune. Some of my friends from America did come to visit. At another time, several other commune projects were started; some in countryside, also one in Tokyo. Visitors came from Europe, North America.

TC: *Your commune project began roughly at the time when the Haight-Ashbury scene in San Francisco was branching into its "back to the land phase." You've often called in at such places on your travels. Have you any sense how successful these communities proved to be?*

NS: Quite a few, I think, are still active. Libre in New Mexico, New Buffalo, Rama Foundation—so, looks like they have good future.

TC: *Nanao, you pack a sparkplug reputation. You get things going. What's it like for you in Japan? Ever any hassle with the authorities?*

NS: Oh, sure. For police, I'm number one troublemaker. "Why you don't agree with these things?!" So always they keep an eye on me, but from a distance. Not so bad. What's important is to speak out. Speak out! Yoshino River dam, for instance—central government still wants to dam this last river, so in springtime we will again organize Walk the River. With a group of people we will have about ten days walking, camping with tents, reading poetry along the river for two hundred twenty kilometers. In Japan, people don't criticize out loud so much. *No!* Already I wrote one poem, "Don't Cry Yoshino River." It's *so* important that we speak out.

TC: *On a personal note, you're a skilled amateur botanist and all-around naturalist.*

NS: No, I just like to know the names of these plants I meet. Same with stars, birds. With some plants I feel like I'm seeing an old friend. Sometimes, same plants even in Alaska and New Mexico. Like kinni-kinnick: "Oh, I haven't seen you for so long time!" Same with stars, birds, mammals: always I'm happy to meet bear, caribou, coyote, eagle. It's good feeling.

TC: *You also have a lengthy association with Zen Buddhism and several of its notable Western practitioners. Any encouraging words from this background?*

NS: Why labels? I never call myself Zen Buddhist, or Beatnik, Hippie—anything. But probably Zen practice is good for Westerners, especially monastery life. So little food! Maybe only 1,500 calories per day, and lots of walking. Western people eat so much. At barbeque dinner last night, so much food was left over. What happens to it? In Southeast Asia many people still have only a little food to eat. So maybe West can give some extra food to other people.

TC: *Anything left you still want to do?*

NS: Yes, visit with Eskimo people in north of Alaska. Maybe next year. Now I have good contacts—same as with Hopi people in New Mexico. I have good relations with them and with [Aboriginal] people in Australia. It's near Taos I lived in a cave—just like ancient time, so cold in winter! And almost fasting: just some brown rice to eat and a little water. Just enough. So now I tell children I want to meet a dinosaur— eat dinosaur sashimi!

Chapter 12

Dangerous Work

The Retirement Interview with Zen Master
Robert Aitken-Roshi

Without a sense of the sacred we are just humanists going through certain intellectual and emotional exercises, that's all.... Thirty years ago, our resident leader at the Maui Zendo came to the end of his patience about the talk he was hearing of nonattachment, and exclaimed, "Nonattachment! Nonattachment! All I hear is nonattachment! If you weren't attached, you'd be dead!"

I was recommended to meet the late Robert Aitken-Roshi (1917–2010) for an interview while in Honolulu with my family in 1996. I prepared for this as if it were an especially tough dokusan, or interview, with a strong Zen master. Aitken-Roshi welcomed me in his robes. We talked first about the local birdlife and he allowed me to look at his bookshelves—I noticed Wordsworth, Blake, and W.S. Merwin's poetry from Maui—and he explained the stories behind several of his Buddhist artifacts from Japan. A searching interview developed. Roshi was patient with my inquiries and spoke lovingly of his late wife, Anne, and of the depth of her contribution to the Diamond Sangha they had founded in 1959. Shortly afterward, a letter arrived from Roshi thanking me for my time and for having organized what he felt were cogent questions for his "retirement" interview. Usually, it works the other way around. On subsequent visits Aitken-Roshi always asked if I'd bring along the children. They liked him and we'd have fun while retaining a certain level of *decorum. Although retired, in 2001 Aitken-Roshi performed the marriage ceremony for my wife and I. It was an event I'd postponed for many years in waiting for the right authority before whom I could make such auspicious vows. Roshi was the authority I'd been awaiting. By then, he was living at Kaimu on the Big Island with a lovely little Zendo. We needed witnesses, so Danan Henry Roshi and two students visiting from Zen Center of Denver were pressed into service. We chanted the Heart Sutra and a rainbow shone forth outside after a sudden shower; thirty minutes later, a pod of gray whales began breaching off a beach nearby: it was always special to be in Roshi's company. His incorruptible commitment to peace, social justice, and interfaith harmony still resonates as a uniquely American contribution to contemporary Buddhism.*

The way to Palolo Zen Center leads up a narrow, hilly lane lush with blooms in suburban Honolulu. The bus drops you off a mile or so away and you wind your way through a tropic landscape, looking back here and there down Palolo Valley at a stretch of the blue Pacific beyond apple-green arboreal canopy and the towered shoreline of Waikiki. Farther along, past shady banyans and a few tight bends, Palolo Zen Centre sits unpretentious before a ridge of heavy verdure. There are few markings, if any, on the typical-looking island house, and on what might easily be taken for a small community hall or rural schoolroom. The quiet is palpable. Only the sounds of birdlife—waxbills, cardinals, and bulbuls—break the stillness. A car or pickup rolls by out front from time to time, and there is the rain, sudden and tropically intense.

Robert Aitken-Roshi, de facto patriarch of Western Zen, lives here. Tall, lean, priestly, he practices in the Sanbo Kyodan tradition (Soto Zen with Rinzai elements, such as koan study). His home is tidy, well-organized, and comfortable. It has a shady feel. The living room floors are of polished wood and cool to the feet. There is a small, rather Japanese view to the greenery out back.

Aitken-Roshi speaks carefully, with great precision. His Asian scholarship and deeply moral nature are renowned, and through the years he has been consulted at crisis periods in American Buddhism. At the age of seventy-eight, he has announced his retirement at the end of 1996. We spoke during the late afternoon.

TC: *Aitken-Roshi, your retirement marks a significant transitional event in American Buddhism. What does this mean in terms of your future activities?*

RA: It has been announced and the phasing-in and phasing-out process has already begun. All the things that are necessary to be in place are now in place, or in train. Nelson Foster, who is one of my dharma heirs and a teacher at the Ring of Bone Zendo in Nevada City, California will replace me. He'll have one foot there and [one] foot here, and be going back and forth.

There is a lot of precedent in Zen Buddhist history for a teacher to have more than one Zendo. Dharma centers are proliferating and there aren't enough good teachers to go around, so we'll have to make do with importing our new teacher here in Honolulu for the foreseeable future. Nelson has led *sesshin* here earlier, so people know him well and are aware that he is the new teacher. I'll be moving to the Big Island of Hawaii and living there quietly near my son, who is a school counselor in [the] Puna District.

TC: *Will you continue to speak or write?*

RA: I'll probably speak occasionally, and the group here wants me to lead a sesshin from time to time so perhaps I'll do that—we haven't decided that yet. I will have a little zendo room in my small house over there that'll seat perhaps eight people and we'll have Sunday morning meetings, but I don't plan to lead retreats at all there. My place won't be a dharma center. It'll just be a house and I'll have a few friends come over. That's the way I visualize it in order to leave a clear field here.

TC: *You established the Diamond Sangha with your late wife. It always seemed a remote but earnest organization. How did it come about?*

RA: We were first established here in Honolulu at Koko An Zendo from about 1955 to 1969. Our function in those days was to serve the Honolulu community. Then Anne and I moved to Maui. Actually, we thought we were retiring at that time but we found ourselves in the middle of the New Age, and gradually set up the Maui Zendo in Paia near the town of Haiku. We were there for fifteen years. Essentially there were two centers: the Maui Zendo and the Koko An Zendo in Honolulu, over in Manoa, one valley west of here.

Then the demography of Maui changed. The old New Age died out and many people moved away to the Mainland or to Honolulu. We no longer had the pool of potential members that we once did there, so we closed and sold the Maui Zendo and moved back here in 1984.

Using the money we'd realized from the sale to buy this property, we started construction all over again in setting up Palolo Zen Center.

TC: *Does the Palolo Center differ from Koko An?*

RA: Koko An and Palolo Zen Center are one organization called the Honolulu Diamond Sangha. Koko An Zendo remains active in Manoa. It serves a group of people who live there and who go out to work or to school in the day, and who keep up a regular practice. They have the house open on Wednesdays and on early mornings. Palolo Zen Center has the function, which the Maui Zendo had, of serving people in training periods who come from away and stay sometimes six weeks or longer before going back home to their roots. We also serve the Honolulu community with our Sunday morning sessions and our sesshins, but we have the facilities for people who want to come and stay for retreats.

TC: *The name Diamond Sangha has always had a lovely far-off ring.*

RA: We got the idea for the name Diamond Sangha from the old days—before the trees and buildings grew up and blocked the view. One could see Diamond Head clearly from the lanai at Koko An. And, of course, there is also that echo from the *Diamond Sutra*.

TC: *Your encounter with Zen came under difficult conditions in WWII. How did you meet R.H. Blyth in the internment camp?*

RA: There's a reprise of all of this in a long autobiographical chapter in *Taking the Path of Zen*, but, yes, I was in Guam working for civilian contractors. I had grown up here in Honolulu, and had developed an interest and studied Japanese and Chinese poetry. I was interned and taken to Japan. A guard who knew of my interests shared his copy of R.H. Blyth's book *Zen in English Literature*, which was just then in print. I became very interested; it opened many doors, which I realized had just been waiting to be opened for me. Then the camps in Kobe where we were separately located were combined and I met him in person. We were together in the same camp from May 1944 until the end of the war. I had a chance to study Japanese language with him and sit at his feet, so to speak. He was a student of haiku and senryu, a satirical verse form, and, of course, had interest in zazen. His zazen was at Myoshin-ji Betsuin, a branch temple of the big Myoshin-ji temple in Kyoto. In those days he was teaching at Seoul National University in Korea, which was then known as Keijo, and practicing there at this branch temple. Just before the war he and his wife, who was Japanese, had moved back to Japan.

TC: *Had you yourself sat zazen before?*

RA: Oh no. I'd not even heard of zazen. It was a totally new subject for me. Although when I went back and looked at some of the books I'd read before the war, for example, Miyamori's *Haiku: Ancient and Modern*, I found references to Zen Buddhism right in the introduction, but it had just gone right past me. I hadn't noticed; it hadn't made any impression. I was just interested in the poetry.

TC: *How did your knowledge and practice develop after this?*

RA: Following the war I returned for a few months to California where my parents had relocated, then I came back to finish up at the University of Hawaii. I'd begun Zen study with Nyogen Senzaki-sensei in Los Angeles who wrote a number of books, and I visited Japan again in 1950 to '51. Senzaki-sensei's books, by the way, were always edited by someone else; for example *Zen Flesh, Zen Bones* was edited by Paul Reps, whose name appears alone on the title page, and who added a chapter of his own at the end. And the book *Buddhism and Zen* he wrote with Ruth McCandless, who was a collaborator in helping him with his English.

TC: *You trained with Japanese teachers in the Zen tradition, but you were raised in Hawaii. Do you have any sense that the overpowering physical beauty of the landscape here may have contributed to your understanding of Buddhism?*

RA: I'm here, I think, by the fact that I grew up here. I feel most comfortable here. I don't feel that I'm really using myself completely when I'm elsewhere. I do feel that if I wasn't living in Hawaii then I might be living in San Francisco, Portland, Seattle, or Berkeley. Those are cities where I have many friends and feel very comfortable, especially Berkeley and San Francisco; they're really Buddha-land. I can speak publicly there and use all the terms I use before my own students and convey the same attitude without explanation, knowing that people are following right along, without having to explain bodhisattva or dharma; everybody knows!

TC: *You've lived in this world now for almost eighty years. Any thoughts on this experience?*

RA: Well, I think we are nearing a socioeconomic-political crisis in the world. The kind of greed that the Buddha spoke about—which has always been an element of concern—seems more and more linked to technology. The human race is using up the world and it's not just a matter of how we use up the earth and its resources, but a matter also of how the people in control are using up the human resources. We have a situation not unlike Germany in 1932, of our government in the United States setting up structures that, for the foreseeable future, can only result in a kind of fascistic regime. At this level, inevitably, the poverty in this country will be such that there will be people watching for the "man on the white horse" to come around and take over for them. I think this is almost inevitable. I don't see the political Left or the people who are even more in touch with political and social realities—the anarchists—having the clout, or even the knowhow and the initiative, to stand in the way of this surge. At the same time, here in the United States I see very promising developments. Thich Nhat Hanh or the Dalai Lama can attract very large numbers of people who are evolving in dharmic consciousness, and in consciousness rooted in progressive Christianity and Judaism also. How rich are these developments going to be for the future? Truly significant, you can be sure; but I am confident things are going to get a lot worse before they get a lot better, and that the engaged Buddhists, engaged Christians, engaged Jews have to hunker down and consolidate—though this may seem like the pessimism of an old man who thinks the world is going to the dogs!

TC: *Regarding matters of form and practice, there's a term you've used with some frequency in your writing—intimacy. Could you enlarge upon your understanding of this idea?*

RA: Intimacy and realization are synonyms in the old Zen texts. By realization, of course, one means the peak experience encountered periodically in Zen practice. As an example from outside Zen practice, somewhere William James quotes a woman saying, "The truths of the Bible seem made for me." This, you see, is the source of empowerment in liberation theology—when the peasants in the barrios of the Philippines in their study of the Bible really grasp the fact that Jesus loves the poor, and that their action indeed is the work of Jesus. Then, that peasant is empowered.

In Zen Buddhism one finds the truth of what one of the old teachers said: "The treasure of the house does not come through the front gate." That is to say the body of teaching is not a truth that comes intellectually; it is not a truth that is "out there," but is one's own.

Work with a teacher is a matter of taking up the old cases of sayings and doings of the masters. When I question my students about a case and a student begins by saying, "Well, I think he was. . . ." I stop him or her right there because *was* places the old teacher back halfway across the world and a thousand years ago. These things are not taken up as "far away and long ago." Rather, the response is to present the story right here and now, in these circumstances. So, improvisation and mime—with or without words—are the proper mode of response in the interview room.

You see, to mime is not to mimic. I always say Marcel Marceau was not a mime. He *was* that butterfly catcher; he *was* that prisoner with the walls closing in. The true actor in *Hamlet* is no one but Hamlet—not a player acting Hamlet, but actually *is* Hamlet. No equivocation there; no qualification.

Now, of course, that actor is Hamlet with his own personality, and there have been some great women who have played Hamlet, but there is an intimacy there: an intimacy whose elements cannot be separated.

TC: *The dancer and the dance?*

RA: Exactly. So in this practice, as Wu-men says in *The Gateless Barrier*, you not only get to meet Chao-chou intimately, but you will walk hand-in-hand with all the successive teachers of our lineage. The hair of your eyebrows will be entangled with theirs. Seeing with the same eyes. Hearing with the same ears. It is not just a matter of solving koans, but of actually being in the place where you know that the other is no other than oneself—with all the complementarity that goes with that: the other is the other, and I am I. To realize that the other is no other than oneself is to realize the hidden half of the complementarity of form and emptiness.

We know very well that the chair we sit on is solid, yet we know that in relation to their size, the particles that make up the chair are as far apart from each other as the Earth is from the nearest star. This is hidden from us; we don't see that emptiness clearly. Zen practice, and I dare say other practices, reveals the void, which is in fact a solid reality like this chair. The void and the solid reality are the same, just as how with light the particle theory and the wave theory are the same thing. Niels Bohr invented this term of complementarity, or at least made it popular, and it's very useful.

TC: *When the Asian masters speak of dualism, they often say that in the West we're burdened by it.*

RA: Well, they're burdened by dualism, too. I think this is a kind of invidious comparison. When the Buddha sat down under the bodhi tree, he didn't see the point right away. He was victimized by the dualism of *his* culture. The Japanese, the Chinese, the Koreans—they have their kind of dualism, too. It may be that when we examine these various kinds of dualisms, some are more fixed than others. For example, if you were to look at Islam, I think you would find a more clear-cut kind of dualism than you would in Christianity. When you look at Protestantism, you find a more clear-cut kind of dualism than that found in Catholicism. It's all relative. But to say, "Oh, you guys are dualistic and we're not"—that's an oversimplification.

TC: *You're a Buddhist teacher who uses the term "faith."*

RA: I grew up in the Depression when many intellectuals I knew were Marxists, or pretended to be, and who were firmly committed to the notion that religion was the opiate of the masses. I came into Zen Buddhism through my interest in poetry, and before I knew it, there I was in a Japanese temple making nine bows prior to a sutra service. What am I doing?! Nine bows? What am I bowing to? I couldn't even answer that because at Ryutaku-ji the image is hidden. Some temples have a screen; you don't see what you're making devotion to. It didn't make sense! As I deepened in my practice and paid attention to the fogged notion of what was happening to me, I realized I was gaining a sense of the sacred. Without a sense of the sacred we are just humanists going through certain intellectual, emotional exercises, that's all.

Now as to faith itself, there is a tendency to be literal about the *Diamond Sutra* and its teaching. People may not have seen or read the *Diamond Sutra* but still been touched by its influence—that there is no concept, no archetype that does not self-destruct. . . . So, the Buddha does not have the thirty-two distinguishing marks of the Buddha: everything is taken down. Every single thing; every concept, every model—all taken down, so there's nothing left at all. Well, this is very healthy. It enables me to say, "It doesn't matter if the Sixth Ancestral Teacher delivered himself of the sermons that are attributed to him. It doesn't really matter if the Buddha never lived at all." What is significant here are the teachings. The dharma itself is a significant thing.

Now, once that is established, I can venerate the Buddha because the Buddha as an archetype embodies the wonderful teachings that I have come to revere. So does Bodhidharma. It doesn't matter if Bodhidharma didn't lose the use of his legs or have them fall off, or any of the things that are attributed to him. It doesn't matter that we have perhaps only one document that can be authoritatively attributed to him.

Did Bodhidharma invent karate? I don't think so, but it doesn't matter anyway; we have karate and wonderful martial arts. It doesn't matter. But we can venerate Bodhidharma as the founder of karate because he embodies that wonderful quality—that archetypal figure created by the veneration of hundreds of thousands, even millions of devoted followers down through the millennia. So there it is.

You know a monk asked Chao-chou, "What is the Buddha?" and Chao-chou answered, "The one in the shrine." The monk said, "But that's only a clay figure. What is the Buddha?" And Chao-chou whispered, "The one in the shrine."

That's the one we've created there. The one who embodies in our hearts the archetype that inspires us. And this is also true of all the many bodhisattvas and the teachers themselves. Faith is all tied up here. There is also faith in oneself. When Hakuin said, "This very body is the Buddha," he meant we are all right *to the very bottom.* In every way, you are okay. So we go on from there and uncover our own Buddha. Without the faith that it really might be possible—that I have this Buddhahood—I think practice would likely be quite flat.

TC: *You've been supportive of incorporating small devotional beauties into everyday practice—chanting, instructing children, and so forth.*

RA: Children love ritual. They dote on ritual; you know—"the little spoon goes outside the big spoon, the glass goes right here." I see children in our own sangha evolving religiously, yet whether they'll actually grow up to be Zen Buddhists, I can't say. I'm not trying to teach them that way. I would like to see them grow up with a religious attitude. So when a family comes here to serve me—since my wife died, the sangha people come to cook for me, or take me out. When a family comes, it's a pleasure to hear a little voice piping up the mealtime sutra. It's really a delight. And they enjoy it so much. Their voices ring out above our own. They greet one with a gassho. It feels good to see children growing up with an attitude of religion.

TC: *The archetypal Asian spiritual training model is that of guru-chela. I know you don't prefer the title "guru," but what are your thoughts on the teacher-student relationship?*

RA: I think it is built on something perennial. In traditional societies the elders were, and still are, venerated by the younger members of the group. As culture becomes more sophisticated, this very natural kind of relationship is established one way or another. In some traditions, in say India or Tibet, you have guru yoga taken to a very literal degree. I tend to say I am not a guru. I'm not one to say to my students, in the way that some teachers do, "Now I want you two to get married." There is a very natural kind of relationship that grows up between teacher and student, which is necessary. If the student is weighing everything I say or do by that student's past experience, we're not going to get anywhere. There has to be a certain transference, a certain trust—an acknowledgment that the other person has been there. And that even though I don't understand why I should do this, I'll do because I'm told to.

You find this kind of attitude in Christianity as well as in Buddhism or any other training. In the Benedictine manuals, for example, you are told that if the abbot tells you to plant tomato seedlings with their roots in the air, that's the way you do it. I don't carry things to that extreme. I don't test anybody for their trust. But if there is that open trust, then there is an openness to the dharma itself. Because the dharma is not anything that one has experienced earlier, except accidently maybe, in a narrow sense. So there has to be a certain naive attitude. Of course, it is this naive attitude that unscrupulous teachers have exploited in taking advantage of their students sexually—betraying their students. I am not one to say that the person who is exploited is responsible for not saying "no."

Naturally there is a naive openness. When it is there, again the dharma has a chance to flow. As time goes on, as the relationship matures, then there is a gradual change so the student is able to say, "You know Roshi, you shouldn't be saying that because it offends people." Or, "I don't see why we should do it this way; why can't we experiment with this?" And the teacher, if the teacher is mature, will respond by listening and being open and glad that the students are standing on their own feet.

So you have the case of a seventy-year-old teacher still listening to a ninety-year-old teacher's admonitions—but listening from a position of maturity. This whole matter of transference is a delicate one, *profound* in its implications. A true teacher is not going to monkey with transference in any way and must be very alert—not only to the avoidance of coarse betrayals, but to other very subtle ways in which transference can be violated.

When Nakagawa Soen-roshi visited us just a few months after we established—he's the one who gave us permission to start up the Zen center here—he said, "How are you getting along in your dangerous work?" I had no idea what he was talking about, but I soon learned!

TC: *In the sense that you're turning people loose into the world, authorized as teachers?*

RA: No, in the sense that I am establishing a relationship with people and don't understand, and can never understand, all the profound implications of that relationship. So I must follow certain rules of thumb, in being exact in not stepping over the line in certain particular ways. I must also be aware and watch for little signs in what I'm saying or doing that might be misunderstood. At the same time, there are places where I must cut through and say "No, that won't do," and let the chips fall where they may.

TC: *Western notions about Zen have tended to popularize the importance of "sudden enlightenment." Have we got the right handle on this, Aitken-Roshi?*

RA: My teacher Yasutani-roshi used to say that *kensho*—which is the Japanese term we use rather than "satori," which has a substantialist and absolutist kind of implication—that kensho is like rubbing a clear place in a frosted pane of glass. You peek through the clear place and that's essential nature, all right. But it's important that we clean up the impurities in the rest of the glass. That's a lifetime practice. Dogen Zenji says that in establishing the ultimate kind of realization and understanding, which he calls "no trace," that this no trace is continued endlessly. He doesn't say, "It continues endlessly." It is continued endlessly; that is to say, by continued practice. . . . There's a saying in Japanese monasteries that the Buddha is still doing zazen somewhere; that he is only halfway there!

So there is no be-all and end-all. There are very important milestones, very important realizations, and one goes on from them. When I look back at what I wrote only five years ago, I think, oh no, that won't do at all! Others have pointed this out, too. My first Zen friend R.H Blyth said to me one day, "I've reached the point where I can now say, 'What a fool I was three weeks ago!'"

In Zen monasteries it is said also that with true realization your skin doesn't stop quivering for three days. The point is, however, that it does stop and you go on from there. In *The Book of Saints* there is the story of a young priest who had a vision of the Virgin Mary. He spent the rest of his life in his cell painting that vision, rubbing it out and repainting it, continually looking back at that old experience he had as a kid. Not moving on.

TC: *Is it possible, do you feel, to visualize these milestones en route?*

RA: With certain points of experience—milestones—suddenly, things are a lot clearer and one feels more a lot more liberated. That's what I mean by milestones. But you forget about those milestones. And you forget that you ever forgot about them.

TC: *We're living in a time of great self-absorption. Further to the matter of enlightenment, Master Dogen observes that as the self advances and confirms the ten thousand things, it is called "delusion."*

RA: What Dogen is speaking of there is the human tendency to name or identify—getting everything squared away, so to speak; getting everything perfect. The first action of Adam was to name the beasts of the field and the birds of the air. That is called delusion. Dogen doesn't say it is delusion. It can be called delusion. In other words, he sets up the distinction as a kind of impersonal, nonjudgmental dichotomy, or directionality. Now, whether the ten thousand things advances and confirms itself is enlightenment, there is no question about that; as with the Buddha, looking up and experiencing the morning star—seeing the ten thousand things.

Now, this seems to be a contradiction with the notion that the treasure of the house does not come in through the front gate—that the morning star enlightened the Buddha. But it is no more than another complementarity; a kind of miracle, so that with the message from the star, the Buddha realized his own dream. This is the co-arising, the simultaneous occurrence of the starshine and the Buddha's realization. Not a cause and effect. The *paticca samupadda.*

The contrast in directionality is Dogen's way of saying that it is in this world that one realizes the treasure of the house. With that realization, as he says, body and mind fall away. The body and mind of others falls away also. No trace of this realization remains, and this "no-trace" also falls away.

TC: *You've long presented the Chao-chou koan inquiring whether a dog has the Buddha-nature as a foundation case in Zen study. Is it your understanding that there is no actual Buddha-nature after all?*

RA: Perhaps it could be explained like that, but only in a very intellectual way. When he answers "*Mu*," meaning "no" or "does not have," Chao-chou is presenting Buddha-nature itself. That is the first basic case of Zen practice in our tradition, and you must pass through that gate before you can take up the rest of koan study. Where is mu? What is mu? Show me mu . . . these are the kinds of questions I ask in the interview room. There is no way this case can be explained; it is such a hard nut that it has to be cracked in itself. Yes, it has something to do with the dog because the dog is the vehicle, the carrier of the story; but the story itself, once it is imprinted, doesn't matter. The question is: What is mu? *Show me mu.*

The student takes that onto the cushions and breathes mu with all possible inquiry. Mu is an arcanum, a single word, a single syllable that carries power to open the heart-mind. Now, it didn't have that potential from the beginning—only from the time of Chao-chou, and from the lifeblood, which countless students have poured into their practice focusing on it. We must not trivialize this case; it is important.

TC: *The first of the Four Vows, "Beings are numberless, I vow to enlighten them," has always appeared to present us with an intimidating task. You've expressed the view that the first vow—to save all beings—means, "I vow to save them in my own mind." Is this a correct understanding of your approach? If so, it's a great relief. We're addressing the very heart of the bodhisattva spirit.*

RA: Sure. I am quoting Hui-neng here: "I vow to save them in my own mind." Where is that mind? Walt Whitman said, "I am large; I contain multitudes." But unless one is totally inclusive, saving becomes a matter of putting Mother Hubbard gowns on Hawaiians. In other words, saving them by a particular view of what it means to save them. My task in fulfilling my vow means to save them for their own sake, by their own inspiration. In the Thai language there is an expression, a very interesting term—*anurak*—which Buddhadasa uses. In ordinary Thai, anurak means preservation or conservation;

however, in the way that Buddhadasa uses it, it means "protection of all beings for their own sake."

I understand Hui-neng as saying, "Saving all beings in my own universal mind, which I have personalized, but which is no more mine than it is yours." Your boundless container includes all beings, including me; my boundless container contains all beings, including you. It is from that realization, that we gain a clearer and clearer sense of responsibility.

TC: *That vow can seem to bear a monumental, unbearable mountain of weight—it's a gigantic vow to try and make.*

RA: Of course it is. Yet it doesn't mean that I am going to lead everybody by their hand to nirvana; it is more that I'll work to save them by their own inspiration.

TC: *In traditional Asian Buddhism there seems to be a distinction made between enlightenment, which appears to be reserved for the clergy, and salvation, which seems to be for the masses.*

RA: Sociologically you can say that, in a general kind of way, we inherit Buddhism as a monastic system. In the Kamakura Period—the twelfth and thirteenth centuries in Japan—there was a great reformation to move Buddhism out of the monasteries and into the marketplace and the home, in the form of the Pure Land and Nichiren schools. However, practice in the monasteries continued, and still does to some small degree. So you can say that realization, enlightenment, occurs among monks, and that salvation—being assured of a place in the afterlife—is for the masses. We have a number of lay practices in Japan, though, and have always had the phenomenon of laymen and women going to the monasteries and doing the same practices as the monks. Chao-chou had many students, including some wonderful women: these are exceptions that prove the rule. When Zen Buddhism has moved to the West, all bets are off. Everything has changed.

TC: *How would you characterize the developing tradition we're seeing in the West, in America? As a reformist school?*

RA: I believe so. I think we're seeing a new Mahayana—the emerging American school of Buddhism.

TC: *More and more, the evolving Western Buddhist tradition is establishing itself as a socially engaged school. Any observations?*

RA: It's not a variant, an offshoot; it's a natural development of one's realization in a Buddhist context that is not confined by a culture of restraints, such as those Buddhism found when it entered East and Southeast Asian countries. In India and South Asia generally there is a slightly dualistic view of the spiritual world and the mundane world. After one had turned life's course—that is, retired—one went to the mountains and did spiritual practice. In China, Korea, Japan, Southeast Asia, and Vietnam, Buddhism was admitted on sufferance. Because the existing traditions were Confucianism and Taoism, Buddhism had to toe the line. The easiest way to do this was stay within the monastery, or else to cooperate fully with the social and political scene, whatever it was at the time. The monastery walls were largely the limits of what was vowed.

In America we don't have any monastery walls. The natural development of our vows has no limit. It fills the whole universe. How do we work this out? How do we invent our way of going about it?

TC: *In inventing this way, do you observe a cross-pollination with Christianity?*

RA: Oh, absolutely. We've learned so much from [the] Christian way of life. I used to hear it said in Japan that "as for Christianity itself, I don't really understand it. But Christianity has taught us how to set up social institutions."

TC: *Work with the homeless, with AIDS, death and dying—much of what America's socially engaged school is involved with resembles what Christian missionaries formerly did in China. Do you have any fears regarding this kind of directional development?*

RA: Not really. The people I know who are involved with the Buddhist Peace Fellowship headquarters are very concerned about their own spiritual practices. They frequently go off to retreats. They do not seem to be running the risk of getting burned out the way a social worker does. That is the difference. Engaged Buddhism is a term coined by Thich Nhat Hanh. His understanding of the term and mine are a little different. Not all engaged Buddhism is BPF.

TC: *It's a material world. . . . Talk about nonattachment has almost become a cliché.*

RA: Thirty years ago, our resident leader at the Maui Zendo came to the end of his patience about the talk he was hearing of nonattachment, and exclaimed, "Nonattachment! Nonattachment! All I hear is nonattachment! If you weren't attached, you'd be dead!" Ha-ha! What is nonattachment? It's a simple answer. It's not being preoccupied with accumulation, with people and pain, with conforming to one's own concept of what they should be. If I have some fixed concepts of how you should be, I'd be stopping you and correcting you every moment. I used to have to correct people a lot, saying, "It's all right to read books. It's all right going to concerts if you enjoy music. It's okay!"

TC: *To conclude, Aitken-Roshi, as someone who's spent a life in this work, what's the great richness of the Buddha Way?*

RA: It is a matter of taking pleasure, of taking delight in this life, and learning when to say *enough*.

Palolo Valley, Honolulu

Chapter 13

Expatriate Passions

Meeting Donald Richie

Have you read Sartre? Well then, you know the temptation of what it is to define yourself as an absolute object. If you can do this, then you're home free, your problems are over. I think everybody tends to want this. You ask them what they are, they name one thing: "I'm a lawyer, a tourist. . . . " In naming ourselves as one thing, we achieve a sort of density that delivers us from doubt. And, further, from "dreadful freedom."

A rguably, Donald Richie (1924–2013) was the finest writer America had on Japanese culture. His métier was film, but Richie's sprawling output of books and journalism demonstrated his comprehension of the deeper structure of Japanese society and customs—yet he was perfectly content to discuss Cavafy, tattooing, French literature, and even European and Asian fashions. Richie appreciated the Buddhist and Animist underpinnings of Japanese life and had quietly been a student of Daisetz Suzuki. This helped him introduce many readers to the subtle underpinnings of Buddho-Shinto consciousness in Japan. During his visit to Simon Fraser University in Vancouver in 2001, I spent an afternoon with him above the harbor and would visit with him again in Tokyo courtesy of his great friend and editor, Leza Lowitz.

For nearly fifty years, no one from the West has written more presciently on Japan and its people than Donald Richie. With an incisive, narrative style punctuated with sharply drawn images from history and contemporary life, Richie's prose leads readers toward small epiphanies in their understanding of Japan's complex human terrain. His acclaimed work *The Inland Sea*—one of the finest Asian travel books extant—became a popular PBS television documentary and follows Richie on a traditional journey through rural, western Japan. While serving as Curator of Film at the Museum of Modern Art in New York from 1968 to 1973, Richie was able to introduce many important works of the Japanese cinema to the West, and his subsequent companion volumes on the seminal directors Kurosawa and Ozu are regarded as definitive. With *Tokyo*, a recent success that the expatriate Richie calls "a love letter" to the city he has called home since 1947, he embarked on a new tack, writing on Tokyo's precocious urban architecture and human portraiture in such felicitous, prickly depth that it earned him at last, inevitably, the sobriquet of "the Lafcadio Hearn of our time." In June, Berkeley's Stone Bridge Press will publish a major survey of his work in *The Donald Richie Reader: Fifty Years of Writing on Japan.*

TC: *You originally went to Japan as a film reviewer for the military paper* Stars and Stripes. *Where do you hail from?*

DR: I was born in Ohio and stayed there sixteen years. When the war came, I joined the Merchant Marine. At the end of the war I understood they were taking people to work in the occupied territories and that one of them was Japan, so I signed up. I went over originally as a typist. Once I got to Tokyo I went to *Stars and Stripes* and said, "You don't have a film reviewer." The occupation was so fluid at that point I was able to be hired. That was 1947. I was at *Stars and Stripes* until 1949 at which time I came back, got my degree in 1953 at Columbia, and went right back to Japan.

TC: *What led you to review films? Was there an absence to fill, or was it a passion?*

DR: Passion. I come from that generation of Americans who spent their life in the dark. From the earliest age I was put into motion picture houses. It kept me quiet and interested, and my parents could do more or less as they wanted. I was always at the movies. It became, as it did for so many people, a sort of preferable alternative to reality.

TC: *With the army newspaper, were you covering American film or Japanese?*

DR: Oh, American, of course. In the occupation the Japanese were invisible, taboo. We were not allowed, not encouraged to learn

Japanese unless we'd learned it in America. There were still signs posted when I got there that said "No fraternization with the indigenous personnel," meaning the Japanese. Everything was off-limits, although I was sneaking into every local theater I could in order to learn something about Japanese film. You had to proceed with a great deal of caution to avoid the MPs. Nevertheless, I did manage to acquire a sort of basics of Japanese cinema. Meantime, I was reviewing Betty Grable films for the troops.

TC: *You settled permanently in postwar Tokyo. What attracted you?*

DR: In 1953 the occupation was over, so it was a completely different place. We'd been delivered from the thrall of the Americans. There was a feeling of something like a Klondike City—you know, fast money, carpetbagging, a lot of get-rich-quick people, including a number of Americans. I needed a job to get in because I was no longer a member of the occupation. *Reader's Digest* was very kind and made a sort of fictitious position for me, so I got my visa that way. Once I was in, I did all kinds of things to earn my living. I did reviews for the *Japan Times*, which I still do. At the same time, a small new company approached me to help them with their English-language correspondence. They were called Japan Airlines. They had about five letters a week in English back then. I also began teaching at Waseda University—I gave Japan its first seminar in Melville, for example. So by doing the various things that I still do, I was able to get together a living.

TC: *You've continued to travel and lecture widely. Are you a settled man?*

DR: Well, I've never had a job. I don't have any set hours. I can do what I want to with my time as long as I make enough to eat. I get up early and by seven-thirty I'm doing my serious work for the day, whatever it is. By eleven-thirty or twelve I go out and make a living. I work at International House. I also do film titles or magazine editing. In the evening I socialize, have dinner with somebody or eat alone, or go to the movies. This is the pattern of my life. I've been married. I'm the kind of man who has an awful lot of acquaintances. Each day's a little bit different.

TC: *You distinguish between foreigners who live in Tokyo and those who go to study traditional aesthetics and so on in Kyoto. Are you a big city person yourself?*

DR: I'm a city person. I love the city. I'm not uncomfortable in the country, but I don't find much to keep me occupied there and I tend to want to get back to the city when I'm bored.

TC: *Curiously, your best-known book,* The Inland Sea, *is rural portraiture.*

DR: That's true. *The Inland Sea* is my favorite of all my books—if the house is on fire that's the one I'll save. It's a book though that's about escape, also about exploration, and is a miniature edition of my life— about getting away from something, running toward something. Usually, however, I write about the city. That's why I wrote a love- letter to the city with *Tokyo,* and I'm happy to say it has sold pretty well and been translated into two or three languages, although that's attributable to the caliber of its publisher. Anyway, as far as the city- country polarity goes, I'm plainly on the side of the city.

TC: *In your first book,* Where Are the Victors? *you talk about a "colli- sion of cultures" between East and West.*

DR: Let me expand. When I wrote *Victors,* Japan was occupied. During such times the occupiers tend to remain visible, while the occupied tend to fade into the woodwork. Now, the Americans were doing their best trying to build democracy and all the rest of it for the people. At the same time, the very fact that the Japanese were a conquered people rendered them invisible; all their decisions were made for them. This happened to suit Japanese character very well because it likes to appear to make no decisions—therefore it has to take no responsibilities. In their peculiar way, the Japanese prospered under the occupation. They were able to take advantage of things to order them to their own liking. The people at American GHQ didn't know what they were doing. GHQ was filled with grandiose ideas of bringing Frank Capra's and Jimmy Stewart's ideals to Japan and they didn't really pay much attention to what was occurring because Yoshida, the prime minister, kept reassuring them all was well. And indeed, U.S. mandates were carried out to the letter, but not the spirit. In the meantime, the true, authentic Japan was burgeoning under the occupation. What happened is that the occupation got hijacked.

TC: *Hijacked in what way?*

DR: At this time, the Japanese were very taken with the idea of becoming more egalitarian and everyone having the vote, even women—things that the Americans were also pushing. Washington, though, had this postwar insight that the real enemy was not the fascist, but the communist countries. Practically overnight the new enemy was Russia and the domino theory was propounded. Japan became not a new democracy, but a "bastion of freedom." This was the McCarthy period and all the new reforms seemed vaguely leftist—little people speaking up, that sort of thing—and thus became highly suspicious. The Japanese were left high and dry with their new democracy and no place to go. The Japanese had thought the point had been the making of a better, more democratic, more egalitarian society. Even now, people in public places speak of their disappointment in America's change of political stance during this period. So this is the crux of *Victors*: it takes place just as all this is occurring.

TC: *It has been said the Japanese and Americans often find exactly what they want in each other.*

DR: I think that's exactly true. But don't we all? I mean, why do you like someone?—because you find what you want in that person.

TC: *In the contemporary sense that, say, the Americans and the Chinese don't necessarily find what they want in each other?*

DR: It depends. Right now, America and Japan are sort of friendly. Currently, America and China aren't at all certain if they want to be friends; it may be more profitable to be enemies, because nothing helps an economy like a war. There's been some sparring around. It depends on your agenda.

TC: *Let's return to you. Henry James speaks of an expatriate conscious-ness that observes and records rather than judges. What would you say has characterized your work over the past fifty years?*

DR: When I write, I don't use Japan as a sort of psycho-theater. I don't use it to dramatize myself. I really try to get out there and observe and record.

TC: *In Tokyo you write that individuality is felt as strongly in Japan as elsewhere, only that it is expressed less directly.*

DR: I'm of the view that Japan is as pluralistic as any other place. It's just that the powers hide the plurality, that's all. The official mind-set, which makes up the national picture likes the idea of a homogeneous culture, all going in the same direction, orderly like fish in a school, all the same hair color. This is perceived as a virtue. However, human beings aren't like that. The Japanese aren't like that.

TC: *That goes against the flow of conventional Western reportage on Japan.*

DR: In Japan some attempt is made to cover things up. The only difference is one of agenda. You won't, however, find the Japanese different, I believe, from any other people on earth—if you can get through the agenda, that is. But they've also got an agenda that's about three miles thick, so you have to live there a very long time and take some trouble to see what is truly there.

TC: *Is the sacrifice of individuality worth the price of social harmony?*

DR: To my lights, no. According to everybody else in the world, yes. Do you ever hear anybody who's anti-civilization? No. Everybody believes it's worth the sacrifice of the individual in order to make the social machine run better. I think everybody believes that—except me. I'm a domesticated anarchist.

TC: *Your new* Reader *contains excerpts from* Zen Inklings. *Are you an enthusiast or have you experienced an actual Zen practice?*

DR: Both, actually. I hanker. My hankering is deep, hence "inklings." We all hanker for some sort of security, and since I've closed the doors of organized religion behind me, the only thing that's left for me are the sort of nooks and crannies of which Zen is one. If you read *Public People, Private People* you'll discover I sat with Dr. D.T. Suzuki. He was a great Zen master and I was his *deshi* (disciple).

TC: *You've stated your belief that Japan is still constructing "masculinity."*

DR: Femininity and masculinity are indeed constructions. To be feminine is a masculine construction. We've made the woman feminine. Feminine means to be ladylike. It means to be constrained. "The female" would indicate the more natural, things the way they really are. To be feminine—and I'm just parroting Simone de Beauvoir—is something men constructed to make women more into chattel. In the same way, men themselves turn into macho to enlarge themselves, to define who they are, to expand their realms, things like that. Japan has always been very adept at being, in this case, a psychologically totalitarian organization, making categories in which the female is turned feminine and the male is turned macho. It makes it much more easy to sort things out; it makes it a lot easier to play a role.

TC: *This issue of self-definition is central to literature. How about film?*

DR: Have you read Sartre? Well then, you know the temptation of what it is to define yourself as an absolute object. If you can do this, then you're home free, your problems are over. I think everybody tends to want this. You ask them what they are, they name one thing: "I'm a lawyer, a tourist." In naming ourselves as one thing, we achieve a sort of density that delivers us from doubt. And, further, from "dreadful freedom"; from this awful idea that everything's arbitrary, like at the end of [Sartre's] *Nausea*. When we manage to completely define our Self, it delivers us from all the terrors of the vague incomprehensibility, which is part of the experience of being human. You notice this in the films of Kurosawa. His heroes have not learned how to do this—but all of his villains have. His villains are one thing all the way through. One definition of the villain in the films of Kurosawa is a man who has achieved his macho status, or a woman who has achieved her feminine status. These people are solid. They know exactly who they are, exactly how they're going to react, because their program model acts this way. Watch the majority of people, watch teenagers—their entire life is spent trying on role models, and at the same time denying their own fluidity. It's a very rare person—Proust, for example—who will encourage fluidity, who will refuse to become the model of the month or the flavor of the week. In Tokyo you'll find people who are terrified of dreadful freedom. They'll lose themselves in work—they'll kill themselves for it. I'm the kind of person who likes to keep things open, but I certainly know what it is like, the temptation to define oneself.

TC: *In politically correct times, you've been honest enough to insist that we must not lightly set aside the sexual in our encounter with Japan. Can you elaborate?*

DR: When we travel we're free of a lot of boundaries that limit us, wherever we come from. We're more naturally ourselves. People on trips are notoriously horny. People who are on vacation always screw more, or want to, than they do when they're home. This is so obvious that no one thinks anything about it. The interesting thing about this is that one becomes so open to certain kinds of experience. Indeed this kind of experience can take over the whole definition of pleasure in traveling itself. If you speak to people who travel to Thailand, for example, it seems an eminently natural thing to do. The other thing is, since we're acquisitive peoples, what do we take home from our encounters? Sex, in a way, makes the ideal souvenir.

TC: *How about expatriates?*

DR: Well, imagine a person who chooses to live his life abroad. We have many examples of this—the Americans, say, in Paris or Morocco. What do they do other than write and screw? Not very much. We have people who devoted themselves—Paul Bowles, whom I knew, Jane Bowles, Robert McAlmon, Gertrude Stein, people like that—in Tangier, in Paris, being able to live their lives sexually in a way they would never be able to in Council Bluffs. So you get people making accommodations with their inner selves abroad. That's why expatriates are so interesting—they've made this leap away from the corporate self. The Japanese have this very much as well, because they don't have any hang-ups on Christian religion, although they have tremendous hang-ups on ritual pollution as in Shinto. But you can go there and take sex trips to Thailand like everybody else. This idea of going "outside" to have your sex life is a very interesting one, and accounts for my statements about not setting things lightly aside.

TC: *In a related vein, you write that the West has created a massive edifice of Orientalism. Yet we now have an institutional academic neurosis about Orientalism courtesy of Edward Said.*

DR: I meant the same thing as Said does, but I meant it benevolently and he doesn't.

TC: *In what way?*

DR: To me the Orient is still this wonderful, romantic place where everything sexy is possible. Orientalism is extremely creative; it's a way of liberating the imagination by illuminating the other. Of course, he would say that I remain an Orientalist.

TC: *Peter Quennell, whom you quote, says that in Japan "vice itself is ceremonial."*

DR: Lovely phrase, isn't it? But first you have to define vice. I think there's a feeling that if you pay money for it, then it's probably vice. So society defines what vice is. It's in all cultures—sex costs money.

We tend to hide it behind certain ceremonial behavior; for example, the ceremony that the grand courtesans would go through with their arcane hand gestures and everything that went on before, during, and after sex. This is all ceremonialized in order to cleanse. It's very Shinto. Shinto ceremonies have this in order to take away the pollution. If the pollution is really bad—for example, menstruation—then you don't take it away at all; but if it's just, you know, coupling, then you're able to clean it up.

What's very common in Japan nowadays, since we don't have courtesans, are the Soaplands. You go in and the woman who is in charge of the man adopts a hearty attitude, a little bit like a school-teacher or a nurse—"Oh, aren't we having a good time?! More to the left!" and "Wasn't that nice?—do come again!" And with this atti-tude, which is ludicrous, we have a nurse-like approach: "You're a sick man because you have a hard-on." And she is the angel of mercy and comes in with her paraphernalia and cures you. This is the social construct that goes on in order to extract, to take away the polluting aspect [of vice]. After all, if it's like a kindergarten, it can't be too polluted, right?

TC: *Would you say there's a similarity with the Mediterranean idea of absolution?*

DR: Yes, it's very like it. You say a Hail Mary and you're clean again.

TC: *A lot of Europe and America missed out on that.*

DR: Unfortunately.

TC: *Switching a little, toward the end of his life the poet Basho devel-oped his fuga, or "Way of the Artist." He's become a touchstone for North Americans looking at Asian art and literature. Do you have any feeling about his idea of* fuga?

DR: About there being "an artist's way"? For myself, I would say yes. Basho and his contemporaries had their own way of doing it—per-haps pretentious to a degree, but however narrow, it offered a ways and means for them. I'm a searcher with all the other searchers. I boast no prior knowledge at all and if I find something in the dark I'm happy, but that's about it.

TC: *Your new* Reader *follows a similar, major* Gary Snyder Reader. *It seems the elders of the East/West tribe are finding honor in their own land.*

DR: It starts to happen if you get old enough. We've reached that time of life and the fruits are ripening on the branches. My work has been to define things that are in the air and give them form. What I am is a definer, although I'm not a purist; I test genre, and some of the selections included in the *Reader* are indicative of this. I'm someone who enjoys writing about things I've learned.

Vancouver

Chapter 14

A Conversation with Andrew Schelling

You couldn't imagine American poetry at present without the influence of Chinese and Japanese models. The work of many fine translators—translators who have done the good job of learning one or more Asian languages—has rapidly and completely altered how we write. Buddhist thought and practice are something else. They will need a much longer time-frame in order to lay down a durable foundation.

In 2001, a painter friend, Arnold Shives, asked if I'd join him at the opening of his international exhibition in Denver. It seemed unlikely. Then a call came from Naropa University in nearby Boulder, Colorado saying that they'd heard I might be in the area. Would I like to visit? I'd long been interested in Naropa's approach to contemplative education and in what I'd heard of the Jack Kerouac School for writers that Allen Ginsberg and others had developed at this Buddhist University. I cashed in my air miles and set off with Arnold. After enjoying the Zen chanting service in English started by Danan-Roshi [then Sensei] at Zen Center of Denver, I drove to Boulder in hope of meeting the poet Andrew Schelling who teaches at Naropa. In anticipation, I brought my copy of Dropping the Bow, his translations of poems from ancient India. As fate had it, Schelling had volunteered to greet the visiting Canuck so we met and I had the benefit of his guidance around the campus. Two years later and after some correspondence we collaborated on this interview via email—still a rather novel approach at the time. Among Schelling's many books of poetry and translation, Wild Form & Savage Grammar, a collection of essays on poetry, ecology, and Asia remains a personal *favorite. Bridging poetics, Beat-inflected ethics, and aesthetics, and a nature wisdom tradition that embraces aboriginal and Asian well-springs, the essays serve as meditations and useful consciousness-raising tools against the worst of what ecologists suggest our time has become— "the Great Dying."*

TC: *Andrew, topographically you've ranged widely in your career. Born and raised on the East Coast; formative years as writer, younger litera-teur in northern California's San Francisco Bay-Santa Cruz area; and resident for some years now at what's close to the geographic heart of America in the Colorado front range country at Naropa University in Boulder. Any sense of what these three experiences bring to your work?*

AS: I could answer this question many ways but let me do it in terms of North American poetry. The East Coast, New England specifically, provided a few heroic poetry figures from the past, but the possibili-ties seemed constricted. Too much Europe, too much English depart-ment, too much Ivy League putdown and depression. I wanted something open, lively, archaic, full of wind and granite. I knew it existed on the West Coast. Pacific Rim culture, the full impact of Asia, and the encounter with vast stretches of wilderness were what I went west for. I was seventeen years in Northern California where the Sierra Nevada and Coast Range Mountains were my singular teach-ers, and I could stand on a crest of chaparral looking toward Asia.

Colorado is something different. It represents a move away from the littoral coastlines, away from the influence of across-the-ocean continents, and a move into the nation's heartland. Living here, the Rocky Mountains—spine of our continent—sets the instinctual compass-points north and south. There's a steady Native American influence, then five hundred years of Mexico. Just south of here it was all Mexico until 1848 when the United States did the big land grab called Treaty of Guadalupe Hidalgo and took half of Mexico. In 1994 I looked at a map and realized the poets of Mexico City live closer to me than the poets of New York.

But this Western land. Half of it is public land. It belongs to the United States people and is technically supervised by the federal gov-ernment. I'm fascinated by and deeply invested in the conflicts over who gets to use it and how. Is public land for the timber companies, for mining, oil, and mineral extractors? Is it for ranchers? Hunters? Hikers and skiers? Indigenous species and threatened plants and animals? Biologists? Is it for the Air Force to do target practice on, the Feds to test outlandishly destructive weapons? For condominiums? Prairie dogs and coyote? I guess you could say this is where I set up my poetry.

TC: *Regarding the East Coast, in your new book* Wild Form, Savage Grammar *you allude to Thoreau. How profoundly do you feel he and the New England Transcendentalists have resonated in the American cultural mind? Is Whitman part of this? Any observation on Whitman taking his show on the road—in the sense that, say, Kerouac and Ginsberg would do later as "stenographers of consciousness," as bard archivists of the nation's life and times?*

AS: Whitman is a great poet. He showed a lot of people the way to break with the formal constraints of European poetry, and to make things out of words that feel like they belong on North American landscapes. I love Whitman. He prophesied the country as we know it today. His America came into existence. This is Walt Whitman's America. Two weeks ago a very conservative Supreme Court surprised everyone by overturning a 1986 Texas sodomy law, effectively saying that whatever any adults do in the privacy of their bedrooms is their own business, and any effort to criminalize their behavior is unconstitutional. After that ruling, I don't think you can find much of anything in Walt Whitman that would be a problem for mainstream Republicans. He was the singer of development, of manifest destiny, of men going to work and building cities. He's out there singing into existence the condominiums and shopping malls, the highways, the colorful throngs of people that flock into ballparks and museums or who eat at Burger King. He's celebrating NAFTA, WTO, and the production of countless high-tech gadgets.

I exaggerate. But I do think it's time to put him reverently on the shelf alongside Milton and Petrarch, a model for poetic craft. He's almost too much the stenographer of consciousness.

Thoreau on the other hand has hardly been digested. He went to jail refusing to pay war taxes on an imperialist grab that Whitman was singing in praise of. It was his essay "Civil Disobedience" that gave Mahatma Gandhi his directive, and then through Gandhi, Martin Luther King, Jr. Comparatively few Americans have caught up with that mistrust of their government's policies, and that willingness to take a stand.

For North America, Thoreau was also the singer of responsible development. He watched the railroad being built and foresaw what it meant for forests, ecosystems, wildlife, and human populations. I bet in a shuddering dream he saw the automobile, the increasing addiction to fossil fuels, and a nation crisscrossed by asphalt highways that would hungrily displace animal migration routes. He devoted his life to a study of Native American lore, hoping to find a measured alternative to the headlong expansion of human settlement, a way to live on the planet lightly. His years at Walden Pond were an experiment to determine what a person actually, vitally required in order to survive. Thoreau became an active and outspoken Abolitionist. All the while he was reading Asian texts—Hindu, Buddhist, Taoist, tribal—and seeing them as more vital to this country than many of the head-trips of Europe.

And he was, importantly, not anti-technology. Most people don't know that he invented the modern pencil, the pencil as we grew up with it. Besides working in his family's pencil factory, he may have been the finest surveyor of his day. But he wanted a technology on the scale of what later visionaries—of the 1960s and '70s—hoped for: human in scale, with self-renewing energy sources. Almost nothing of his vision has been put into place; what little has crept through (like Emancipation, or the vote for women, or the Wilderness and Endangered Species Acts) has been brought forward by struggle, and still isn't firmly established. Thoreau is the "other" America, the one that hasn't come into existence yet.

TC: *As a younger buck back east, did Kerouac or his companions register on your radar screen at all?*

AS: Hardly. East Coast establishment buried most of it. A few magazines like *Ramparts* could be had. I'd heard of Ginsberg and Ferlinghetti but knew only a book or two. The one poet of that crowd I read with great attention was Leroi Jones [Amiri Baraka]. Then just before I left New England I started to read Chinese poetry in translation. That was when I encountered Gary Snyder's *Cold Mountain Poems*. Those hit me, along with a lot of India material I was turning on to, and I went off to Asia. I was twenty. When I returned it was to California.

TC: *You turn up in the S.F. Bay Area studying Sanskrit at university. That's uncommon enough to be worthy of attention. What event(s) stimulated this turn of mind?*

AS: I'd been reading Hindu and Buddhist texts in translation for a long time and even tracked a little Sanskrit. I loved the thunder and hurtling winds, the surging mountains and voluptuous deities, the folkloric humor that comes in from Paleolithic backgrounds. A dear friend, Bhuwan Joshi, who had been raised in the Kathmandu Valley, helped me work through some Upanishads and he made the old poems come totally alive. So I kind of raided the University at Berkeley to learn Sanskrit, wanting to read deeply into those texts. I never did get a degree. It became clear eventually that my motive was to learn how to read certain core books in the language, not become a professional. Bhuwan had encouraged me to study Sanskrit, and sadly he died the year I formally began at Berkeley. But in the sinews of the old language I began to find fantastic material for poetry—as he told me I would—as well as to witness a magical transformation of the old books.

TC: *Was there any significant spiritual dimension in this Indic interest or was it more secular? A literary interest? Some combination? Had you grown up in New England with a sense of religion?*

AS: I'm not sure I believe in these as separate dimensions any longer. At the time I would have said my interests were spiritual. I'd grown up with no religious allegiance whatever. My first contact with any meaningful sense of spiritual awe or ecstatic union came first through an early love, then through contact with some rugged backcountry. A sense of the spiritual came more formally through the sculpture of India and the ink paintings of China and Japan. I found these art works in the museums of Boston and Cambridge. They were images of consciousness for me—places I wanted to be, spiritually. Notice that in Indian sculpture religion and sexuality are often intertwined, as in China religion and wilderness are often inextricable.

Later, as my confidence as a poet grew, and I realized the spiritual call of literary work, I began to search out India's poetry. But at the start I wanted to understand the kinds of things said in Buddhist sutras and Hindu texts, things that accorded with my own experience and instincts. Like many people, psychedelic drugs opened some doors, and the vast speculative mind spaces found in Asian texts were useful guides to what was going on.

TC: *In your essay on William Everson we get a look into the development of your own mind at what appears to be a pivotal time in your career. Did he carry with him any of the old politics of his pacifist WWII years? Any of this rub off? How about the heavy influence of Jeffers on Everson: have you a sense that Jeffers still sings to people?*

AS: Bill was a perfect example of Yeats' "Why should not old men be mad?" Here I take mad to mean something like "wild." Bill's politics, his pacifism, had been deeply etched into his dramatic life. The political stance rubbed off through simply being around him. Most of our friendship was based on a regard for craft not politics though. I worked with him on a letterpress book at the Lime Kiln Press and we looked over another of his projects, *American Bard*, together. We talked about women, love, the writings of Ananda Coomaraswamy, forest fires across the bay at Big Sur, and we sat quietly on the porch of his Kingfisher Flats cabin and smoked cigars. He was getting old, the Parkinson's disease was just becoming evident, so he was entering that ruminative phase that comes with advancing age. His wildness lay coiled up within him. The Whitman beard and hair, the wide-brimmed hat, bear-claw necklace, buckskins—these were like monk's robes to him. Outer evidence of his inward quest. I guess I'd have to say his politics were not organized or dogmatic or particularly articulated. They were the outcome of his religious discoveries, his struggle with Catholicism.

Jeffers was the master poet for Bill. In terms of West Coast poetry, and its effort to get the staggering land forms into verse, Jeffers remains the most powerful expression of what Bill called the Western archetype. I guess Jeffers still sings to people. Stanford has published his collected poetry in four huge expensive volumes, and recently brought out two volumes of selected poetry. He's got what Melville called the wild game flavor—like venison—lean and untamed. It won't be to everyone's taste. I have been writing a poetry sequence that wrestles with Jeffers, I try to lighten him up a bit, make some fun with his gloominess. Bill wrote much of his own poetry wrestling with Jeffers. It was like a struggle of giants. Face-to-face Bill was a deeply humorous man, but in his poetry he has the crashing granite, terrifying Pacific coast storms, and sacramental violence Jeffers kept writing about. It's not a taste our urban, educated, professional classes have cultivated.

TC: *Moving out of your acquaintance with Everson, your excellent essay on the continuing relevance of the small press tradition offers a furtherance of this attention to craft. You're involved yourself now in fostering this tradition at Naropa with students. Can we speak here a little about lineage? The notion of lineage-bearing looks to have slipped a point or two in Western culture, although it would appear to be a core tenet at Naropa.*

AS: You're right. The idea of lineage remains central to Naropa's Jack Kerouac School. Poetry is a weave of lineage with no time or place constraints. You may not meet masters in daily life, but that doesn't mean they aren't there instructing you.

Our postmodern condition is that each of us has our own lineage—individual and precise, instructive, full of direct transmissions of consciousness. I see a good poem as an embodied state of mind. At any moment you can slip right in, or through. The secular perspective says, "Well, he's self-taught. He's an autodidact. He didn't get it from anyone else. He found his voice." That's what the books say of Kenneth Rexroth for instance. I think that view is bullshit. The other side says: I have direct access to the mind of Aeschylus, to Sappho's mind, to the thoughts and ardor of the early Sanskrit poets, to Tu Fu, Shakespeare. Only the thinnest veil divides me from Lady Murasaki. "All times are contemporaneous in the mind," Ezra Pound wrote. When I read and translate the poems of Vidya or Lady Shilabhattarika in Sanskrit, I'm receiving direct transmission through the body of language.

"The body of language." That, by the way, is a term I learned from Bhartrihari—he lived about eighth-century India. "Body of language." He whispered it in my ear through a poem 1,300 years ago.

TC: *Let's talk linkages. Something brought you to the West Coast and kept you there for seventeen years. Something brought you to Colorado. We've touched upon some of the formative literary elements in your life back east, the centering experience of Sanskrit study, and your learning to work with fine press techniques. How was your development as poet coming along? Were the various streams intertwined or have they necessarily run along parallel tracks? Inevitably, they seem to converge, but in terms of process were you obliged to compartmentalize different parts of your life?*

AS: I was writing all along. It wasn't until my mid-twenties, though, that I realized how central the writing had become. It's a funny development. I had been supporting myself by work in a bakery—this was in the mid-'70s. I'd turned myself into a pretty good innovative baker, working in a California establishment with natural foods—whole wheat flour, honey, organic butter—and decided to write a baking cookbook. I spent a lot of time in the library investigating the origins of baking. The more I worked at the cookbook, the more I found my real interest was not really baking but writing—study and writing. When I saw this clearly the cookbook dropped along the wayside and I turned to poetry. I made the gesture of seeking out Bill Everson. It was a way of saying to myself, I'm a poet and I want to meet the lineage holders who are still alive. I want to know their minds. So I turned my love of craft from the bakery to the print shop.

Studying Sanskrit at first was a separate activity; I didn't know quite how it hooked up. When I stumbled upon the impossibly complex, elegant poetry tradition of classical India I began to see how the work of translation could be central to my commitment as a poet. Virtually nobody outside India knew Sanskrit poetry at the time, so I happened on it cold. By 1978, when I set out to study Sanskrit in earnest, well-read Americans knew Basho, Lady Murasaki, Tu Fu, Po Chu-i. No one had heard of Bhartrihari, Yogeshvara, King Hala, or Vidya. This was the best lesson I have ever learned about poetry: the real work may lie where you aren't expecting it. The lesson is about accident, happenstance, synchronicity, magic. World folklore points this out time and time again. Sometimes I think of it this way, an image that came through a dream. The scholar goes out tracking his prey, knows its habits, where it wanders, uses skills precise as a hunter's, and brings the animal down. The poet releases his arrow but often misses his prey. He is obliged to plunge deeper into the forest in search of that arrow, and there he finds the unexpected.

That's why I love the account of Kurt Schwitters' discovery of chance operation. Frustrated with one of his drawings because it looked so conventional, so boring, he tore his composition apart and tossed away the shreds in disgust. When he looked down he saw an unexpected beauty: a new configuration on the floor.

TC: *Looking back, do you have a sense of how your poetry was coming along?*

AS: I had to learn that lesson first. About chance, and about heartbreak. About missing the target. Then I had to learn about cut-up, bricolage, and the ideogramic method of Pound. It was slow learning. I had to learn how to think like the poets of ancient India so I wouldn't just repeat what had been done by Bill Everson. Or by Baraka or Niedecker or Snyder or any of the poets I admire. I had to speak every day with dead poets—"all times are contemporaneous in the mind"— argue points of craft with them, fill up notebooks with ideas and words I had stolen. I had to figure out how to go forward with no preconceptions. This makes it sound close to Zen practice. Basho wrote, "Don't follow in the steps of the old masters; seek what they sought."

TC: *The other chief informing element in your mature work is what I suppose we used to call "natural science." By this I mean there's been a progressive sharpening of attention to ecological detail in your work. There are times in* Wild Form, Savage Grammar *where the narrative voice is so thoroughly imbued with place, with a kind of systems theory awareness of local ecological inventories that, in a deeply appreciative sense, we can practically hear Gary Snyder in there. Can you comment on this development in your work: Was there a triggering moment for you when you decided to know the names of the birds and trees in your community terrain? What part of your living experience led to the kind of bioregional awareness that turns up in your letter to the government requesting that Christo's proposed "eco-wrap" project be directed elsewhere?*

AS: That's a personal and pretty complex question. How can I answer except by telling stories, or pulling together a few threads of thought? As I said, in California the mountains were my great teachers. In Colorado I do my apprenticeship with the Rockies. The eco-zones and watersheds are what I've come to love. It all happens in the details, so, of course, I learn what I can. "Details are the life of prose." That's Kerouac. The same for poetry. Same for ecology. Maybe I got my interest from too much time in Thoreau territory as a kid! I used to swim in Walden when it was forbidden and get chased off by rangers.

On a more sober note, the planet's ecosystems are now our neighborhood, our house, our home. Inside a home you give things the dignity of their names. I don't generally call my daughter or my girlfriend "hey you" or ask them to pass the whatsit. Names are powerful, full of magic. They call things otherwise unseen into existence. There is a politics in this, too.

As for Christo's wrap of the Arkansas River, I don't want it directed somewhere else, I want it rejected because of its potential for hazard. If Christo wants to wrap something up in synthetic fabric, make it a building or a bridge or a refrigerator, not a fragile ecosystem. I'd be glad to walk the high country with him, check out a few plants and animals, and together we could talk about why sinking steel anchors into rock in bighorn sheep territory isn't a good idea.

TC: *Given the state of the world this eco-mindedness is important, so let's develop it further. It seems pretty clear that writers from out of the Beat culture have had an outsized impact in fostering improved environmental awareness in our time. Is it a basic social justice/leftist/community-mindedness that may be inherent in the Beat ethos that's helped spawn this? What aspects of Beat culture would you say led to this form of awakening? Is it as simple, maybe, as there being a preponderance of Beat poets who went camping with their folks when they were kids and had at least some basic forest/wilderness savvy, or is it deeper? Since the NYC contingent of Kerouac, Ginsberg, Burroughs et al. were essentially, though not exclusively, urban (at least early days), were the West Coast/ S.F. Renaissance personalities key, the Oregon/Washington State band of Welch, Whalen, Snyder or. . . . ?*

American academic culture has had fits with the Beats, notably so with its ecologically attuned dimensions. I'm thinking here of the old East Coast put-down of Snyder's poetry as "the bear-shit on the trail school" (which of itself is a remarkably perceptive epithet!). Nowadays it's not unheard of to hear Wendell Berry, Wes Jackson, or Snyder and others brushed off as Neo-Luddites (which again can be seen as spot on). What is there in this form of put-down, do you think?

AS: These are big questions and I'm not an expert. But I think the emergence of an environmental movement, an ecologically sound approach to life and the arts, and the development of bioregional consciousness—these are huge matters of human consciousness. This is a critical and strangely exhilarating moment in human history. The chance to ruin or retrieve the planet as a viable sphere of life is in front of us. Do poets create these recognitions, these shifts in consciousness, or simply announce them? Or document them? Anyone paying a bit of attention recognizes that the Earth's amazingly resilient biosphere has met its match in contemporary human populations and technologies. With or without the poets, questions about clean air, clean water, chemical and nuclear contamination, vanishing wild life, compromised wild lands, and so forth, will be hugely debated.

At the moment the real leaders are not in the developed world. They are in India and Chiapas. What the Beats did was to make issues like these appear in American poetry. They made poetry serious, bringing an activist approach to crisis, as Ezra Pound did by leveling his gaze at economics and war.

As for the put-down of poets, it always happens. There are many ways to make a poem, many things to write about, many sympathies and ideas to explore. Most of the celebrated poets of the past hundred years, and nearly all the academics and critics, have been urban dwellers. They want something else from a poem than bearshit on the trail. Fair enough. But if poets took put-downs too seriously we wouldn't have any durable poetry at all! What if Catullus had listened to those temperate citizens of Rome when they said, you can't write shit like that about love affairs and politics, someone might have you assassinated. What if Anna Akhmatova had listened to the Stalinist censors? Chaucer is very funny, dramatizing a big put-down of his skills in *The Canterbury Tale*: "your rhymes are not worth a turd." It's true. You and I could be out making real money, Trevor, not following this thankless path of poetry.

TC: *The next obvious point crops up during your essay discussion about how certain American, particularly Pacific Northwest poets/translators, develop a yen for classical Chinese/Japanese aesthetics in art and poetry. This has tended to fit hand-in-glove with an interest in Buddhism and Taoism. As interest in Buddhism is undergoing a boom in the West do you have much sense that influence from Beat-affiliated writers continues to play a role in this? Have we reached a point where knowledge of the Dalai Lama, Thich Nhat Hanh, Chogyam Trungpa Rinpoche, and others may have sufficiently mainstreamed that* The Dharma Bums *isn't as central as it once was? Your professional experience at Naropa makes you uniquely qualified to address this point.*

AS: You couldn't imagine American poetry at present without the influence of Chinese and Japanese models. The work of many fine translators—translators who have undertaken the difficult study of one or more Asian languages, often old literary languages along with contemporary spoken ones—has rapidly altered how North Americans write poetry. Buddhist thought and practice are something else. These will need a longer timeframe in order to lay down durable foundations, and possibly they will require that temples, monastic settings, colleges, and other institutions survive for generations. The Buddhist teachers you mention are instrumental; there are many, many more, and quite a few effective ones with no celebrity recognition at all. It is lovely to have North America able to support Buddha halls where poets can come and go at will—like Tu Fu and Li

Po did, Basho, Sei Shonagon. But thinking back to an era when few temples existed here, in the annals of American Buddhism the Beat poets will necessarily figure as wily, savvy, quixotic Buddha ancestors.

I hope one day everyone will see *The Dharma Bums* as a first great book of American Buddhist poetry. Let's imagine that for a thousand years it spurs readers to emulate the masters of the past: to write poetry, to practice zazen, to take vows of creativity and restraint. To study big Mind, to lock eyebrows with Bodhidharma and Han Shan, to drink tea with beloved companions. To head on foot into the mountains with a rucksack full of books. To cultivate visions, to practice love. *Dharma Bums* is a big brave book, which most American should read. It is full of pain and fuck-ups, too, alcoholism, tragic affairs, and a suicide. So I have one word of caution about the Beats. It's from Basho. Don't follow in the footsteps of the masters; seek what they sought.

TC: *Further to the links between poetry, ecology and Asia: you discuss the resurgent idea of cross-species empathy on the part of eco-activists and formally name it "jataka mind." It's a brilliant declaration. Can you summarize the understanding this represents?*

AS: I drew the idea from a number of related studies in ecology, art, and psychology. The word *jataka* is Sanskrit; it means birth, or life, as in lifetime. *The Jataka Tales*, originally oral tales then written down in Pali, are early Buddhist stories. In them the Buddha—long before he is born Prince Siddhartha—shows up in former lifetimes, most often in animal form. In each story he makes some extreme sacrifice, often to save the lives of critters of another species. Have you ever seen the rabbit in the moon? Go out and look closely at the full moon and you'll see the imprint of a rabbit. It's there because long ago the Buddha, living as a rabbit, couldn't bear the hunger of a group of unsuccessful, starving hunters. He jumped into their pot to feed them. To commemorate the act, one of the old gods, Indra, mightily impressed at the show of compassion, put that rabbit's image on the moon. "The hare-marked moon."

My essay simply observes that creatures of divergent species—including we homo sapiens—have an inherent empathy for one another. Buddhists are familiar with this, theoretically at least. So are Jains, Hindus, Taoists. Christians have charity, though many seem unsure what do with St. Francis when he extends his good will to nonhuman creatures. In our own day I see it most among people who get pegged as animal rights or ecology activists. I like to think that they are also pioneers toward a new spiritual sense of our place on this planet.

When I wrote my essay it was partly to celebrate the bravery of the Redwood Summer activists who were putting their lives on the line for old growth trees, spotted owls, salmon, the entire understory of the forests of the Northwest, and related ecosystems. I had not yet read Edward O. Wilson's *Biophilia Hypothesis*, which is a proposition by a respected scientist that matches the poetry speculations my essay got into. Wilson's sound biological ruminations are where I'd go next. From the standpoint of deep time—the point of view of evolution— all species are fellow travelers in complex ecosystems. Different animals aren't simply a colorfully benign costume for the planet that we humans get to groove on—or snuff out if they get in our way. Diverse species are intricately woven into our lives along metabolic, ecological, and spiritual pathways. We utterly depend on each other, not just for food and fertility, or clothing, but for companionship. It will be a very lonely planet for everyone when the last elephant has been hunted down for its ivory, or if we lose the grizzly bear and the wolf.

These creatures, as world folklore repeats again and again, are our sympathetic teachers. More than that, they make us. When you're wandering up a hiking trail and the buzzing of a small rattler's tail makes you leap backward—that's because we have co-evolved. Our brain is structured the way it is partly because snake lives out there in the bush. Didn't snake provide us humans with coolly alert senses, able to note a slight quaver in the brush at our feet, able to leap aside without having to calculate? Snake gave us the skills we hone in the martial arts dojo. We owe much of our psycho-physical competence to Snake Old Man! So, recognizing and cultivating those old contracts of respect, admiration, companionship—this would be the hip, archaic, far-seeing, and lovely new way to be human. A rattlesnake isn't bad. It just wants respect. Not to be trod upon. It gives us a quick lesson, and then does its job of cleaning up the vermin, aerating the soil, and possibly leaving the poet with a crisp little song.

What I call Jataka Mind would be the deep-level recognition that these connections exist, are ultimately important, and that in the large picture no one—no species—is dispensable. We have to take care of one another. This is a sensibility we can cultivate and pass on to friends and children. Studying ecology is one way in, meditation might nail a few things down, but stories and poems are the best way to celebrate interspecies kinship. Why do kids want to hear animal stories? Same reason that the early stories of every culture have animals showing up in them. Humans have been profoundly curious about other beings—they are our teachers—and it's reciprocated. Animals are helpers, assistants, companions. Some extend real friendship toward humans. They like us, you know. We're weird and interesting to them. They come around to check out the crazy things we cook up.

TC: *A longish, compound query: In your essay "Notes on Form & Savage Mind" you remind us that the essential patterns of nature constitute "a far-reaching grammar"—to paraphrase Chuang-tzu, one that picks up where words leave off. Later, you note that "Dream like evolutionary theory predicates shapeshifts and transformations." Shapeshifting is a recurrent theme in the bardic tales of the old Celts—psychologists have a field day with Cuchulain's adversaries becoming scary monsters, what have you. I note occasional Celtic references in your book. Perhaps as a bridge here, we could point to your interest in interglacial age cave-art where the shaman-artist seems to serve an intermediary role in striking connections between "wilderness/wild mind" and, say, dream. And if it's not too far a reach, in your Indian ventures you've observed sadhus as envoys of this eternal-moment Deamtime here and now. Interestingly, you dedicate this key essay to poets Robin Blaser and Joanne Kyger. Blaser, of course, has affiliation with the Robert Duncan-Jack Spicer stream, and Kyger with her own manifold poetic linkages.*

AS: I love it that ecology is scientifically confirming what poetry, dream, and stories always told us. Things change, people change, landscapes change, everything shape-shifts in meaningful and sometimes unpredictable ways. In the old time, animals were people and people animals. No paleontologist has ever found an indication of anything else. All living creatures are on complicated journeys from form to form, and the postmodern poem has to deal with it. The postmodern mind has to deal with it!

Celtic material is something I've just started to dig into. You know, it is very, very close to the old stuff I find in India. Like I say in a poem, "Banaras to Dublin to Boston, it's an Indo-European thing." Here I'm thinking about language per se, and the grand playful shifts that happen through time. I recently went on an exploration of the Aran Islands off Ireland's west coast—looking for old tombs, forts, hermit hutches, holy wells, and other sites. I used Tim Robinson's good, detailed map, and read his two-volume *The Stones of Aran*. His work shows how in Ireland every rock, every little inlet or old tree, each cliff face or rock outcrop, has a name. Every name has a story, and every story has a history or legend. It's like going on a nature walk with a good biologist—in six hours you might not get past the weed-lot twenty feet from the classroom door. I mean if he's a *good* biologist.

Some of my poetry gets into this for Colorado. One poem I did with Althea, my daughter—she was about ten—we pulled out a Colorado gazetteer of place names. The poem includes a list: "A town called Gothic. A town called Troublesome. A canyon called Chaos. A rock called Elk Tooth." We were laughing and rolling around with the map. Talk about "a far reaching grammar!" She was a little sha-maness of place names: "A town called McCoy. A gulch called Skeleton. A peak called Quandary. A town called Rifle. A park called Interlocken. A peak called Thunderbolt." The poem ends, "a bar called Rocky Flats."

TC: *Thinking specifically of your poetry, there's an abundance of erotic imagery in your work. Is this organically Schelling or might it arise from your compelling interest in Sanskrit poetry wherein ripeness and fecundity often verge on carnality? Is there a special gift the Sanskrit offers our time?*

AS: Erotic energy is the energy of the planet. It is playful, loving, polymorphous, it is also dark, brooding, fecund, vegetative. The tricky thing for a poet in Western civilization is to find a language that can express this range. I don't need to go into the history of it, but for a long, long time in the West the language of sexuality was in the hands of the medical doctor or left out in the street. We don't have a tender, literary vocabulary for erotic love. It has been hard to depict love with lightness or vulnerability. What McClure and Lenore Kandel did, and writers like Joyce, Lawrence, Gertrude Stein before them, was very brave.

So a special gift left us, among others, by the Sanskrit poets of a millennium or two ago: erotic poetry that gets the lightness, the juice, the passion, the special human ways of courtship and consummation. You find it in Sappho and the other early Greeks, too. But in old India the "language of love" was entrusted to the poets. In King Hala's *Sattasai*, a nearly 2,000-year-old anthology, an opening verse criticizes anyone who would claim to know something about love without reading poetry. Poetry is where you go to learn this stuff. It was commendable to study love in those days. Somewhere Kenneth Rexroth writes that in Sappho's culture the pursuit of sexual pleasure was totally respectable, the way making money is in our culture. I know where I'd like to live. What about you? A world where the discoveries of love define our lives? Or where the NASDAQ Index does?

TC: *In "Allen Ginsberg Death Notes" you observe, "Dour white Protestant America needed a touch of music and ecstasy, and Allen helped bring that." You were privileged to work with Allen for many years at Naropa. What was it like to be in his presence over an extended period of time? Did you sense any deep dichotomies between the public and the private man? Was he comfortable in solitude or did he generally prefer to be among the company of others?*

AS: I knew Allen from about 1990 until his death. Hundreds of people knew him much better than I did. He put up with me in a way that was sometimes grumbling, sometimes sweet-natured. But I did get to see him in ways that he's not generally portrayed—sitting through long tasking administrative meetings, designing curricula for a writing program, or brainstorming ways to raise funds for Naropa. He had a good head for that kind of thing. He took it seriously. Our relationship was mostly built on practical jobs. We did teach or perform together at a number of poetry programs over the years. I don't think he cared too much for my poetry.

I also knew him in the waning years of his life. He had a lot of ailments and had to treat his aging body with enormous care. Special diets, lots of macrobiotic food, probably heaps of medication, insulin, chairs that didn't hurt his creaky back. I don't think his thirst for public life, or simply the presence of other people, ever dropped off though. A lot of folk loved him deeply, and he cared for so many! Underneath I always sensed something sadly far-off or alone. Bluesy.

My essay on him was not about any special intimacy. I just thought my Sanskrit studies, and conversations with him about that kind of thing, haiku and Buddhist practice, had generated a few curious anecdotes that people who weren't there might enjoy.

TC: *Re. Naropa and Kerouac School. One essay mentions Harry Smith with the Grateful Dead in the same breath, a lovely little parable. A very* *tender photograph of Harry appears in Allen Ginsberg's photography edition,* Snapshot Poetics. *How are these three linked?*

AS: Harry was an old friend of Allen's. Allen brought him to Naropa—the story is he found Harry nearly dead in the Chelsea Hotel, cleaned him up—and Harry Smith lived his final years in a tiny clapboard building on our Arapahoe Street campus. He was there when I arrived, a kind of obscure elderly Dada coyote. He always had a gentle cult of students who were terribly loyal, and he was fun to seek out and talk to. He was like an oracle, I mean he didn't talk the way anyone else did. You'd say something and he'd come up with a kind of impenetrable aphorism. You'd say something else and he'd come out with another weird speech object. Conversation with him was like making a mosaic out of found objects.

Harry had put together the important *Anthology of American Folk Music* in the '50s, from which the big generation of rock-and-roll people learned traditional American music. Blues, Appalachian fiddle, work songs, ballads, hollers, all that great vernacular shit. So someone got the Rex Foundation—the Grateful Dead's benevolent society—to put up some money to keep Harry alive. Rent, food, a little bit, you know, some grass, a lot of books.

TC: *Writing schools are a new growth area for academia. There's controversy about this, but the proof does seem to be there in the surprisingly talented graduates who are emerging. Canadian literature, at least, is the richer for them. If it doesn't sound naive, how do you view the role of Naropa's celebrated Kerouac School these days? Has there been any change in operative mood since Allen's passing?*

AS: It changes all the time! Because poetry changes. Some people were nervous when Allen died. "Uh-oh, that's it, how will the school continue? Allen is dead." But you know, it ain't a school, a university—a serious place of study and work—if it's dependent on the personality of one figure. That would be a cult. If it's a real place, with energy and vision, and accomplished faculty, and brilliant courageous students, it ought to get along simply because poetry is a craft that requires solid training. You can train alone, or you can train with other people. If you want to train with other people, a school is a noble place to do it.

The writing office keeps a list of accomplishments by students—mostly books, but also grants, gigs, service, reputations, an impressive list. I can't tell you how edifying it is to read the Chinese translations of Mike O'Connor, or Shin Yu Pai's excellent new book of poems, or the nonstop magazines and journals and chapbooks begged or borrowed or stolen into print by students. The letter-press print shop, which we named for Harry Smith—man, you can't keep up with the beautiful items it produces: broadsides, chapbooks, postcards, book-art objects, odd little collaborative accordion poetry things.

TC: *As someone on the ground at the Jack Kerouac School you've witnessed encounters with a phenomenal plurality of poetic and creative personalities, from the Beats, the New York and San Francisco schools, and major jazz and visual artists, through to language poets and religious masters. The lot. Are there some pinnacle moments or encounters with particular individuals from this rich, unfolding tapestry you can share?*

AS: My philosophy—that's not the right word; my instinct, that's better—in my gut I regard poetry as a communal effort. Language is communal. It is made by hundreds, thousands, millions. Some are known people who got famous, many are quiet, hardly heard of, but everyone indispensable. There is a huge psycho-conspiracy in this country, wrapped up in scandalous ways of making money, which pretends that the world is populated by a few geniuses, and the rest of the population is there to be inspired, exhilarated, thrilled, or instructed by these heroes. Namely, to pay for tickets to events, buy big selling books, consume CDs and celebrity magazines, whatever. I find this attitude ugly, stupid, reactionary, and infuriating. The only revolution will involve everyone when it arrives, not just the media stars. Marx saw this. Plants and animals included! (I don't think Marx saw that.) But the children do.

Hundreds of memorable people have come through Naropa, the roll going far deeper than the big names. Much of it has been audio or video taped, and there's a large archives project in place now, with help from the NEA and elsewhere, to get this material secured, digitalized, made available. Remove a single visitor from the archive and the archive ecology is violated.

Okay, having given my rant, I can quiet down and mention a few notable moments. Hearing Carl Rakosi in his nineties engage in deep gossip about the Objectivists one hot afternoon was a high point. He told how he made the long trip out to Black Hawk Island, Wisconsin, to visit Lorine Niedecker. He'd never met her in person.

She said, "Louis Zukovsky is the greatest living poet, isn't he?" Carl said no, I don't see it that way, and went out and spent the afternoon painting the shed with Lorine's husband Al, or something like that.

Meeting Miriam Patchen and watching her deflect any suggestion that she might have been partly responsible for her husband's poetry, was a high point. I found her fearless, acid-tongued, bitingly humorous. We met a few times, wrote to each other, and had a funny relationship. She'd see me and start right in—"You can't be a poet if you're in a classroom! How can you waste yourself like that?" She'd write me, "Schelling, are you still in that classroom? You'll kill any poetry in you." That kind of thing. It kept me on my toes. I really loved her. Then her house in Palo Alto got wiped out in a flood and she died shortly after.

Any one of Lorenzo Thomas's lectures on the blues, on racial identity, on whatever. To hear him chuckle with rich good-natured humor. Joanne Kyger never stops surprising me with her wild syntax and dry eco-humor, and I hope Harryette Mullen will keep her thing going for decades. One precious event I don't think got onto tape was about 1989: Gary Snyder and Peter Warshall debating the Endangered Species Act, with Gary taking the part of the ranchers and loggers. Most ecology activists were pretty myopic in those years. Like, "Bring in the ranchers and see what they want? Fuck that." So Gary took the rancher-logger side. I bet he converted a few people that day. He was not just rooting into his upbringing in the Pacific Northwest, but seeing the seed of the future. Because the ranchers, the loggers, the salmon fishers, have been here a long time.

I remember that debate, because ten years later I had to organize a crew to shut down plans to construct a telecommunication tower near Trout Creek Pass in central Colorado. An international conglomerate, which puts up cell phone towers in sixty countries, was going to wreck some good high-altitude forest territory with a poorly thought out construction that violated zoning ordinances. They tried to play up the scary side of no cell phones: what happens if your grandchild has an accident and there is no cell phone service. Guess who we had on our side—this was 2001—in front of the Board of Adjusters in Fairplay? A rancher, a retired military officer, an accountant, a fieldworker for the U.S. Geological Survey. The rancher hated those towers, they were going up on all the ridges around Park County. He pulled out studies and testified that half the towers were there not to deliver signals, but to block service from rival companies!

Like Whitman said, "The United States are themselves the greatest poem."

TC: *And a last question. The literary sensibility is perennial, but from the mixing of Eastern and Western literary/creative/esthetic traditions, do you intuit any specific school or wave evolving out of this cross-pollinating intelligence? Something that might in part be heir to the Beats, as they acknowledged others before them—Imagists, Symbolists, Pound, Lawrence, Baudelaire—a kind of "new world dharma" perhaps?*

AS: New world dharma! I love that. It would be the hip side of globalism, wouldn't it? I just don't want to lose the local though. I mean the details. I hope we can reverse the trend of animal and plant species extinction; also language and poetry tradition extinction. So I think—if we're lucky—we'll head into a poetry that is conversant in many, many languages. And that people will wake up and start translating like crazy.

When I went to Mexico City in 1994 I visited with a number of poets including Elsa Cross and David Huerta. Hearing them talk I realized, *they know all the USA poets!* Up here in El Norte we read or know of hardly anyone south of the Alamo. Octavio Paz. Who else? That's why I designed a translation concentration for the Kerouac School. I'd have to say, if you're going to be a poet of the future, learn another language. Translate. Ezra Pound said in *The Cantos*, "It can't all be in one language." What I'm talking about is committed, long-term conversation between traditions. Who can discuss these things in Basque? Hopi? Gaelic?

I'd like to see dharma in there, too, but not as a standardized religion or set of poetry protocols. Religion makes me anxious, ever since 1993 when I went to India and the adherents of three religions were slaughtering each other. So just to suggest a few values: human intelligence, cross-species compassion, some wise elderly women who remember what it all means, wine, song, wilderness, confident children. Maybe a Buddhist economics of simplicity or restraint, like E.F. Schumacher imagined several decades ago, but such a thing looks like it's way off in the future.

Meanwhile, give poetry room to play, lots of leeway to make up the future. There are so many different ways to make a poem, so many reasons, and the more range the better. But young poets will have to give up the idea that it's a good career move. We should shut down the big publishing house dinosaurs and celebrate that a thousand small presses have bloomed. Another thing Pound said: "Poets are the antennae of the race."

The race as always is between the tortoise and the hare.

Boulder – Vancouver

Note

Since Andrew Schelling and I spoke, several substantial anthologies of Mexican poetry have come into print. Meanwhile, Rodrigo Toscana, and Kristin Dykstra's journal *Mandorla*, a kind of yearly anthology, does a fine job of bridging English-Spanish or North-South borders, and brings in Cuban poets, too.

Chapter 15

Notes from the Gone World

Lawrence Ferlinghetti on Street Smarts and the Poetry Revolution

There's a reason why poetry is important to young people. . . . It's still the only rebellion around.

L awrence Ferlinghetti has been one of America's preeminent post-WWII literary and countercultural figures. He served in the navy during the war and in 1947 moved to Paris where he earned a doctorate from the Sorbonne. In 1953 he settled in San Francisco where he co-founded first a magazine, then City Lights Books, and soon branched into publishing poetry and international literature. His own first books Pictures from the Gone World and A Coney Island of the Mind were both immensely successful. City Lights Books' fourth Pocket Poets title Howl became a sensation following its obscenity trial and helped catapult both its author Allen Ginsberg and Ferlinghetti /City Lights to national attention. An outspoken liberal political activist, he has also written works of political satire, plays, film scripts, and fiction. While initially wary of some Beat-era writers' early fascination with Asia, his poem "A Buddha In The Woodpile" that laments the civil crisis disaster at Waco, Texas exhibits Ferlinghetti's deep-seated compassion and pacifism that rests at the heart of his work. While coordinating the Calgary Olympic Winter Games literary festival in 1988, I was able to invite him as a literary representative from the United States and his polished reading was a triumph. During an *assignment in San Francisco in 1996 I spoke with him regarding his civic street-renaming project discussed here. At the time of writing, aged ninety-five, he remains creative, defiant, and a beloved elder of his city's old Italian North Beach district.* His opus Poetry as Insurgent Art *he says, "is still a work-in-progress."*

It may have brought the world Bondage-A-Go-Go, but, happily, the great city of San Francisco is abloom again with a rush of creative vitality currently unrivalled anywhere save New York. Still a Victorian architectural jewel, the City by the Bay has endured earthquake, the scourge of AIDS, aftershocks from the Rodney King riots, and growing U.S. urban malaise to continue thriving as a city of neighborhoods par excellence.

The once-mangy South of Market Area (SOMA) with its new Museum of Modern Art draws all the raves, but it's North Beach, the town's eternal Latin Quarter that fits as comfortably as an old raincoat—and no visit here is complete without a necessary pilgrimage to City Lights Booksellers, the shrine to literature that Lawrence Ferlinghetti built.

City Lights isn't hard to find. At the corner of Columbus Avenue and Jack Kerouac Street, it's across the way from William Saroyan Place. Alternately, walk up from Mark Twain Plaza on the east side of the unmistakable Transamerica pyramid. Chinatown browsers nearby can hang a right at Kenneth Rexroth Place. Jack London Street or Isadora Duncan Lane are a little off the mark, but Dashiell Hammett Street is a good spot to find your bearings and work your way back through Chinatown and home free. It isn't every town that bears this sort of homage to its native authors and artists—few towns are lucky enough to have had so many, even fewer a Lawrence Ferlinghetti. These literary street names and more were his brainchild. Seven years ago it was his energy that pulled off the street renaming project, which brought twelve such streets into being. This year, 1996, Ferlinghetti himself will be honored with a street bearing his own name.

For forty years Lawrence Ferlinghetti has distinguished himself in this most beautiful of American cities. Poet, publisher, translator, and editor he has remained consistent in an ethical, outspoken activism that began in 1956 when he put money, reputation, and civic liberty on the line to publish Allen Ginsberg's *Howl*. The rest is history. The ensuing legal battle became a test case in freedom of speech, ultimately helping topple America's censorship laws.

Synonymous with the Beat generation—a cultural hybrid that took root when Ginsberg's New York gang of Jack Kerouac, William Burroughs, and Gregory Corso encountered a San Francisco literary and arts community in renaissance—Ferlinghetti continues to look upon the Beat movement in the present tense.

Regarding the current worldwide "poetry boom," the term may be a misnomer, he says, adding that it may be more appropriate to regard it as the latest affirmation of the poetry renaissance that grew out of the San Francisco Bay Area's own unique poetic and cultural lineage.

"Poetry boom?" he clarifies. "I didn't know there'd been an explosion. Poetry is something that's steady here; always has been.

"There's a lot of talk, but I don't think what's going on now is a revival," he adds. "We sell an astounding amount of poetry at City Lights every month. We've always done well with it, and we even have a separate poetry room in our store for it because we need one.

"You know, if you think of what's happening now, with all the reading series, book and poetry events, you need a newspaper to look after it all. There's an *enormous* amount of activity out there, especially in San Francisco. There's also a publication here, a monthly called *Poetry Flash* that you can pick up free; it details what's taking place in San Francisco and beyond. The scene has certainly expanded and grown but it seems to have been a steady growth because all that began here in San Francisco, in North Beach, in the 1950s."

Ferlinghetti remains active as both poet and painter. A year ago his longtime New York publisher New Directions released *These Are My Rivers*, a selected edition that reminds one how familiar so much of Ferlinghetti's work has become. Characterized by clear speech, sharp painterly images, and equal admixtures of wry humor and breathy sensuality, his work—more than any other poet of his generation—was taken up by teachers eager to transmit its contemporaneity to students. As retired teacher and author Sam Roddan puts it, "Ferlinghetti came along and he wasn't bombastic; his poems were simple; not monosyllabic, but simple—almost crystal clear. They could be political, yet there was something universal and illuminative about his work."

In 1955, Ferlinghetti published *Pictures of the Gone World* with his fledgling City Lights Press. The first of what would become the "Pocket Poets" series, the collection has seen twenty-two printings and has never been out of print. To celebrate City Lights' fortieth anniversary of publishing, Ferlinghetti has just released a new expanded edition of the work with eighteen new poems. In true Pocket Poets tradition, at $6.95 it is also affordable.

Additionally, a major show of his paintings is currently on exhibit at the University of Maryland in Baltimore.

"You know, the Beat writers—we're all still very active," Ferlinghetti relates. "The Beat movement isn't something out of the past: it's now. Burroughs, Corso, Ginsberg, me—we're all still publishing: there's a stack of Gary Snyder's new book right near our front counter."

About the enduring attraction of the Beats to younger North American's readers, Ferlinghetti is candid. "There's a reason why poetry is important to young people," he says: "It's still the only rebellion around." And that brings up Ferlinghetti's naming of names— street names, that is.

"It was my idea, and City Lights and I did it," he says flatly without self-congratulation, though it is known the project is especially dear to him. "We had a small group and we kept quiet about what we were doing—no publicity. We wanted to honor the writers and artists who contributed to this city, and we knew that to accomplish a street-naming, we'd have to work quietly with few people in on it. We'd also have to pick quiet streets.

"We got mostly disreputable alleys, streets where there wouldn't be too many people to oppose the name change. [They missed on three streets where too many people protested.] Then we got the San Francisco Arts Commission to agree to our proposal, and got a letter of support from the Tourist Board. We were able to take these letters to the City's Board of Supervisors, who had the final authority. When it was all finally approved, there was quite a celebration down here."

For anyone who might be interested in the idea Ferlinghetti suggests that the best advice he can offer is, "Don't go after publicity. The more people who become involved—no matter how good the idea is—the more they'll find reason to scratch their heads and wonder. Just pick your objective and work toward it quietly."

Happy fortieth anniversary, City Lights. . . .

San Francisco – Vancouver

Chapter 16

Beloved Renegade

With Allen Ginsberg at Cortes Island

A llen Ginsberg was one of the genuine larger than life characters in
American culture from the 1950s onward. I began reading him
seriously as a student in the early 1970s. Ginsberg's voice rang true to
me and there was plenty of experience in it that felt familiar—he
incorporated Hindu and Buddhist mantras, references, and prayers in
his work and having knocked about India myself, I appreciated this.
While working in a graveyard near Vancouver in 1978, I learned of a
reading he would give and was able to meet him briefly afterword. The
advice he offered, which follows, floored me. Seven years later,
I attended a workshop-retreat he was leading at Hollyhock Farm on
Cortes Island. Ginsberg's generosity and teaching style has been a profound influence ever since. He loved William Blake and his root
teacher/dharma teacher was Chögyam Trungpa Rinpoche. At our last
meeting in Santa Monica in 1994 three years before he died, he mentioned his association with Gelek Rinpoche of the Jewel Heart sangha
who he became associated with in the late 1980s, and who was with
him at Allen's final breaths. Ed Sanders relates a story about Allen late
in his illness at the emergency ward in Beth Israel Hospital in New York.
There's Allen on the way in, and a ward doctor recognizes Ginsberg
and gives him a poem. Allen's maybe dying but the doctor asks if
Ginsberg can read it and offer any suggestions. Allen did this on the
spot. He said he thought that he was able to improve a few lines; that
he was pleased to do so for a devotee of Ascelpius. That was the bodhisattva dimension of Allen Ginsberg.

Howl, Kerouac and the Beat gang, anti–Vietnam War leader, free speech, Chicago Seven, No Nukes!, flower power, Merry Pranksters, gay lib, embracing the Buddha dharma . . .

I was meditating on these things one morning at the low-budget end of Vancouver's airport. It was May 1985, and I'd just returned from Asia. Rex Weyler had called: Allen Ginsberg was flying in to lead a retreat at Hollyhock Farm on remote Cortes Island off the coast of British Columbia. Was I interested in a fellowship? I could fly in with Allen himself. As I stood there, wondering how I'd approach my poetic hero, a familiar character appeared out of the airport crowd that didn't recognize him: Allen Ginsberg, shuffling his way down the gantry like a dancing bear.

I loved Allen Ginsberg. I'd read and studied his work for years, and had met him once before in Vancouver at a bash in the '70s. Ginsberg had read *Plutonian Ode* that night and led us on an intergalactic excursion. He worked with a rocking guitarist and they got down like crazy on Blake's *Tyger Tyger!*, on olde English verses like "Sumer Is A-Cumen In," and his own dharma poetry. It was marvelous—loose about the edges, magnetized at the center, and riveting with music-poetry.

Ginsberg blew the crowd away. When the reading ended, he hopped down off the stage onto the auditorium floor and began mixing with people. He seemed completely approachable, yet I had sat there. I desperately wanted to ask him a question—not just any question, a *good* question. Meanwhile, a gaggle of local literati surrounded him and kept him busy for a long time.

I sat alone, trying to think of something profound to say while the heavyweights fenced him in. Then, with the hall pretty much emptied, I noticed Ginsberg work his way to the exit where a last hanger-on or two waited. I caught up with him a few steps from the door. The wisdom pregnant on my lips burst forth. "Excuse me," I asked. "Will you sign my program?"

He looked at me intently, then obliged in a kindly way. The question that burned inside me blurted loose: "You're probably asked this all the time," I said. "But have you any advice for a young writer with ambition?"

I must have looked forlorn, or obsessed.

"So you're a young writer, are you?" he asked professorially.

I nodded.

"And you've got ambition, have you?"

"Yes."

"Well, my advice is to forget it. Forget about ambition," he said flatly. "Just write for yourself and for your friends and anyone who'll listen. Forget about ambition. It's better to be a loser."

I stood dumbstruck. *It's better to be a loser?* With that, my hero—the world's best-known poet, Allen Ginsberg—walked out the door. I meditated for years on what it might mean.

I still do.

We stood chatting, boarding last. He looked weary behind those familiar steel-rimmed glasses of his that had always personified an air of alert wonder. His beard was a little shorter than in the old days, still thick but shot through with gray. He wore an old black leather jacket and khaki trousers. His banged-up harmonium was plastered with concert-tour stickers: Bob Dylan: All Access Backstage, the Clash, Rolling Thunder Revue. I motioned toward the aircraft door.

There were only fifteen or so others on the small coastal prop-engine. Allen took a window seat up front and asked if I'd like to sit with him. As the plane taxied and left the ground I peeked to see if he had any special rituals for takeoff—prayers, mudras. If so, they were invisible to me. We looked out the window quietly as the plane climbed higher. I pointed out the Cascade Range, the Fraser River and the delta lands, downtown Vancouver, the Indian reserves, precious Wreck Beach.

"You really know your city," he said. "That's good. Not common. Do you know much about Cortes?"

Allen's reading had been jubilant. The event was held at a cavernous high school auditorium on the older, affluent side of the city. People lined up excitedly for tickets, laughing, greeting old friends and smoking dope. One character clowning in line grinned and said, "Makes me feel like dropping acid again."

Inside the hall, heavily amplified rockers jammed for the growing crowd. Booksellers flogged volumes of Ginsberg, Beat Gang poets, and leftist studies. Folkies and hippies milled and swilled, searching out faces in the crowd. A table was piled high with Ginsberg's acclaimed *Collected Poems: 1947–1980*, and the handsome new editions in red were selling well at $40 apiece.

The art crowd had dressed in its best funky chic for the gig. A tide of longtime West Coast faces passed by, forever cool. Vancouver's glitterati of academics, critics, and self-conscious, fragile sylphs hob-nobbed among college kids and unreconstructed hipsters. Here and there, older poetry lovers almost curiously out of place in their tweeds and gabardine threaded through the mob. Thorazine-dazed casual-ties shuffled among skinhead tribals. It was more than just another reading; it was a gathering of the clan, a communion ritual: *Allen Ginsberg's back in town.*

Ginsberg read and chanted, accompanying himself on harmo-nium, while a hometown guitarist thumped along in time. The eve-ning flowed and Allen offered stories and background to many of his poems—of old loves, frequent travels; of meetings with well-known Beat Gang personalities: Jack Kerouac, Gregory Corso, William S. Burroughs. Interwoven, too, were unvarnished accounts of painful confessions, of sexual liaisons in lonely hotel rooms. There were people in the audience who got up and walked out, and few who remained could not have helped wondering what it meant to be in a room with a man who had chosen this path as vocation.

Then it was penitence and taking refuge in the compassionate heart of the Buddha before another shift of gears and years brought homage intoned reverently to Blake. We heard song as poem and poem as calypso with "Do The Meditation Rock": "If you want to learn / how to meditate / I'll tell you now / 'cause it's never too late. . . ." The evening went on. Allen hollered through "I Fought the Dharma and the Dharma Won." Then it was "Father Death Blues": "Hey Father Death, I'm fly-ing home / Hey poor man, you're all a-lone / . . . Hey old daddy, I do thank you / For inspiring me, to sing these blues." And we were crying.

As the early buzz evolved further and deeper through poem after poem, the evening became a kind of darshan in the way that an Indian audience loves basking in its guru's mana, or spirit. It was my wife's first experience hearing Ginsberg and she was moved, even strangely charmed as I hoped she'd be. It's like holiness, she said, except for the one character sitting too nearby who smelled terrible. Somehow that fit, too.

Warren Tallman, Vancouver's Beat-professor and an old pal of Ginsberg, was our boozy host for the evening. We were there, he reminded us, for a night of poetics, benevolent Buddhism, and witness to the Wages of Noble Poets; which, he duly noted, at $40 for Ginsberg's *Collected Poems* covering thirty-three years, worked out to about $1.22 per annum.

Ginsberg had already worked the dharma trail nearly a dozen years by the time I'd been introduced to his *Howl* by an adventuresome English instructor in the '60s. Now I was sitting with Ginsberg on a light aircraft, heading for an island on the edge of the world.

We landed at Campbell River. I scuffled up my bag and saw Allen welcomed by Catherine Ingram, dharma journalist and Hollyhock resident. Already directing traffic and organizing people around himself Allen made introductions, noting that Catherine had a taxi waiting outside. We could share

We caught the government ferry to Quadra Island where the local lighthouse-keeper obliged us with a lift cross-island to a second ferry terminal. We'd be island-hopping, moving onward to Cortes, a second, smaller island within the Inside Passage that leads north to Alaska. Cortes lies out of sight of the Big Island and veers roughly northeast back toward the wild, snowbound peaks of the BC mainland.

The three of us stood leaning against the railings on deck as gulls trailed the ferry's wake looking for handouts. In the stiff salt breeze I noticed Allen's right eyelid was lazy, a little weepy. Somewhere I read he'd developed Bell's palsy.

The ferry chugged on. Allen stood looking at the chain of islands beyond, then back across to the big island's Beaufort peaks. He excused himself with that and went inside to rest. Catherine followed his progress with a glance and smiled. "How was your journey up?" she asked. "You two seem to be getting along fine."

I nodded agreement. "He's amazingly generous with himself," I said. "He really listens to what you have to say. It's as if even small talk is precious to him."

Catherine bundled up against the wind. "I think it is," she grinned.

Hollyhock Farm sits above a fine, wild stretch of shoreline surrounded by woods. A former resort, it has undergone numerous transformations since Richard Weaver, a visionary from Alberta, established it as Cold Mountain Institute in the consciousness-raising days of the late '60s.

The principal structure is a two-storey lodge that serves as great hall and general learning salon. Upstairs there are guest rooms and a spacious seminar area. The lodge hall offers sweeping water views, a heavy fieldstone fireplace set off to one side, and a piano. There is a large kitchen, and outside a covered deck leads to a coopered cedar hot tub, wood-fired and big enough in the open air for half a dozen soakers.

Behind the lodge is a lush kitchen garden under heavy organic cultivation that supplies much of inventive fare the farm's table is noted for. Guesthouses are located in the woods; there is an old-timey beach cottage; and a wander up the forest trail leads to Kiacum, a serene meditation and practice hall.

Following dinner, the half dozen or so participants drifted upstairs for Allen's initial discourse on "Inspired Poetics." With the unfamiliarity of a first session together and people still weary from travel, Allen suggested confining discussion to matters of general poetics and to sounding out the ground we'd be covering in the next five days. He began by remarking on the origins of his own poetics, tracing a line from William Blake through Walt Whitman, Emily Dickinson, William Carlos Williams to Kerouac, Snyder, Creeley, and himself. His observations ranged free-form, encompassing considerations of breath, poetic form, structure and content, correlations between meditation and poetry, Buddhist sitting meditation as a review of consciousness, haiku technique, and something he called "esthetic mindfulness."

I wondered what esthetic mindfulness might mean, but didn't wish to seem ignorant. Doggedly I made a note, determined to catch up on it later, and observed how Ginsberg peppered his discourse with anecdote and lore concerning particular writers, techniques, and styles. Glancing occasionally from my notebook, I saw the others absorbed in his effortless, scholarly dialogue.

Speaking, Ginsberg sourced an encyclopedic torrent of literary reference. Time and time again he referred to the work of Kerouac, Burroughs, Gertrude Stein. In particular, he offered a matched pair of admonitions. Essential writerly advice no matter what the form of one's writing, these were: Kerouac's "*Cut out unnecessary syntactical fat!*," and Burroughs' "*Condensation is the key to solid prose; pack it up tight like boxcars!*"

Allen continued to sit cross-legged on the floor, supported by a firm meditation cushion. He spoke carefully, attentively, with only nominal gestures of his hands, containing his energy. He was still wearing his leather coat and its darkness lent him further physical authority. He declared that the lineage he evolves from as poet begins with Homer or some aboriginal cousin, and it dawned on me through my fatigue that this man spoke with three thousand years of poetic history behind him; that our enterprise at Cortes was not simply to be about Allen Ginsberg, or English and North American literature but about *poetry* itself, as history and lineage, as an identifying signature of our human engagement with civilization.

Forcing myself to pay closer attention, I listened as Allen explained his view of how modern poetry in English comes sharply into focus with the concise imagistic clarity of William Carlos Williams. Williams' alchemical preoccupation with measuring a line of verse starts it all, Ginsberg pronounced:

"From there—Williams, Olson, Creeley—a lot of it is just intuition and flying by the seat of the pants stuff."

At this, we advanced upon consideration again of "esthetic mindfulness," with Ginsberg describing it as, "Writing our own mind. Writing down what we see when we see it, what we feel when we feel it."

I had a date with this term, and apparently was not alone in my unfamiliarity with it. Rex Weyler intervened, inquiring, "Okay, Allen; but is esthetic mindfulness a purely contemporary idea? What was it that Keats and the Romantics, say, were trying to accomplish—what makes their work especially esthetically mindful?"

Without blinking, Ginsberg steamed forward again: "Well, they worked in comparative obscurity for one thing," he said. "And Wordsworth sets it out in the *Preface to Lyrical Ballads* what he was attempting to do. How does it go—'Fitting to metrical arrangement the real language of men in a state of vivid sensation'?"

Leaping further, like a musician extending his reach up the keyboard while holding to his thread of melody, Ginsberg explained how the poet's work is to use real language to present incidents and various phenomena from common life in a spontaneous way; in a way that reflects his or her emotions at the time in which the poet actually becomes aware of them. So we can see from our reading how figures like Keats indeed bring mindful attention even to the crafting of classical works such as *Ode to a Grecian Urn.* Here I am, I thought, studying Wordsworth and Keats with Allen Ginsberg. Who'd have thought?

Allen ploughed on, explaining the importance of knowing what it is that we do as poets.

"Recollecting in tranquility?"

"Well, Wordsworth makes his position clear, doesn't he?" rejoined Allen. "'Poetry is the spontaneous overflow of powerful feelings that takes origin from emotion recollected in tranquility.'"

This led organically to the subject of meditation, and to certain fundamental correlations between meditation and poetry. Buddhist sitting meditation and Wordsworth's idea of "recollecting emotion in tranquility"? *Bing!* Suddenly the light went on: the link was obvious. Allen smiled knowingly at what had just been discovered. Then he began to let this critical idea grow in front of us.

"By its very nature, human consciousness is discontinuous," Allen said, illustrating this with the example of sitting meditation. "Inevitably, when we sit and empty our mind for example, randomly and unbidden the mind begins throwing up disconnected flows of illogical images on our inner screen. This illogical flow of images—the working process of mind—is revealed in modern poetry by Eliot's *The Wasteland.*

"Close your eyes and be still," he continued. "What happens? The mind's eye, stillness, is punctuated by the flotsam and jetsam of the unconscious. . . . *The Wasteland* with its fragmented universe accurately reflects what enlightened masters have been telling us over and over again through the ages," he went on. "That there is no final perfection, no idealistic, nirvana-like still point. *Satori*—enlightenment— is just ordinary mind. Real enlightenment comes in mastering the disorder of daily existence."

With that, the evening drew to a close. There was little else to do but sit in admiration. People began straightening up, tidying cushions, gathering notebooks, stray glasses and cups. Readying to leave for his room down by the beach, Allen exchanged a few last words with one or another of the group. I gathered up my things, thinking about the haiku exercises and compositions we were scheduled to work on next day.

As Allen called it a night, I stood on the porch watching as the journeyman poet picked his way carefully down the trail to his cabin.

Cortes, 6:35 am.

Outside, pine boughs bathed in amber cathedral light.
Slipping downstairs quietly, I nod to the cook already at her work. Outside, the dewdrop world is one great lungful of air. I take my stance near a brace of trees in a clearing beyond the lodge. The trail into the woods slopes nearby.

A quarter hour later, Allen arrives from his beach house walking up the rise from below. Moving slowly I see his grizzled hair and glasses glint in sunlight as he circles up the path. A respectful distance away he takes up a spot. We nod briefly, without speaking. He looks somnambulant.

Allen faces the ocean and begins his tai chi straightforwardly, occasionally forgetting a step or two, but accounting himself as a good determined learner. He wears black cloth Chinese shoes in the still damp grass, but this seems no hindrance. Ten minutes later, he leaves as respectfully as he arrived.

Working with my sword I catch an eye or two glancing out from the lodge. Putting them aside, I play through to completion. The heron dance, tai chi.

The breakfast table at Hollyhock is pure Breughal: baskets of hot muffins and breads, fruits, honey, and yogurt, earthen jars of steaming porridge, jugs of juice, pots of coffee. We load our trays, greet one another, remarking on the day, the landscape, the night past. Already some are tucked in and yakking by the window. Allen is roaming the kitchen as I arrive and says hello. I make for the porridge, ladling it into a bowl.

"Just what I ordered!" he exclaims, rubbing his hands with delight. "I especially asked the cook last night if it was on!"

I thought of the seedy all-night Times Square cafeterias memorialized by Kerouac, Holmes, Burroughs, and Huncke: Allen Ginsberg loves porridge!

"I've been wanting this since I left London," Ginsberg yawns.

At nine o'clock we move upstairs fetching second and third cups of coffee. The library is still shady and cool; shafts of light filter through the windows. Allen has suggested we bring pillows and begin each day with a period of sitting meditation.

"For those who may find it new, I suggest sitting forward on your cushion, crossing your legs and raising the spine as vertically as possible," he instructs, delivering instructions patiently: legs folded, eyes straight ahead, looking downward at a spot about nine feet in front. Hands resting on the thighs. Back straight. Seat raised up for comfort. Breathing easily into the abdominal cavity. Head supporting heaven.

He stands and checks our postures individually. I feel him tilt my head slightly, adjust my mid-spine, lightly tuck my backside in; already my spine has straightened dramatically.

Ginsberg sits once more, quietly still, then continues: "It is now 9:08. I propose sitting until 9:30, followed by ten minutes of walking meditation, then another fifteen minutes sitting. That should bring us to ten o'clock.

"Begin."

Staring ahead: no other focus than the sitting. Water beyond the windows. Allen advises that, as we sit, it's natural for distracting thoughts to arise in mind. No sweat. In the Tibetan tradition, says Trungpa Rinpoche, we acknowledge such thoughts in a friendly manner and dismiss them, returning our focus to the in-breath, the relaxing stroke.

Twenty minutes pass effortlessly. It feels perfect, as if I could sit comfortably all day. Then *kin-hin*, walking meditation, clockwise in a circle, eyes down, breathing easily, hands folded, the right resting comfortably in the palm of the left. Giving the legs a rest.

We finish sitting. It feels great, exhilarating. Rex mentions that he hasn't sat in a while; he too thinks it might feel great to sit the whole day. Catherine Ingram looks on. "Nothing *but* sitting all day in Asia," she cautions, smiling.

Down to the business of poetry. Ginsberg addresses the notion of "present consciousness in composition," the root of his dharma poetics.

"The correlation between meditation and poetic practice," he says, is simply in the developing of awareness of our own mind; and in sharpening up awareness of what is outside our mind. So is there a mode or meditation common to poetic practice and meditation? Yes, there is—by noticing what we notice, and by sharpening up awareness of our own perception.

"In poetry, the key is waking up."

North America's best known poet sits before us enunciating with conviction his views on poetic form, technique, and aesthetics. The official party line.

"In meditation, the lack of distraction—our stillness, our rootedness—gives us greater awareness of the phenomenal world: the patter of rain, birds in flight, cocks crowing," Ginsberg notes. It sounds like haiku—pouring out of him unconsciously.

"The stuff of poetic imagery," someone interjects.

"Right," Allen agrees. "What do you remember especially well from your sitting this morning? Was it a seagull flying above the water? A log drifting past outside?"

My mind locked onto his thought like a laser beam: so here's how it works, at last.

"By sitting, by stilling the rush of images our mind throws up on the screen, we can hone in on specific things that come to our attention," Ginsberg continues. "We can also deal with unnecessary distractions that arise."

I'm thinking it's Wordsworth recollecting in tranquility; but more than that: it's taking a pair of sharp scissors and cutting away everything that doesn't matter—*Snip Snip Snip!*

Allen carries on again: "In sitting, we also can appreciate the review of consciousness that's happening all the time in our mind. As poets, we can simply write our mind. It's the same for meditation and poetry.

"Meditating, we keep up an awareness of the distractions," he continues. "As they arise, we embrace them in a friendly fashion. It's the same when we write—keep your notebook and pen, your 'axe' *ready*. Have a good one for dignified notes and a cheapo extra for loosening-up exercises. That's where you get wild and be raunchy, jot down random flashes of mind in a kind of spontaneous, imagistic journalism."

For novices, first-timers, those new to the craft, the time-proven method of learning how to write, Ginsberg says—whether poetry, prose, you name it—*is to read a lot.*

Allen invited me to meet him on the beach in the afternoon for a one-on-one tutorial examining the poetry manuscript I'd brought. It was precisely the session I yearned for. Some of the other participants had apparently spent similar private time with Ginsberg, but, curiously, none of them were much inclined to discuss what had taken place during their meetings.

I had lugged my manuscript across the peaks and troughs of East Asia for the past four months, constantly fine-tuning the work in hope of seeing it through to completion as a book: my first book after five years of journalism. A freelance professional, I felt reasonably secure with my material. There were difficulties, I knew—problems of resolution with certain key poems, but I felt that advice and encouragement from Ginsberg would quickly get the material over the top.

Accordingly, I made my way to the beach searching for a log to rest my back against. Checking through my work one final time I noted my apprehension at the intended meeting.

Allen arrived on schedule clad in his old leather car coat. He camped on a drift log and with a minimum of chat asked to see my collection. I handed him the work and he began to read. There were two dozen poems. As Allen read he made notations in pencil. Leaving him to the work, I gazed at the sea, waiting.

For ten minutes he leafed through the manuscript, silently underlining phrases, jotting question marks beside lines and words, noting space breaks.

Time passed. Whatever dreams I harbored of being discovered as Allen Ginsberg's new protégé looked to have gone awry. Rather, more dauntingly, this poet whom I admired seemed more and more a stern, foreboding teacher, or so I felt as he read and marked my work on and on. I felt amateurish. A sham.

"What do you mean here, this sentence?" he pointed, breaking silence, glancing at me carefully. "I don't know what you're trying to say." His tone was kindly, helpful.

I looked at the page. It was my weightiest effort—a poem I'd struggled with for years. Begun shortly after I'd left university, it aspired toward Eliot-like narrative and lurched dangerously near Corinthian self-importance. Ginsberg had ferreted out my weakest spot.

Built on a prose line, the poem went *"Time past/is past./The continuum, irretrievable;/the garden paradise/forever gone/yet not irredeemable . . .* leading to something about Time, lost Eden and the possibility of redemption. I began my explanation: "Well, it's about. . . ."

Allen heard me through, underlining questionable phrases. "Then why don't you write it down like that, just the way you've told me?" he said. "I have no difficulty understanding that. It's as though you're trying to be deliberately ambiguous, or write like T.S. Eliot. Look at these phrases: so many words—'The ripple of water beneath a low, red bridge/shining carp that lay suspended/among the stones of an old green pond.' Can you see the superfluous language there?" he went on. "Too many descriptive adjectives: too wordy! Look at these articles: 'the' ripple, 'the' stones. . . . 'The' everywhere—cut them out. Keep the images clean, tight. Keep the language simple, so we can understand it."

My face burned with embarrassment. He flipped through other poems: on almost every page I saw his corrections, noted with a small "x" beside each flawed line.

"And here," he pointed out again. "What do you want to say in this line? What's this poem about?"

Another explanation. More fraternal criticism—keep it lean, keep words active, keep it simple. Then he turned to a favorite piece, a tai chi poem I knew inside out. More correction. Finally, I moved to defend myself:

"Keep it simple? Sure, you can say that," I exclaimed, "but it isn't poetry then. It's just language. . . ."

"*Ahhhh,*" he interrupted. "'*It wouldn't be poetry. . . .*' Don't you see? As soon as we get hung up on the idea of writing 'poetry,' language automatically becomes something else, something grander, elevated. That's what gets in the way of clear writing. We get caught up with the idea of poetic form. What we need to do is make it easy for people to understand our thoughts. Do you want to make it difficult or easy?"

There was nothing I could say.

"*Look*, let's go through this here. . . ."

For an hour Allen Ginsberg took me through the traces. Consideration of titles: "Give every poem a title—it'll help make clear in your own mind what you're thinking about."

On line breaks: "Work with your breath to pace the line. Read your work aloud. Even better—get someone else to read your own work back to you!"

Punctuation, capitalization—"Be *relentless* in seeking clarity." Avoid stylized, neoclassical language. No mercy. In some poems he found merit in a line or phrase and verbalized its strength relative to the poem. More frequently, it was excision and trimming: *snip snip snip!*

"What's your intention with this work?" he asked. "You write prose, don't you?"

"Yes, or I have done for the past few years. Sixteen months ago I left commercial publishing though to return to poetry and fiction. What I want to do is publish a book."

"A book? Poetry?"

"Poetry, right. These poems I hoped." I laid it all out. "It's what I want to do now: publish a decent book of poems, even if it's a long shot."

Allen listened with concern. "Why a long shot?"

"Well, isn't it always hard to publish poetry?"

He shrugged. "Just do it yourself. . . ."

"But that'd be vanity publishing," I countered. "No one takes it seriously."

"Who says? Vanity publishing is when you publish *anything*. When you take time to work at something, devote yourself to it—to the craft—that's not vanity. It's self-publishing and it is an old tradition among poets: Chaucer, Virginia Woolf, Whitman—they all did it. Anywhere in Asia poets still have to self-publish."

Ginsberg spoke reflexively. "I self-published my own first work in New York. A lady helped me, although everyone seems to think my career began with *Howl*. What you should think about is completing the work on these poems until you feel they're ready, then publish them yourself."

I sat listening, dumbfounded.

"It's important to achieve a sense of completion with your work," Allen continued. "It's useful for a poet to get it out for a number of reasons; one of them being the tendency to keep reworking old material that's jammed up inside us. Don't block the flow. Get the inside stuff out; get on with the new. You'll learn more from self-publishing one book yourself, than having two or three published by someone else. Okay?"

The session was over. Allen headed off to his room. I sat dazed, mulling over what had happened. He'd said *us Writers together*. Admitted me as a student. But still lots more work ahead.

Back on the Buddha Trail

On the ferry back to the mainland I asked Allen if he'd sign my copies of his books. I'd bought a beat-up copy of *Howl* once for a nickel and he turned the faded price into a sunbeam: *Ferry to Quadra Island, BC. 10:10 am. Sunny Clouds, for . . .*

At Campbell River we were met by two or three people who'd driven up from Victoria to transport Allen south. One of them announced himself as a journalist and began chatting up The Man. Promptly, Allen was appraising the experience at Hollyhock. It was a restorative visit, he confided. Very healthy and restful, great food. He confessed that he'd developed erotic crushes on several of his students—"trim athletic fellows, good bodies."

"And?" the reporter waited hopefully.

"Unfortunately, none of them wanted to swing."

With last good-byes and hugs we made our leave. I watched Allen head off south for the capitol. I caught a lift to the airport. The flight back home felt emptier than I expected.

At the terminal I bumped into my former publisher. "Allen Ginsberg?" he said: "Write up those journals! Don't lose 'em!" I felt in my bag for my notebook.

At a phone booth I called my wife. She'd bring lunch, she said. Thirty minutes later in Vancouver we picked our way together down the Buddha Trail to Wreck Beach.

"Allen said I should bring the Tang masters down here," I said as we clambered through dense underbrush.

Kwangshik cleared her way through a tangle of wild rhododendron that clung fiercely to the radical incline down the cliffs. Already her legs and back in all their angular strength were bronzing up in the early sun. She wore a *karateka*'s headband and her teeth flashed in a beaming smile. In her hiking boots and cutoff jeans she looked ripe and beautiful. Then she turned, and in that instant I wanted to share with her an epiphany I recalled: Allen reciting the *Four Vows* one morning at zazen.

It seemed precious to me now, here, above wild Wreck Beach, the vows ringing in mind like a meditation bell. Is this what Allen was somehow working toward showing us in his own way? I knew now that the greats were all filled with crazy wisdom, with their own doubts, passions, eroticisms. And that surely when someone of Ginsberg's stature draws near and displays all their personality, then our own personality too, flaws and all, is on display, and it is this that we must finally confront.

Kwangshik waited at a lookout clearing. I stood beside her, over-looking the waters of Georgia Straight. A flood of images arose—Allen reading "The Bricklayer's Lunch," a week's close proximity to what I understood as sainthood, "The Nurse's Song," Allen eating porridge, playing tai chi, our session on the beach. As distractions arise, embrace them in a friendly way, he'd said: return to concentration on the breath.

This was his gift. I filled my lungs and repeated the vows after Allen's example:

Beings are numberless, I vow to enlighten them;

Obstacles are endless, I vow to cut them down;

Dharma gates are manifold, I vow to master them;

The Buddha Way is endless, I vow to follow through . . .

Cortes Island – Vancouver